D0884339

6

Women at War
with America

305.409
C152

Women at War with America

Private Lives in a Patriotic Era

D'Ann Campbell

Harvard University Press
Cambridge, Massachusetts
and London, England
1984

WITHDRAWN

LIBRARY ST. MARY'S COLLEGE

158739

Copyright © 1984 by the President and Fellows of Harvard College
All rights reserved
Printed in the United States of America
10 9 8 7 6 5 4 3 2 1

Publication of this book has been aided by a grant from the
Andrew W. Mellon Foundation.

This book is printed on acid-free paper, and its binding
materials have been chosen for strength and durability.

Library of Congress Cataloging in Publication Data

Campbell, D'Ann, 1949–
    Women at war with America.

    Includes bibliographical references and index.
    1. Women—United States—History—20th century.
2. World War, 1939–1945—Women—United States.
3. World War, 1939–1945—Social aspects—United States.
I. Title.
HQ1420.C32   1984   305.4'0973   84-6566
ISBN 0-674-95475-0 (alk. paper)

Designed by Gwen Frankfeldt

To my father and mother,
Bernard and Eleanor Campbell
       and
To my mentor, George E. Mowry

Acknowledgments

Archivists and librarians throughout the country helped me locate and photocopy material for this book. Their many efforts made my research much easier. Special thanks to Dean Allard, Susan Boyle, Rudolph Clemen, Martha Crowley, Martin Gordon, John Jacob, Patricia King, Nancy Noel, Henry R. Shaw, and Earl H. Tilford, Jr. It is a pleasure to acknowledge the assistance provided by the library staffs at the following institutions: Maxwell Air Force Base Library, Montgomery, Alabama; Department of Archives and History, Montgomery, Alabama; WAC Museum at Fort McClellan Army Base, Anniston, Alabama; University of Arizona Library, Tucson; University of Central Arkansas, Oral History Collection, Conway; Colorado Historical Society, Denver; Estes Park Public Library, Estes Park, Colorado; University of Colorado, Boulder; Western History Collection, Denver Public Library; U.S. Coast Guard Academy, New London, Connecticut; Yale University School of Nursing Library, New Haven, Connecticut; American National Red Cross Headquarters Library, Washington, D.C.; Library of Congress, Washington, D.C.; National Archives, Washington, D.C.; U.S. Navy Department Library and Historical Center and Operations Archives, Washington, D.C.; Chicago Historical Society; Chicago Public Library; Illinois State Archives, Springfield; Northwestern University Medical School, Evanston, Illinois; National Opinion Research Center, Chicago; The Newberry Library, Chicago; University of Chicago; University of Illinois, Chicago and Urbana; Indiana University,

Bloomington; Indiana Historical Society, Indianapolis; Indiana Extension Homemakers Oral History Project, Rushville; Indiana State Library, Indianapolis; Iowa Historical Society, Iowa City; Iowa State University, Ames; University of Iowa, Iowa City; Dwight D. Eisenhower Library, Abilene, Kansas; Frontier Nursing Service, Wendover, Kentucky; Kentucky Division of Archives and Records, Frankfort; Kentucky Historical Society, Frankfort; University of Kentucky, Lexington; University of Louisville, Louisville, Kentucky; National Library of Medicine, Bethesda, Maryland; U.S. Naval Institute, Annapolis, Maryland; Boston University Nursing Archives, Boston; Arthur M. and Elizabeth Schlesinger Library, Radcliffe College, Cambridge, Massachusetts; Sophia Smith Collection, Smith College, Northampton, Massachusetts; Walter P. Reuther Archives of Labor and Urban Affairs, Wayne State University, Detroit, Michigan; Michigan Historical Collection, University of Michigan, Ann Arbor; University of Missouri, Columbia; Harry S. Truman Library, Independence, Missouri; Nebraska State Historical Society, Lincoln; Columbia University, Oral History Collection, New York; Franklin D. Roosevelt Library, Hyde Park, New York; Duke University, Durham, North Carolina; North Carolina Division of Archives and History, Raleigh; University of North Carolina, Chapel Hill; Ohio Historical Society, Columbus; U.S. Military History Institute, Carlisle Barracks, Pennsylvania; North Texas State University Oral History Collection, Denton; George C. Marshall Research Collection, Lexington, Virginia; State Historical Society of Wisconsin, Madison; University of Wisconsin, Madison; University of Wyoming, American Heritage Center, Laramie.

Several historians commented on the lectures drawn from earlier drafts of this book or offered suggestions on the manuscript. For their generous and most helpful criticism of the entire study I want especially to thank Constance Dyer, Glen H. Elder, Jr., Elizabeth Fox-Genovese, Susan Hartmann, Richard Jensen, George E. Mowry, Walter T. K. Nugent, and Glenda Riley.

Helpful comments and valuable material for particular chapters were provided by Marie Bennett Alsmeyer, Karen Anderson, Eleanor Arnold, John Bodnar, Elise Boulding, Susan Boyle, Jo Ann Carrigan, Harvey Carter, Ruth Carter, M. C. Devilbiss, Peter Filene, Sherna Gluck, Nancy Goldman, Cynthia Harrison, Reuben Hill,

Darlene Clark Hine, Joan Hoff-Wilson, Maureen Honey, Richard S. Kirkendall, Susan J. Kleinberg, Sheila Lichtman, John Lovell, James Madison, Rosemary McCarthy, Waddy Moore, Bettie Morden, John Nelson, Nancy Noel, Janice Reiff, Leila Rupp, Frank Ryan, Daniel Scott Smith, Ronald Spector, Judith Stiehm, Eleanor Straub, and Russell Weigley.

Special thanks to John Wickman, the Dwight D. Eisenhower Library; David Harvath, the University of Louisville Photograph Archives; Vern Brown, the Des Moines *Register and Tribune*; Barry Edwards, King Features Syndicate; and the Library of Congress staff for their help in securing the photographs for this book.

Thanks are also due the California State University Foundation and Sherna Gluck for permission to include material from the *Rosie the Riveter Revisited* oral history project, a copy of which is at the Walter P. Reuther Archives of Labor and Urban Affairs, Wayne State University.

I am indebted to Rhonda Ferber, Office for Women's Affairs, Indiana University, for drawing the figures and to Elizabeth Suttell, Harvard University Press, for copy editing the manuscript. Aida Donald of the Press has also been invaluable during the entire publication process.

Throughout the seven years it took to research and write this book my husband, Richard Jensen, has been the finest possible scholarly critic and emotional supporter. Without his help I would never have had the positive reinforcement necessary to complete this project.

The book is dedicated to my parents and to my mentor. These unselfish people continue to provide me with a special education. Their support, advice, and faith have always given me a special edge.

Contents

Illustrations

Assembly-line workers at a midwestern munitions plant turning out 37 millimeter antitank shells, 1942. Courtesy of King Features Syndicate, Inc. Photographer unknown.   *1*

At Fort Des Moines, Iowa, Wacs take over clerical duties, July 1943. Des Moines *Register and Tribune*, courtesy of Dwight D. Eisenhower Library, Abilene, Kansas. Photographer unknown.   *17*

The emotion-charged capping ceremony at the Johns Hopkins Hospital Nursing School, May 1943. Office of War Information, Library of Congress. Photograph by Ann Rosener.   *47*

Red Cross volunteers folding bandages at Bayway Community Center, Elizabeth, New Jersey, April 1944. Courtesy of Standard Oil of New Jersey Collection, University of Louisville Photograph Archives. Photograph by Esther Bubley.   *63*

The vast majority of factory jobs were not at all glamorous. A bag factory in Louisville, 1945. Courtesy of Canfield and Shook Collection, University of Louisville Photograph Archives. Photographer unknown.   *101*

The friendly unions allowed women to become members but not leaders. Sheffield, Alabama, June 1942. Office of War Information, Library of Congress. Photograph by Arthur Rothstein.   *139*

Housewives waiting in long queues explained the intricacies of rationing to each other in New Orleans, March 1943. Office of War Information, Library of Congress. Photograph by John Vachon.   *163*

Trailer homes were a way of life for many servicemen's families as well as other families who had to move frequently. Jim Hogg County, Texas, June

LIBRARY ST. MARY'S COLLEGE

Women at War
with America

Introduction
Rediscovering the Women of the 1940s

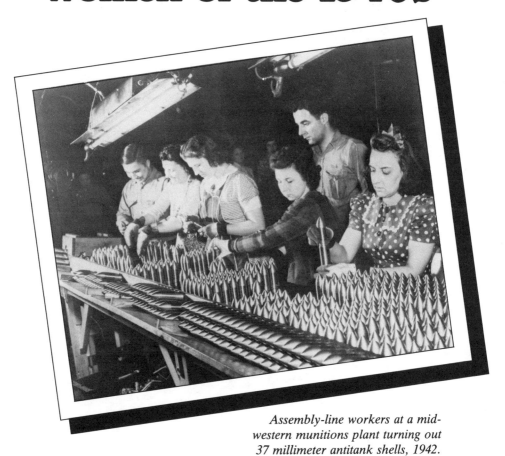

Assembly-line workers at a mid-western munitions plant turning out 37 millimeter antitank shells, 1942.

In the 1970s and 1980s the status of women in the United States underwent a revolutionary transformation. Traditional restrictions on education, careers, sexual behavior, and political activity were challenged. Values, roles, and the relationships between men and women shifted. In 1970, when asked to name the two or three most enjoyable things about being a woman, 53 percent of the women polled spoke of motherhood and 43 percent of being a homemaker. Only 9 percent mentioned careers and jobs, only 14 percent general rights and freedoms. In 1983, women gave radically different answers to the same question: 26 percent spoke of motherhood (down 27 percent), 8 percent of being a homemaker (down 35 percent), while 26 percent cited careers (up 17 percent) and 32 percent pointed to general rights and freedoms (up 18 percent).[1]

What accounts for these large disparities in women's attitudes? William Chafe gave one explanation when he focused on the upsurge of paid employment by married women during World War II. Jobs outside the home were seen as inherently liberating. He hypothesized that a "time bomb" was ticking and that it exploded a quarter century later with the woman's liberation movement.[2] Chafe's interpretation reflected the optimism of the early 1970s—a time when feminists believed that outmoded traditions restricting the sphere of women would soon be brushed away, a time when passage of a constitutional amendment guaranteeing equal rights seemed imminent.

Later in the 1970s, when it became clear that traditionalism retained a powerful grip, the mood of historians grew more pessimistic. Attention turned to the reaction after 1945 that negated wartime gains. The government, corporations, labor unions, and especially the mass media were portrayed as the reactionary forces of the late 1940s. While Chafe had cited heroic role models, and had pointed to liberating programs like child-care facilities, the pessimists were reading another lesson from the 1940s. Only concerted political action based on heightened feminist consciousness and knowledge of the adversaries would allow the woman's revolution to proceed.[3]

While building on the research of historians during the 1970s,[4] this study takes a different approach. The wartime emergency did lower certain traditional barriers. It also caused severe disruptions in women's roles as wife and homemaker. The question is how women—and men—reacted to the situation. The argument here is that their reactions were produced primarily by their attitudes and values, especially those expressed in the interaction of women and men, rather than by material factors such as paychecks. Wartime experience did set the stage for the future, but only for the 1950s and 1960s; it did not set in motion the liberation phenomenon of the 1970s and 1980s. The "suburban" ideal of companionate, child-centered marriages, with little scope for careerism, can be seen as a major result of the interaction between the values of the people and the disruptions of the war. The suburban ideal—Betty Friedan called it the "feminine mystique"—was a major target of feminist reformers of the 1970s. In retrospect, the war helped create a society that flourished for a quarter century and now has been left behind by the daughters (and sons) of the war generation.

In 1942 women went to war "with" America: in army barracks, at nursing stations, on assembly lines, in typing pools, in home kitchens, and in shopping queues, women contributed in all manner of ways to their country's effort. And yet many of these women were also "at war with" America. They perceived war in general, and this war in particular, as threatening to their values—the values of peace and of undisrupted private lives. They could and did rise heroically to the imperatives of patriotism when it required that they save and do without; they had less enthusiasm for the risk to the lives of their husbands, sons, brothers, and sweethearts. The departure of their men meant not merely the fear of loss but also the daily problems of coping. Were women really needed or wanted in those huge new tank factories, ordinance arsenals, and bomber plants? Who would care for children if their mothers worked? What would happen to women, married and single, who took on traditionally male jobs? Should women follow their husbands and fiancés to distant army camps? How could housewives provide adequate food, dress, housing, and medical care for their families in the face of shortages?

In the 1940s American women of all classes and ethnic groups faced the challenge of finding a new balance between their private and public roles. Throughout the decade, most women saw their basic roles as those of wife and mother, and that of their husband as primary breadwinner. But the meanings of marriage and motherhood were changing for younger women. Many women still espoused the traditional view that "what is good for my family is good for me"; nevertheless, younger, better-educated women were seeking less passive, more egalitarian, and more emotionally satisfying companionate marriages. Very few women at the time claimed to want independent lives, but the younger generation wanted to adapt the old roles to new personal aspirations. They sought to transform the roles of wife and mother, and to improve the quality of personal relations in the face of disruptive forces—the draft and migration to war centers—as well as new advantages, especially the availability of well-paid jobs and the higher levels of education and personal competence of the younger generation.

The lives of different classes of women were also shaped by two forces: the new affluence and the legacy of the depression. Affluence eased women's customary responsibilities for home management, budgeting, shopping, food preparation, and cleaning, even though wartime rationing and shortages imposed new problems. For too many the hardships of the depression persisted, and despite improvements in the welfare system, millions of families still had to support or shelter elderly parents, married children, and down-on-their-luck in-laws. In coping with these responsibilities and uncertainties, women drew on, and contributed to, support networks composed of friends, kin, neighbors, and coworkers. Above all, women sought guidance in making sense of rapidly changing circumstances, in devising strategies for weathering current difficulties and formulating dreams for the future. Inescapably, these private concerns intermingled with the public events that were pressing so heavily on their lives.

The war forced consideration of public affairs at every level. Women participated in these affairs through community activity, paid employment, and interaction with the war government. Millions of families faced the uncertainties and fears occasioned by a loved one in military service. When would he, or occasionally she, return, if at all, and in what condition? Every family, no matter how isolated, had to come to terms with rationing, taxes, shortages, transportation difficulties, and the rapidly shifting patterns of employment. The nation's urgent need for women's support in the war effort provided the principal catalyst for change. Community groups were drawn into civil defense, and the female employment rate soared; women supported rationing, taxes, the draft, and the nation's war goals. But women had little or no opportunity to direct policy, even in those areas that so directly touched their lives.

By 1940, American women had enjoyed suffrage for two decades, but, apart from a few prominent figures around Eleanor Roosevelt, had not effectively attained political office or leadership in public affairs at the national, state, or local level. When the federal government discovered its need for women war workers, men made all the decisions, ignoring even Frances Perkins, the token woman, who, as secretary of labor, had nominal responsibility in such questions.[5] From the heights of national policy to the intimate circle of the family, men *talked* politics to women but seldom *listened* to them.[6] Twenty years of the vote had apparently not earned women any serious modification of the traditional view that politics was preeminently a male prerogative.

Mobilization for total war, as leaders in Washington were quick to recognize, posed a new challenge. Successful prosecution of the war required a total popular commitment. Pearl Harbor guaranteed that virtually no overt opposition to the war effort would surface. But there were other dangers: passive resistance, quiet pacifism, reluctance to sacrifice. The Office of War Information, which closely monitored the national mood, found disquieting evidence that the nation's women were much less enthusiastic about the war than the men. Was women's weaker enthusiasm related to their lack of identification with the direction and execution of public policy? Still primarily devoted to private, domestic values, women, not unnaturally, sought to protect those values.

Throughout the war, women remained more dovish than men. Two months after Pearl Harbor, 57 percent of the men, but only 36 percent of the women, favored all-out war against Japan, "even if our cities would be bombed." By 1942, whereas nearly half the men surveyed by the Office of War Information (47 percent) talked about the war in terms of military offensives, only 28 percent of the women did. As a group, women expressed more pessimism about the war than men, feared a longer war, distrusted the Allies, and were less convinced of the wisdom of a postwar United Nations. But women also differed among themselves. Farm wives proved especially dovish, while higher income housewives and younger employed women expressed more personal commitment to the war. Level of income, marital status, and moment in the life-cycle influenced women's views, just as they influenced women's experience of and identification with public events. Most single women had only a remote sense of the importance of the war to them personally. Married women, on the other hand, more readily identified with the war effort. By contrast, being married or single scarcely affected men's strong sense of identification with the war. It was a man's war. Married women, being in closer contact with men, were therefore in closer contact with the war than single women.

Women, conforming to a proper feminine role, paid much less attention to military themes and to national and international events and personalities. They relied on sketchy radio bulletins rather than fuller newspaper accounts. Only 45 percent of the women who looked at the *Columbus Dispatch* on May 7, 1942, read the banner headline story on the fall of Corregidor, while 72 percent perused "He Puts Spare on Parked Baby." Women did follow news of rationing, but less carefully than men. They talked less about the war than men and looked to their husbands for opinions on public affairs. Some avoided war news and war talk out of a sense of anxiety; most conceptualized the war in terms of the possible threat to their families. Yet even these personal responses had public consequences: mothers' opposition to the use of eighteen-year-old draftees forced the Army to promise they would not be sent overseas.[7]

Public policy during the war presented a strange contradiction to women. The media, closely following directives from Washington, glorified martial values, and saluted women chiefly when they took on traditionally male roles as soldiers, fliers, or riveters. Those women who received acknowledgment and celebration of their efforts on behalf of the war were those who entered the world of war directly, who stepped out of their traditional roles. Yet the opportunities for women's participation in the male world of war and politics remained sharply curtailed, and even where manpower imperatives dictated urging women to enter the public sphere, the women who responded to the call rarely enjoyed positions of power or leadership. Whether in the military or in industrial production, women faced traditionally male worlds in which they were being asked to fill in, but with which they were not invited to identify. Their motivation was supposed to be devotion to their nation's war effort, not the establishment of their own permanent presence in roles that had previously been closed to them. Furthermore, in spite of the massive influx of women into new war jobs, the vast majority of women contributed to the war effort in less glamorous and, above all, less touted domestic roles.

The patriotic impulses of the 1940s contrasted sharply with the privatistic tone of the 1930s. Whereas the war focused attention on public events, the depression had focused attention on the private sphere, on the quetions of food, clothing, housing, and family stability. During those years, housewives had not confronted unemployment directly. Since they had not worked for a wage, they did not have a wage to lose. In fact, their work load increased with the need to shop on a meager budget, mend outworn garments, feed extra relatives, provide emotional support to a husband whose role as breadwinner was threatened, and hold their families together.

However, just as the dislocations caused by the depression had forced millions of women to change their plans—to put off marriage, postpone children, or forego material possessions, so too the war years forced millions of women to hold off a little longer on their private needs and dreams. Constant anxiety became a habit. During the war most Americans feared that peace would bring another depression. Wisely, they saved and planned for yet another rainy day. Happily, they discovered a postwar world of spreading affluence, a better chance to realize their dreams than they had known in many years. How did the wartime experience reshape those dreams, by strengthening—or changing—the values of American women? To understand we must first explore the wartime experiences these women encountered. Then we must attempt to assess how and in what ways, if at all, the war experience altered women's and men's perceptions of women's roles and aspirations. We must, in short, consider women's private experiences in the context of public demands and public opportunities.

Five principles have guided this effort to recapture the full lives of the women of the 1940s. First, I try to be comprehensive, to consider a representative sampling of all American women. Second, I argue that it is misleading to seek "the American Woman"; there were 50 million different women, with different values, needs, resources, and obstacles to overcome. Third, to best illuminate individual experience, I group women according to the roles they played and the resources they possessed. Fourth, I attempt to write social history from the perspective of the people themselves, rather than from that of the government or some other formal institution. Fifth, and finally, I have worked on the assumption that people—all the people—contribute to making history. "You *do* make the rules," Amanda Bonner (Katherine Hepburn) told her secretary in *Adam's Rib* (1949)—"we all make the rules."[8] Although women were systematically excluded from the formal decisionmaking mechanisms of government, they nevertheless played a central role in shaping and supporting popular values and norms of behavior. In short, I have attempted to write a history of American women during World War II that takes into account not merely the diversity of those women, but also their own perceptions and determinations and efforts, through the roles available to them, to create their own history and influence that of their families, communities, and nation.

Writing the history of ordinary people poses tremendous problems of conceptualization and the use of sources. Some historians have attempted to study the image of the American Woman by analyzing media representations or government policy. Indeed, both the media and government impinged more and more on the lives of all women by the 1940s. Doubtless the image of Woman that was presented to

Media

the public bore some relation to the experience of American women, whether as distorted reflection or prescription or ideal, and few people were unaware of those images. Yet studying the image of the American Woman, whether that projected by the movies, soap operas, novels, billboards, women's magazines, daily press, or government propaganda, only offers a very indirect access to American women's actual experiences.

Similarly, access to actual experience through biography addresses only the experience of a very small, highly atypical elite. The women for whom sufficient materials exist to permit a biography can almost by definition be taken as exceptional, and their lives can safely be assumed to have departed in significant ways from those of the majority of women.

Increasingly, oral history is opening new avenues to the study of the lives of ordinary people. Several large-scale projects are successfully compiling oral history archives for the decade, and I have used some of these interviews.[9] But oral histories dealing with memories of forty years ago do not constitute reliable samples of the population and require very special techniques of interpretation. Therefore, I have drawn primarily upon sources that were created during the 1940s and that, whatever their special biases, accurately reflect the concerns of the period—the topics on which various groups concerned with shaping or studying opinion felt it important to collect information.

In the 1940s, Congress, federal and state bureaus, state agricultural research stations, and specialized media like consumers' magazines and trade publications tried to obtain a comprehensive picture of what was happening in their domains. They all recognized the war's massive effect on society and the economy; their reports are revealing and have been cited extensively. The elaborate manpower planning and public opinion polling by the government was not, of course, a disinterested effort to gather materials for future historians. The government wanted to stress public roles and convince people to suppress or postpone their private needs. Likewise, the thousands of pages of official histories (mostly unpublished) of war agencies, state defense councils, the women's services, and the Red Cross were written to strengthen the public sphere next time around. Fortunately, it is not necessary to share those motivations in order to utilize the information so conveniently collected.

At about the time the war began, American social science was developing powerful survey techniques, based upon large-scale samples, personal interviews, and systematic coding. These techniques, employed by the Census Bureau, the Woman's Bureau, the Office of War Information, the Army, the Roper and Gallup polls, and various other governmental and private agencies, generated huge amounts of information on the social and economic conditions of American women, their attitudes, behavior, and values. In addition, the extensive collection and analysis of case files by social workers and sociologists generated a rich body of information about the experience of families coping with poverty, psychological stress, and the loss of husbands and fathers to the military. I have relied heavily, but not uncritically, upon these sources. Before using any results, I evaluated their methods and findings; in some instances I obtained copies of the original IBM cards and surveys and reanalyzed the data with modern computer and statistical techniques. In the case of Census reports, I have usually selected, regrouped, and retabulated the original statistics to highlight the significant patterns I think were there.

Any effort to utilize primary data sources presupposes some theoretical premises. My work has been guided by the assumption that women's access to resources and acceptance of specific roles provide the best principles to use in grouping and understanding the experiences of innumerable individual women. But as is well known from the complex issues that cloud any simple attempt to group people by class according to objective criteria, neither resource theory nor role theory provide clear and simple patterns, all the more since access to resources and access to roles cannot be precisely correlated with each other. The issues of classification become more difficult yet in the case of women. Each woman, whatever her access to resources, played many roles in relation to her family, her friends and neighbors, her employer (if she had one), her community, and her country. To date, no one has successfully catalogued all the roles available in a complex modern society, although Robert and Helen Lynd, W. Lloyd Warner, Robert J. Havighurst, and other community sociologists of the era made a start. And identifying the roles only constitutes a beginning, for there remains the thorny problem of ranking them according to their importance in the beliefs and behavior of the women themselves.

I have also attempted to define the roles according to the perspective of the women themselves, rather than that of the agencies that collected the original data, or the society at large. In doing this, I have tried to avoid identifying as heroines those women whose values I most agree with and celebrating women's every breakthrough into the public sphere on the uncritical and ahistorical assumption that those breakthroughs were of primary importance to the majority of women at the time. I remain primarily concerned with how women in the 1940s saw the demands of their private and public roles, and how they tried to balance them. To the extent that this book has heroines, therefore, they are those women who coped most successfully with the challenges they encountered according to criteria of time and place.

Women's own perceptions in time and place permit us to recover contemporary attitudes toward women's lives, responsibilities, opportunities, and external constraints. In this respect, they constitute an essential component of any historical assessment of women's experience. They do not, however, provide an adequate source of information for assessing change and continuity in women's public and private roles during the period. Yet change and continuity, for good reasons, constitute dominant themes in women's history. On the face of it, a study limited to half a decade must inevitably emphasize continuity. Yet such a brief period, when it includes a major war, can also reveal significant change. The task is to compare short-term upheaval with secular change, to assess the significance of the war itself—the short-term upheaval—in altering, accelerating, initiating, blocking, or remaining irrelevant to long-term change. Debate remains fierce as to whether the war constituted a watershed in women's, especially married women's, participation in the labor force; whether it inaugurated a change in values, and, if so, in what direction. Did the war, for example, foster a renewed emphasis on the values of domesticity, including larger families, or did it provide an impetus toward higher divorce rates and smaller families? The answer depends at least in part on whether one considers the impact of the war from the vantage point of the 1950s or the 1930s or the 1980s. The issues are complex and any attempt at resolution is surely premature. I have, nonetheless, made every effort to identify any indications of both change and continuity that did occur.

The importance of perspective can be illustrated by the debate over day care, a program that was operated without ever consulting the chief beneficiaries, the mothers and children, and thus eventually failed. Numerous special interests seized on the issue of public day-care centers to manipulate women. The program in operation was simplicity itself: hiring women to look after small children in public buildings. Yet the debate was more complex than that on the atomic bomb because motivations varied drastically. The War Manpower Commission favored day care because it wanted more mothers to take jobs; its surveys indicated that millions were tied down by child-care responsibilities. Factory managers, as well as leftists concerned with aiding the Soviet Union, thought centers could cure the problem of high absentee rates and thus increase the production of munitions. Community councils saw the promotion of centers as a way to rally support for the war. Socialites sponsored them as part of their volunteer efforts. Some social commentators, alarmed at reports of "latch-key" children left to fend for themselves, decided that if mothers worked they must have a place to leave their children. School boards saw an opportunity to expand their kindergarten and after-school programs. Feminists at the time welcomed the opportunity to relieve women of family burdens, while feminist historians in recent years have argued the importance of paid jobs in liberating wives. The WPA, which operated a network of nursery schools, saw them primarily as a means to employ women on relief. The Federal Works Agency, which controlled Lanham Act funds to build centers, saw them as emergency construction projects that aided overcrowded boom towns. (Lanham was a southern congressman who did not feel mothers should work, or that "his" money should go for day care.) Catholic clergy, alarmed at the threat to the family posed by working mothers, stood opposed. Union leaders were afraid that company-run centers would indoctrinate the children (but only a handful of leaders suggested alternative day-care arrangements). The Children's Bureau, interested primarily in the welfare of children, wanted to emphasize elaborate child-care procedures, including the professional training of suitable staff workers. They vigorously opposed the all-out-for-the-war attitudes of other federal agencies, until President Roosevelt ruled against them. State governments wanted to coordinate all civil defense activities, and not allow the federals to deal directly with communities. Social workers wanted to interview all applicants, so as to provide "necessary" expert intervention in the affairs of families with problems. They argued that many, if not most, of the women who would use the centers had troubles, especially in relating to children. The social workers preferred foster family solutions.

Most mothers, employed or not, saw child care as their major responsibility, enjoyed it, and thought that preservation of the American family was the purpose of the war. Very few working mothers actually used day-care centers—they recoiled at the "relief" image, the inconvenient locations, the high weekly charges, and the risks involved should the child be sick. Nine out of ten made alternate arrangements, usually with other family members. (Most mothers who took jobs did so to help support disabled husbands, elderly parents, or other dependents, who usually lived with them.)[10]

The day-care experiment in World War II was ultimately a failure because the vast majority of women did not wish to give up their children to public institutions. They resisted arbitrary public demands in the name of private values. They made history by refusing to participate in a revolution in patterns of child care that challenged their own primary self-identifications and social role. Even government policy was unable to overturn the norms rooted in individual and community experience, norms reinforced through personal contact and transmitted from generation to generation.

Similarly, when the government systematically tried to change the norms regarding women's work roles and women in military service, all of its advertising drives and persuasion efforts failed because most people did not want to accept the new norms. The government considered coercion—a national service requirement for women, a draft for nurses—then backed away. The Army discovered that even its coercive control over servicemen could not change their strong beliefs about the place of women. Government and "society" could set some of the options and the constraints, but it could not control people's values. In a democratic society the government was unwilling to use its coercive powers to force women to behave according to edict.

The task of the historian is not to pretend that women did something else, or to hypothesize what the future would have been like if people had different values. Rather it is to discover what did happen, explain why it happened, and relate that explanation to the values, resources, and constraints of the people at the time.[11]

To recognize the limits of the ability of government policy to shape women's lives is not to claim that women could achieve anything they wanted. Women established their priorities and fought to realize them under specific conditions over which they frequently had little or no control. Women's access to the resources of wealth, knowledge, skills, family, and even individual personality varied greatly. I have tried to take account of these variations by paying attention to differences in women's race, class, age, education, marital status, and identification with a specific community. My analysis necessarily remains incomplete, in part because the surviving information is incomplete, in part because to tell the story of even the principal groups of women as defined by race and class would require as many books. It is, nonetheless, essential to recognize that the conditions that limited women's choices frequently operated differentially. If some constraints affected all women, as women, many others affected specific groups of women more than others.

History for some people means entertaining stories about the past, for some pure scholarship, and for many a morality tale that ought to instruct us on correct beliefs and proper behavior today. History means all of these things to me as well, though my main concern has been to set the record of the 1940s straight rather than to entertain or reform people today. If this story carries a lesson for the 1980s it is that the problems and opportunities of the 1940s were those of the people of that era, reflecting their culture, society, and values. The feminist revolution of the last fifteen years was in large measure a reaction against the suburban family ideal that fascinated the war generation and become so prevalent in the 1950s. That ideal was a product of different circumstances—war and depression—and of a people less sensitive to individual needs, aspirations, and abilities, and yet more sensitive to the private demands of family and the public demands made by the nation in the name of patriotism. The challenges of the 1980s would have been incomprehensible to them; my goal is to make the challenges they faced comprehensible to us.

1.
A Crushing Defeat in This Man's Army
Wacs, Waves, Spars, and Women Marines

At Fort Des Moines, Iowa, Wacs take over clerical duties, July 1943.

Making women soldiers was the most dramatic break with traditional sex roles that occurred in the twentieth century. During the war the major powers did it to meet the needs of all-out warfare.[1] Yet American women never comprised more than 2 percent of the military; they were hardly indispensable. Furthermore, most Wacs and Waves had been holding civilian jobs, some of which were as important to the war effort as the jobs they were assigned by the military. Why, then, were the women's services created?

The United States proposed to win the global war through maximum utilization of manpower, technology, and industrial capacity. Twelve million soldiers and vast quantities of equipment had to be coordinated. Millions of letters, personnel files, repair manuals, equipment specifications, vouchers, planning documents, transfer orders, payroll slips, requisitions, medical records, budget summaries, priority authorizations, and any number of other kinds of documents had to be dictated, typed, copied, delivered, responded to, and filed away. Total federal civilian employment leaped from 1 million in 1940 to nearly 4 million on VE-day, of whom 1 million were civilian clerks (mostly women) working for the War and Navy Departments. Despite the help of civilians, much of the paperwork was handled by men in uniform—23 percent of the Army was assigned to clerical work in 1943, 35 percent in 1944.[2] The generals and admirals were pained that office duties kept so many of their good officers and men from fighting, yet the inner processes of modern bureaucratic warfare forced them to assign an increasingly larger number of soldiers to clerical duties. Civilians could not do the whole job because commanders insisted upon the importance of military discipline: they demanded workers who would work as many hours as necessary, move from station to station immediately, and not quit. Women in uniform provided a solution, partial to be sure, but essential nonetheless. The war allowed and encouraged bold experimentation.[3]

High-ranking officers in the Army Air Corps had expressed interest in using women volunteers ever since the favorable experience of Britain and the United States in World War I. Over 11,000 American women had served then as nurses or as Navy "yeoman (F)."[4] During the 1920s and 1930s, Army Air Corps commanders had commissioned staff studies that recommended the extended use of women in future conflicts. By Pearl Harbor, England and Canada were again recruiting women. Rear Admiral Randall Jacobs, chief of naval personnel, was among the high-ranking officers who visited the British and Canadian women's units while reviewing Allied troops and drafted a preliminary plan for an American women's unit.[5] However, the creation of a women's corps bogged down in Congress. At one point, according to Colonel John Hilldring, General George C. Marshall "shook his finger at me and said, 'I want a women's corps right away and I don't want any excuses!' "[6] In March 1942, Congress finally passed the Women's Auxiliary Army Corps (WAAC) Act and for the first time gave women partial military status. The Navy drafted its own legislation, and by the end of July 1942 women were accepted on the same basis as male Navy reservists. Primary support for the WAVES (Women Accepted for Volunteer Emergency Service) legislation came from Admiral Ernest J. King, chief of naval operations and former chief of the Bureau of Aeronautics, Admiral Arthur Radford, chief of naval aviation training, and the ranking officers in the Bureau of Aeronautics.[7] By November the U.S. Coast Guard had created the SPARS (for *Semper Paratus,* the Coast Guard's motto). The Marines, giving their women no nickname, followed suit in February of 1943. In June 1943, the Women's Auxiliary Army Corps became the Women's Army Corps (WAC), gaining full military status. At peak strength 271,600 women served in some branch of the military; a total of 350,000 women voluntarily entered the services at some point during the hostilities.[8]

While some high-ranking officers were lobbying for women soldiers, others remained skeptical. General Thomas Holcomb, commandant of the Marine Corps, was one of the reluctant generals who needed proof. He soon discovered, however, that "there's hardly any work at our Marine stations that women can't do as well as men. They do some work far better than men."[9] General Dwight D. Eisenhower was another key convert. When he was put in charge of the troops in North Africa, Eisenhower ordered WAC Director Oveta Culp Hobby to send him 5,000 Wacs immediately and prepare to send more. General H. H. Arnold, head of the Air Corps and a long-time supporter of women in the military, boasted that "in the fields for which a woman's civilian training best fits her, a woman can do the job of two men." He warned his officers:

> As we ship men to the theatres of operation in increasing numbers, it becomes . . . essential to recognize and use the skill and training of women to the maximum extent possible. If there is a man [who] does not train and use the available Wacs . . . to the fullest possible degree, he will shortly have no one to do his job—if there is such a man, he is a definite danger to the continuing successful and efficient operation of your organization.[10]

Releasing men to fight was the most important objective. The second wartime commandant of the Marine Corps, General Alexander A. Vandegrift, assured his women Marines that they were accomplishing that objective, and that "they could feel responsible for putting the 6th Marine Division in the field . . . Without you, we would be seriously handicapped."[11] More and more generals and admirals went on record in praise of women soldiers.[12]

Resistance among the general public to the idea of women in uniform was surprisingly weak when the units were being created. Perhaps the sense that the military is always right, or at least should get whatever it wants, helped to mute public criticism. The idea of having women take on men's military roles alarmed Catholic leaders, however, who denounced the WAC as "neopagan" and more fitting to the "spirit of Communism or Nazism than to a Christian concept of life." The Catholic bishop for the Army told his soldiers that although they may not like peeling potatoes, darning socks, or sewing buttons, "I think that for the sanctity of the home you would rather

do these things than have them done for you by women in the army."
After a year or two of observation, however, the Catholics not only
dropped their criticism but even began to applaud the servicewomen.
As one chaplain observed, after the war the women veterans would
"naturally transmit much of this . . . respect for authority, discipline,
scrupulous regard for promptness and exactness and execution of
detail to their children." Surely, he added, "this will make for a
much better disciplined generation."[13]

All services required women to be twenty years old to join, whereas
men were drafted at eighteen. Throughout the war, younger women
or their parents pleaded for a lower age limit. One parent wrote
Eleanor Roosevelt, "If girls 17 were allowed to enroll in the last
war, could it be possible for a girl 19 to enroll in the Marines today?"
Another parent, a Distinguished Service Cross holder, wrote, "As
I have no sons to give to the Marines, I would be more than happy
if you . . . would recommend my daughter . . . She will be 18 this
June." Pressure mounted and at one point Congressman Everett
Dirksen even introduced a bill, but it was quickly defeated. The
minimum ages for men and women remained different. The military
felt eighteen- and nineteen-year-old "girls" would cause too many
additional problems. Military leaders reasoned that the eighteen-
and nineteen-year-old men they recruited were at their peak physical
form and thus made prime candidates for combat duty. Women
recruits were to be selected on the basis of maturity not youthful
zeal. Consequently, the median age for enlisted Wacs was twenty-
five; for women Marines it was a year younger. Officers were a few
years older, but women over thirty-five were usually rejected, except
as candidates for the most senior leadership positions.[14]

The services varied in the amount of education they required. For
some, high school background was preferred, for others it was required. For officers, the services generally wanted college graduates
or women with two years of college and two years of work experience.
Educational backgrounds of men and women officers was comparable, but enlisted women were much better educated than enlisted
men (see figure 1). The women's services were highly selective and
took only those candidates with strong educational backgrounds or
work experience. Men were drafted and taken if at all possible, so
the range in their educational backgrounds was greater than for

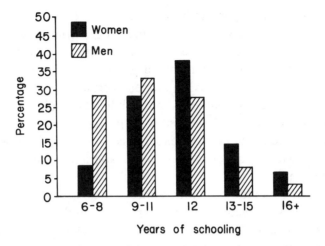

Figure 1. Education of enlisted Army men and women. Source: Samuel Stouffer, "The American Soldier in World War II," Surveys S-194 and S-205, 1945, Roper Center, Williams College, Williamstown, Mass.

women. Of the enlisted Wacs, 42 percent had a high school diploma and 20 percent had some college education or more. In contrast, only 28 percent of the Army's enlisted men had high school diplomas and 11 percent had some college experience.[15]

Wives in general and mothers in particular were not welcome, and no dependency allowances were given for children or for husbands. As a result, in 1943 70 percent of the Wacs were single, 15 percent were married, and 15 percent were divorced, widowed, or separated. By 1945, 16 percent of the Wacs were engaged and half were single with no marriage planned for the hear future.[16]

Women from rural areas and small towns in the North were overrepresented, at least partly because military recruiters did not have to complete directly with industry for available women workers.[17] On the other hand, there was an underrepresentation of women from the South, where military service was a high prestige male career choice. Indeed, southern men had always been overrepresented in leadership roles in the military. In 1935, 56 percent of the Army's top-ranking officers and 38 percent of the Navy's were southern born. Being a military wife was a high prestige role for a southern woman. Consequently, they might have been encouraged less than their regional counterparts to become soldiers. "Service in women's military organizations is a newer idea in the deep South than in other parts of the country and more at variance with their customs and traditions," concluded the director of the women Marines.[18]

Occupational backgrounds of women recruits were as varied as their educational backgrounds. About half had held full-time clerical or sales jobs. Less than 10 percent were professionals or managers, and only 5 percent had no work experience (see figure 2). The Spars reported an average of seven years work experience in education or government jobs.[19]

Women who had full-time jobs before enlistment were paid about as much as WAC privates as they had received in their civilian jobs. However, women with college degrees and work experience in education or government had not been paid as well for their civilian jobs as men with similar backgrounds. Thus, those who became officers made almost twice as much on the average as they had before. The pay differential was an incentive to join for a woman with a

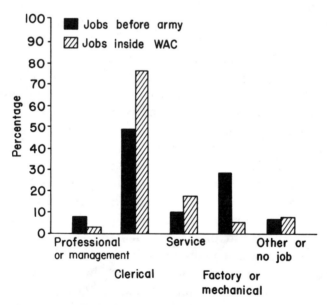

Figure 2. Jobs before and after enlisting in the WAC. Source: Samuel Stouffer, "The American Soldier in World War II," Survey S-194, 1945, Roper Center, Williams College, Williamstown, Mass.

higher educational background. Save for the unemployed, blacks, students, and farm laborers, the men were paid much less in the military than they had been paid before. While the men grumbled about their bad pay and loss of civilian opportunities, the women were enjoying the best pay they had ever known.

None of the services were eager to recruit black women, but national policy considerations eventually forced them to relent. The WAC allowed blacks to serve in segregated units and set a 10 percent ceiling, but it was never less than 94 percent white. More than 4,000 blacks served in the WAC, including over a hundred officers. The WAVES, Marines, and SPARS were all-white organizations until late in the war. The Navy justified its policy by explaining that all WAVES had to replace men to enable them to go to sea. Black men were eligible to enlist for only a few types of positions in the Navy, so black Waves were not needed. When in 1944 FDR demanded that black women be recruited, the WAVES accepted two black officers and seventy-two enlisted women, the SPARS took four, and the Marine Corps none.[20]

To add prestige to the fledgling units and to attract the "right type" of recruit, the services carefully chose their corps directors. Advisory committees, drawn from the ranks of deans of women and women presidents of elite colleges, assisted in the process. The WAAC/WAC and Marines selected prominent club women from southern and eastern high society. The WAVES and SPARS went to Purdue and Wellesley to find their directors.

Oveta Culp Hobby, director of the WAAC/WAC, was thirty-seven at the time she was appointed, the wife of a former governor of Texas, and the mother of two children. She had served as newspaper and radio executive, publisher, lawyer, writer, president of the Texas League of Women Voters, and civic worker in numerous state and city organizations. Hobby had helped with the drafting of the WAAC legislation and had created and directed the Army's Bureau of Public Relations, Women's Interests Section.[21] Ruth Chenery Streeter of the Marines, a Bryn Mawr alumna, had experience in civic activities such as public health and welfare, unemployment relief, and old-age assistance in her home state of New Jersey. She had served on the board of many community and philanthropic organizations. In 1941 she was the only woman member of the Committee on Aviation of the New Jersey Defense Council. She had learned to fly the year before.[22] Streeter and Dorothy Stratton, director of the SPARS, were both enrolled in the first class of Waves. Dorothy Stratton had been a dean of women at Purdue and was serving as a senior officer in a training program in Wisconsin. Stratton was recommended by Mildred McAfee, who had also been a dean of women before becoming the president of Wellesley and then director of the WAVES. McAfee was one of the few women college presidents or deans who was young enough to qualify for the low rank of lieutenant commander, which was the highest rank a Wave could hold.[23]

In selecting a woman college president, the Navy wanted to reassure parents that their daughters would be well looked after and that the project was respectable. McAfee and Stratton had another advantage: both knew the problems and needs of college-age women and had worked in bureaucracies designed to accommodate and model impressionable young women. Both also were part of a larger network of women educators. In fact, the Navy men complained that too many schoolteachers were signing up for the WAVES. Hobby and Streeter had a different set of advantages. Both were experienced in dealing with influential male leaders and in organizing volunteers. All four women left their mark on their respective organizations. Hobby went on to become a powerful newspaper publisher and, under her old comrade Dwight D. Eisenhower, Secretary of Health, Education, and Welfare.

Unfortunately for all the women's corps, its women leaders were not able to draw upon a leadership heritage within the military. All encountered major problems with their male counterparts and at times had to handle difficulties with their immediate male superiors. Luckily, each woman leader was able to find a senior ranking man who would run interference for her. The four also met frequently and formed their own support group. Shared information helped each to develop similar or improved programs.

Women in uniform posed a new challenge for military leaders: how to modify the rules and customs designed for an all-male institution. Planners grappled with questions of sexual behavior, uniform design, housing, and discipline.

Relationships that might naturally form between men and women gave the military planners special trouble. Should male officers be allowed to date enlisted women? What rules should govern the behavior of enlisted women and officers? The custom soon emerged that a male supervisor should not ask a woman subordinate for a date, nor should the woman accept. The Navy said its male officers could fraternize with enlisted women; the Army said no. Neither situation worked well. Navy enlisted men resented having officers encroach on "their territory." Rumors disseminated that certain enlisted women were favored because of their connections with officers. On the other side, Army officers resented being cut off from what they considered one of the few attractions of the war. Rules had to be bent for those who were engaged before enlisting and for siblings. Morale problems caused by the social caste system of officers' privileges were made worse when relationships between the sexes became involved.[24]

Marriage was an issue that military leaders took years to resolve. Ideally all women enlisting would be single or at least not married to a serviceman. However, women with service husbands often made the best soldiers. The Pentagon first ruled that a woman must not have a husband in any branch of the Armed Forces. This rule was later modified to require married women to join a service other than that of their husbands. If a woman in service married a man in the same branch, she was the one who had to resign. The Marines considered allowing wives of Marine POWs and those listed as missing in action to enlist. But many felt that when the men returned, the women would quit. Restrictive marriage rules were costing the services some of their best women, so near the end of the war most rules were relaxed. Women married to servicemen could remain as long as both parties realized that they would get no special privileges such as being stationed together.[25]

The proper response to pregnancy also baffled the planners. They finally decided that it was a medical not a moral problem, and both married and unmarried pregnant women were honorably discharged for the benefit of the service. Few were discharged because of pregnancy before 1944, but by the end of the war the Marine Corps was reporting two hundred pregnancies a month. (Getting pregnant was the easiest way to "devolunteer.") In the Army the pregnancy discharge rate was seventeen per thousand women in 1943, forty-nine per thousand in 1944, and sixty-eight per thousand in 1945. It must be stressed that the great majority of the pregnant women were married. Pregnant soldiers had to pay all their own maternity expenses, whereas wives of soldiers were treated free. Not until the end of the war did servicewomen receive maternity benefits.[26]

Abortion presented an even thornier issue. Although abortions were never numerous, a woman was to be discharged if she "is or has been" pregnant—with the objective of discouraging abortions. The Navy first tried to discharge women if there was legal evidence that an abortion had taken place; if upon examination the woman was not pregnant and no evidence of an abortion was discovered, she could remain in the service. It soon proved impossible to find legal evidence short of a confession, so that part of the law was quietly dropped.[27]

Homosexuals were treated as undesirables and discharged as soon as they were discovered. The rigorous screening process that each volunteer had to undergo was designed in part to detect and reject lesbians and prostitutes. The official Army and Navy histories merely state that homosexuality was not a problem. The Marine Corps director was more precise. Homosexuality was determined by overt acts or by psychiatric reports, and 20 women out of 23,000 were dismissed as lesbians. Rumors and gossip circulated widely to the effect that the women's units were havens for lesbians. Some people, baffled by the apparent incongruity of women in soldiers' uniforms and by the manifestations of comradeship among unmarried women that involved hugging and kissing, concluded that sexual perversion must be the explanation. Investigations by the Army indicated that lesbianism was less common in the military than in civilian life. The women's units were more cognizant of the emotional needs and styles of women, and therefore were less fearful of signs of homosexuality than the military generally.[28]

VD caused more casualties than the V-2 for men but was a rare problem for women soldiers. Only women, however, were at risk of menopause. Some men urged that women be retired at age thirty-eight to avoid menopausal medical problems. At the end of the war the surgeon general had to testify that most women were not incapacitated for the rest of their lives because of menopause in order to prevent women from being dropped from the service in their late thirties. He explained that men go through a similar process, a remark which inspired appropriate comments whenever any general behaved in a cranky way.[29]

Military discipline of women posed delicate new problems for the services. The whole point of having women in uniform was to subject them to military discipline. Yet the rules had been written for men, with the implicit assumption that discipline in battle was an absolute necessity. Would the rules for an infantryman be needed for a typist? The women's services decided no and adopted a different model of discipline, that of *in loco parentis,* with confinement to quarters and expulsion the major disciplinary weapons. Such an approach reflected the experience of women college deans who served as advisers to the women's services.

Although courts-martial were rare, they did occur and required the formation of a complex set of rules and punishments. Among the 23,000 Marine Corps women, there were 7 general courts-martial, 80 summary courts-martial, and 227 deck courts. Half the offenses were for absences, 31 percent were regulation violations such as disobedience or disrespectful language, 9 percent were for forgery of passes, 8 percent were for intoxication, and 2 percent were for theft. Of the seven general courts-martial, three resulted in dishonorable discharges, and four in bad conduct discharges. Under the undesirable category, besides the twenty discharged for homosexual tendencies or commission of overt homosexual acts, twelve were let go for repeated infractions of discipline, nine for immoral and promiscuous conduct, two for fraudulent enlistment, and two for concealing police records.[30] During the first year in the Navy, no WAVES officers were court-martialed, though five had been asked to resign for disciplinary reasons. There had been five summary courts-martial of enlisted women, no general courts-martial, and only two bad conduct discharges.[31]

The WAVES director asked that a WAVES officer be present when any discipline was issued. Her objective was not so much to protect the women as to uphold naval standards, for male Navy officers were often more lenient than Waves toward women. The offenses frequently seemed more like student pranks than aggressive acts. On one typical Saturday night at a center in the Fourth Service Command, with almost 10,000 WAC trainees, the military police reported eleven delinquencies:

2 kissing and embracing in public
1 no hat on
2 injured in auto accidents
1 without ID card
1 walking with officer on street
2 found intoxicated
1 AWOL returned
1 retrieved from Halifax River in an intoxicated condition[32]

The Navy was more apt to discharge a Wave under unsatisfactory conditions than to repeat punishment. The WAC could restrict a woman to her barracks for thirty days, but neither the Navy nor the Army sent women to the brig or prison. When a punishment would normally call for the brig, the woman was discharged. Since postwar civilian women job applicants were not usually asked to account for how they spent the war years, honorable discharge papers were not important. Going AWOL or breaking a major rule or faking emotional unsuitability would only lead to what they wanted by the end of the war—getting out. The women were volunteers, had been carefully screened upon enlistment, and were closely monitored by maternalistic officers. Although women who were dissatisfied with barracks life could get discharged by committing deliberate infractions (unlike the men, who would be sent to prison), there is no evidence that even one woman in a hundred followed this route home.

Once the women were recruited, trained, and transferred to the bases or posts, what jobs awaited them? While estimates by the services were very conservative on how many women they could use in the beginning and in what capacity, once women arrived their usefulness grew exponentially. In some jobs classified as women's work, such as stenography or typing, women could often replace two men. In areas more traditionally considered men's jobs and requiring heavy lifting, it might take two women to replace one man. The Marines developed a simple classification scheme: jobs where women (1) were more efficient, (2) were as good, (3) were not as good, and (4) could not or should not be substituted for men.[33]

As the war progressed, more and more opportunities opened. In some manual jobs, such as parachute rigging, special tools were designed to help shorter, less powerful women. Soon, just as in industry, both men and women used the tools and increased production. The Navy took its mandate literally and at first only allowed women to replace men transferred for sea duty. As the paperwork grew, just as many women were needed to fill new billets as to fill existing ones. In the Twelfth Naval District, by September 1945, 8,239 Waves held 30 different rates and performed 130 different activities. Women comprised over half of the uniformed staff in the Navy Department at the Pentagon and six out of seven of the enlisted personnel in the Marine Corps Headquarters.[34] The admirals were happiest when they could claim that women took over an entire onshore operation. A major source of pride for the Spars was their participation in the top-secret project LORAN—Long Range Aid to Navigation. Unit 21 was at first manned only by men. Within a month Spars completely staffed the unit except for one veteran radio technician who acted as their instructor. Six months later he also shipped out.[35] The Marines filed a similar report. At Cherry Point, by August 1944, all the Link airplane instructors were women Marines. They took almost complete charge of the photography department and film library, did 90 percent of the parachute packing, and conducted 80 percent of the landing-field control tower operations. Women Marines comprised from one-third to one-half of the post troops at representative Marine posts and stations. Some women handled mail, others the radios and the storerooms, still others trained pilots or were mechanics.[36]

Successful achievement in jobs that had traditionally been closed to women made for dramatic publicity photographs and fostered an image of "wonder woman" in khaki, but it raised doubts on the homefront about the wisdom of having the nation's future mothers and homemakers in service. However, it was easy for the services to reassure parents that their daughters would not lose their femininity by joining the Armed Forces. Overall few women served in jobs different from what they did as civilians (see figure 2). In fact, more women were channeled into clerical positions than had been trained for such positions in civilian life.[37]

More women were trained than could be used in some areas, such as storekeepers, stenographers, medical technicians, and machinist mates. In addition, women were not always assigned to positions to which their background and training suited them. A WAC survey in February 1945 reported that of those who had received special training, one in five said that they never used their training, another 14 percent said hardly ever, and 12 percent said about half of the time. Therefore, only half of those trained by the Army used those skills all or most of the time.[38] Women were most often misassigned in projects that were shrouded in secrecy and difficult to monitor. For example, serious morale situations developed in the Pasco and Los Alamos atomic bomb units, where Wacs were habitually used as babysitters, servants for civilians, and in other nonmilitary jobs.[39]

A second area of misassignment involved Wacs who had been induced to enlist with the promise of being trained as medical technicians. Many who volunteered were highly intelligent and had college educations. These Wacs soon discovered that nurses and male corpsmen outranked them, and that they were being used as charwomen. The informal practice was formalized at Fort Jackson, South Carolina, when the commanding officers issued the order that "All WAC personnel will be used entirely for cleaning of wards." As one Wac grumbled, "If I had only known before I joined what I know now they could have shot me before I would have ever joined. Your people at the recruiting office show a beautiful film that shows the girls at work really doing things for the boys . . . We scrub walls, floors, make beds, dust, sweep, and such only . . . They should stop this farce of recruiting 'medical technicians' and ask for 'mop commandos.' "[40]

By summer of 1944 the problem grew worse. Over 1,200 women were assigned as orderlies or nurse's aides. It was more convenient to use them than to hire unskilled women. Male orderlies worked twelve-hour days, seven days a week. The officers, nurses, doctors, and civilian women all worked eight-hour shifts. How long should female orderlies work? If the shifts were eight hours the male orderlies would complain; therefore twelve-hour shifts were assigned. The Wacs vigorously protested. A representative of the surgeon general defended the twelve-hour work policy explaining, "I don't think any of them work as hard as they will when they become housewives and mothers." WAC Director Hobby reasoned that if this were a true emergency, her Wacs would sacrifice health just as men sacrificed lives in combat. But men were not sent to their death unnecessarily, so women orderlies should not be subjected to poor health conditions unnecessarily. Hobby suggested that the female orderlies work the same number of hours as the nurses. In a crisis, nurses would also be working twelve-hour shifts.[41]

A woman's issue could become a racial problem. At Lowell General Hospital, Fort Devens, Massachusetts, sixty black Wacs went on a sit-down strike protesting that they were given menial jobs and treated badly because of their color. All but four finally went back to work; those who refused were court-martialed for disobeying a superior's command and sentenced to one year of hard labor and a dishonorable discharge. When the national black community staged a loud protest, the Army backed down and sent the four back to their posts, nullifying the trial on a technicality.[42]

Some jobs never went to women even though there was no official ban on women holding them. For example, chaplains decided that they did not want women as their colleagues or aides. It would complicate the counseling of the men, they explained. However, chaplains welcomed women soldiers in chapel because they drew men to services. On one Naval base in Hawaii where religious services were poorly attended, a knowledgeable visitor warned that chapel facilities would have to be expanded as soon as the first Waves arrived. Indeed, facilities had to be enlarged threefold for the sailors. Likewise, police officers were male except where such employment was more or less necessary to avoid embarrassing male police. Women were assigned to clerical positions in the Provost Marshall's offices, and they assumed custody of women. No employment involving the carrying of weapons was officially authorized for Wacs.[43]

A critical area of concern for all branches was the caliber of women who became officers. The Marine Corps director concluded from her experiences that up to half of all women Marine officers should not have been put in leadership positions. Doubtless the problem was a common one for men and woman officers, but with women there was not the built-in cushion given to men. Many ensigns or second lieutenants were the senior ranking women at the post or base. A young male ensign or lieutenant always had the security of many high-ranking male officers who could serve as mentors and teach him the ropes. But senior men rarely served as mentors for the women officers.[44]

The women had to figure out by themselves how to become military leaders, and they had to do it in a matter of weeks, not years. They had to make do with no heritage of women in military service, no leaders with decades of experience, no traditional training schools, no well-worn paths to advancement, no expectation of glory on the battlefield to drive them on, and no convenient dumping grounds for failures.

What qualities made a good woman officer? In the beginning when men were doing the picking, they tended to look for masculine features such as loud voices and assertive behavior. Women with soft voices and reserved demeanor were often preferred by enlisted women but passed over at first by the male-controlled selection committee. The dominance of the women's services by college educators meant that academic credentials often carried more weight than leadership ability. Perhaps because many officers were former schoolteachers, the enlisted women complained that they were being treated like schoolgirls. Most Wacs accepted and respected their leaders, confiding personal as well as professional problems to them. However, the enlistees were almost as educated and skilled as their officers. Some college alumnae signed up for the enlisted ranks when the WAVES quota for officers had been reached. The officer corps lacked stature in terms of age, experience, and knowledge of how the military system worked. Furthermore, the men, both officers and enlistees, often ignored or denigrated the women officers, none of whom were allowed to command any men. The miracle is not that the learning experience was so painful, but that so many outstanding women volunteered and blossomed overnight into effective leaders.

Women officers regularly ran into opposition from their male commanders, who automatically assumed that they had little talent. Some WAC officers even reported being assigned to clerical duties. It was particularly difficult to explain to men that women officers should be assigned to staff jobs in technical fields in the same way that men with technical backgrounds were assigned.[45] Other complaints against the men revolved around charges of favoritism and sexual harassment. The senior women in the Pentagon did not have direct control over units in the field, and could only use persuasion with the appropriate male commanders when problems arose. In camp the enlisted women were often critical of their male trainers, few of whom had their background and education. It was startling indeed for a schoolteacher on her first day in service to hear her male instructor's opening order, "Put dem hats on dose tables."[46]

The transition from WAAC to WAC in 1943 highlighted the importance of job satisfaction in maintaining high morale. One-fourth of the WAAC failed to revolunteer for the WAC. In some units half the women quit and went home. The chief reason given for not reenlisting was the inefficient use of the women's time and abilities.[47] Assignment to a job with little visible relation to winning the war, such as scrubwoman, beauty operator, or personal servant, could produce low morale. In the WAVES, units assigned to largely dull, meaningless, monotonous jobs had the lowest morale. Assignments were most popular when a person's importance to the war was most readily apparent. When a volunteer prepared documents for a plane and watched it take off, an overwhelming sense of pride and satisfaction overtook her. By February 1945, 59 percent of the Wacs were satisfied or very satisfied with their jobs, and an equal number felt that their job was worthwhile and as important as any other job. They volunteered to do a job that needed doing, and as long as they were busy and felt needed, their morale was good.[48]

Women soldiers were not rotated as often as men; indeed, the Navy and Marines tried to make a woman's first assignment hers for the duration. From the bureaucrat's point of view stability was an asset, but low morale could develop, especially if the soldier was misassigned or denied the opportunity to serve overseas. Slow promotion rates likewise caused morale problems, although some entire units were promoted faster than others through the special efforts of a commanding officer. The no-fraternization policy of the Army also depressed many an enlisted woman, not to mention male officers. Lack of privacy, poor uniforms, inadequate laundry and ironing facilities, and poor recreational facilities rounded out the factors leading to bad morale.[49]

On the positive side, support from senior male officers could make all the difference on a base. The Army Air Force, which more readily accepted women and provided them with a sense of belonging, lost the least number of recruits in the WAAC/WAC transition. Surprisingly, close-order drills were one of the most effective morale builders. Many wrote home about the sense of pride they experienced participating in the Saturday review during training. College women seemed to adjust better and more quickly than other recruits. Perhaps they had already adjusted to dorm living, with rules and regulations about closing hours and meal hours, and could better handle the ambiguities of a complex new situation.[50]

Why did some American women enlist, and why did most not volunteer? Patriotic reasons for enlistment dominated every survey. Emotional comments were eagerly seized by publicity bureaus: my husband (brother, fiancé) was killed at Pearl Harbor (the Java Sea, Salerno), or is a prisoner of war; sons are fighting and I want to get this war over as quickly as possible. The Pentagon seemed to agree that women with this background made some of the best workers because their psychological involvements were so high. On the other hand, more than one woman stopped in the recruiting station to get out of the rain and found herself in the service.[51]

The Marine Corps conducted one of the more systematic surveys. It asked, "While we recognize that most of you volunteered to help serve your country, what was the next most important reason you joined?" One-fourth of the women surveyed joined for negative reasons: to get away from something such as a boring job or family difficulties. About half the women enlisted because they had men in the service (35 percent) or were from families with no men to send (6 percent) or wanted revenge because their men had already been killed (4 percent). Of the remaining third, half enlisted for adventure (15 percent) and the remainder to benefit themselves.[52]

The more critical consideration is why more women did not enroll. The Navy, Marines, and Coast Guard kept their quotas low and filled them, and British and Canadian women were highly responsive, but the Army had a frustrating time filling its quotas. As the generals kept asking for more Wacs, standards had to be lowered, though they always remained well above those required of male draftees. Madison Avenue advertising agencies helped coordinate intensive nationwide media campaigns; censorship prevented unflattering stories or photographs from appearing. As an experiment, the Army beseiged the citizens of Cleveland to see how many women could be recruited in a saturation campaign. A total of 74,000 families were interviewed, 8,253 eligible women were acquainted with the opportunities for women in the Army, 427 signed up, but only 168 enrolled.

At that rate of response, the Army would have had to personally contact more families than lived in the entire United States to meet the quota. Six out of seven Americans knew that the Army needed more women. But the vast majority of eligible women failed to volunteer. Why? A 1943 Gallup survey found five reasons: apathy, fear of Army life and regimentation, misunderstanding as to the jobs the WAAC did, opposition from loved ones, and the hostile attitude of the Army.[53]

A nationwide underground slander campaign painting all women soldiers as sexually promiscuous began in 1943, at about the time of increased government publicity emphasizing how badly women were needed to release men for combat. Armed forces nurses and Canadian and British servicewomen experienced similar smear campaigns. The Pentagon called in the FBI to see if any of the rumors were true or if they could have been planted by Nazi agents. They determined that American servicemen were inventing and spreading these false rumors. The Army recruiting campaigns never fully recovered, and all services suffered at least a temporary setback.[54]

To explain this intense hostility toward women in the service, the attitudes of military leaders, soldiers, and the general public must be separated. Senior servicemen originally did not want women in uniform. Maleness was synonymous with the military. Some joked about orders from women generals; others feared women would have a softening influence on their soldiers and weaken their fighting abilities. Virginia Gildersleeve caught the attitude: "If the Navy could possibly have used dogs or ducks or monkeys, certain of the older admirals would probably have greatly preferred them to women."[55]

Yet when they saw firsthand the British and Canadian women's auxiliaries, they quickly realized that they also needed women to do the paperwork. The nature of war had changed and for every man fighting there were three others in noncombat duties. Much of the clerical and administrative work in the civilian world was considered women's work. Seeing an eligible combat-trained man with football fingers poking at a typewriter instead of working on an airplane was depressing to these generals and admirals. One by one they were converted to the idea of recruiting women. They were simply recognizing that clerical work was traditionally women's work. From the Pentagon's perspective, the formation of the WAC and the

WAVES was not a radical departure at all, but a conservative reflection of civilian life which kept the sex roles in balance by employing both sexes to win the war. The more military life resembled civilian, the less men would grumble and the more efficient would be civilian skills.[56]

The question of trading women's lives for men's never arose. In common with the British, the United States refused to station women where they might become prisoners of war. (Nurses were captured at Bataan, Wake, and Guam, but that was utterly unexpected.) The Navy refused to allow the Waves to leave the forty-eight states until late in the war. On the other hand, the Army was not reluctant to send women to areas in Britain, Italy, France, India, and the South Pacific where there was a small chance of enemy bombardment but no risk of capture. Exposure to bombing was not a threat to traditional sex roles; after all, most of the bombing victims in European and Asian cities were women.

But in sharp contrast to Germany and the Allies, the United States adopted an explicit policy (one that remains in effect forty years later) that women were not to hold any combat positions, nor any positions in units with a combat mission. The rule kept Waves off ships and restricted Wacs from drills with real weapons. The image of fair damsels engaged in hand-to-hand combat in trenches and jungles was a terror and fixation that drove Americans to endorse the rule, regardless of its meaning in practice.

In Britain and Germany women served with high distinction in antiaircraft batteries (usually as spotters, radio and radar operators, and messengers). Newsreels and movies made highly visible their role in the operations room at Fighter Command during the Battle of Britain.

Alerted by Eisenhower that the British use of women in combat antiaircraft posts had proved successful, Marshall embarked on a top secret experiment. In late 1942, 400 WAAC officers and enlistees were integrated into antiaircraft batteries around Washington and four other major cities. Their performance was closely monitored. The experiment was a smashing success. The women "exhibited an outstanding devotion to duty, willingness and ability to absorb and grasp technical information concerning the problems, maintenance and tactical disposition of all types of equipment." They worked smoothly with the men, and "no serious moral problem" arose. Furthermore, they proved "superior to men in all functions involving delicacy of manual dexterity, such as operation at the director, height finder, radar, and searchlight control systems. They perform routine repetitious tasks in a manner superior to men."

Major General John T. Lewis, the commander of the Military District of Washington, asked for another 2,000 women for combat duty. The General Staff was now confronted with a major policy decision. It rejected Lewis's request, ordered the women dispersed, and ended the experiment. The main explanation given was that there were too few women available, and those were needed for clerical duties. But there were also legal barriers. The judge advocate general ruled that congressional legislation clearly prohibited women from combat roles, and then helpfully sent along a suitable amendment to Public Law 554—77th Congress: "Nothing in this act shall prevent any member of the Woman's Army Auxiliary Corps from service with any combatant unit with her own consent." Marshall and his aides felt that "national policy or public opinion" was not "yet ready to accept the use of women in field force units," and that such use was not "presently necessary." They ruled that no further experiments be attempted. Marshall felt he had pushed as hard as he could to win acceptance of women in noncombatant roles. Lacking the sort of urgent need felt by the European armies, he refused to push on. America had drawn the line on sex roles.[57]

The response of rank-and-file servicemen to the enlistment of women ranged from enthusiastic reception through amused condescension to open hostility, mostly the latter. One Army survey reported 84 percent of the men expressed disfavor and most would advise a woman not to join. Some threatened to jilt a fiancée, divorce a wife, or disown a sister if she joined. Scuttlebutt had it that the women were assuming unnatural male roles and had volunteered only because of sexual hyperactivity one way or the other. Two Waves discovered that some sailors really believed that the Waves were government-issue concubines. When they attempted to politely spurn the advances of two sailors, "one of them sought out the MP riding the train and demanded that we be forcefully compelled to carry out our military assignment. When the MP attempted to correct the obvious misconception the old sailors were crestfallen and incredulous." Such an interpretation was popular among men with stereo-typed, highly traditional sex roles in mind, those who felt the need to prove themselves "real men" and to fight for "motherhood and family." It was important to them that the women they fought to protect back home stayed back home. On the other hand, women in uniform meant that men would be moved out of safe "women's work" and reassigned to the battlefront. The women thus posed more of a threat than the Luftwaffe. The Spars had a ready characteri-zation: "It was natural that the swivel-chair commando should rail against the pretense of the little lady who had come to release him for the briny deep." In addition to those who would prefer pecking at a typewriter to dodging bullets, "there was many a man whose ego was punctured when he found his place could be so easily taken by a woman." Nurses and Wacs and Waves in the medical services also experienced hostility when they came in to take the jobs of corpsmen who were then shipped out to a real war.[58]

As a result, the original release-a-man publicity campaign had to be stopped. Too many men and their spouses, girl friends, and par-ents did not want men sent to the front and perhaps killed just because women were supposedly able to handle some of the safe jobs. The women soldiers were hurt and angry. The Spars circulated a story that took some of the sting out of being a threat to men's lives when serving as replacements. A lady seizes a Spar by her lapels and cries, "You sent my son away . . . you released by son and sent him away . . . I won't see him for months and months now, and it's your fault." The Spar finally gets up enough nerve to ask where it was her son went, thinking that it must be some remote battlefront. "Idaho!" wails the mother. The Marine Corps women's reserve di-rector complained that opposition by male Marines hurt recruiting, since they often had to stop work to "sell" the basic idea to the men. The commanding general of the Fourth Air Force Base agreed that "one of the most important recruiting obstacles is the attitude toward and influence on prospective applicants of men in general and men in uniform in particular."[59]

An Army survey in June of 1945 revealed that the men had firm notions about the place of women. Sixty-four percent definitely would not, and 20 percent more probably would not, advise their girl friends to join the WAC. Almost half of the soldiers felt that women could do more for their country working in a war industry; only 18 percent thought they could do more in the WAC. One-third of the soldiers felt it was "pretty bad" for a girl's reputation to be a Wac; one-fifth thought it was very bad. Almost half concluded that the WAC was no place for a girl to be. A third believed that WAC officers did not deserve to be saluted just the same as men officers.[60]

Wac leaders hoped that when the men actually saw what women could do, the opposition would diminish. Indeed, according to one Army report, the unfavorable comments dropped from 90 percent before Wacs arrived to 28 percent after several months in the station. In Australia favorable comments increased from 30 percent to 70 percent in soldiers' correspondence from the time the Wacs arrived in May 1944 to the time they disembarked in August 1945. But favorable observations about the performance of particular Wacs or Waves did little to affect popular thinking about the dangers women in uniform seemed to pose to the values and the lives of the men.[61]

What sort of explanations are possible for such behavior? Sociologist Judith Stiehm, in studying the reaction of Air Force cadets to the admission of women to the academy, states that "male sexism seems to have (at least) two components: chauvinism and chivalry." Despite the conventional wisdom that ignorance is the source of most intergroup prejudice, Stiehm notes that contact sometimes *increases* prejudice. Hostility is increased when (a) the contact involves direct competition (which seldom occurred in World War II); (b) the contact is involuntary (as was usually the case); (c) male prestige is lost by the contact or the woman is of lower status or weaker in any relevant characteristics such as fighting ability (the latter was apparent); (d) the dominant male group is generally frustrated (the usual story in any war); or (e) the sexes hold different moral standards (as was the case with respect to sexual conduct, dirty language, and rough behavior). Contact tends to decrease prejudice when (f) an egalitarian relationship exists (nominally true, but men often refused to acknowledge women's ranks); (g) authority encourages friendliness and egalitarianism (which it did, but the fraternization rules caused trouble); (h) background is similar (generally true, except for the relative scarcity of black and working-class women); and (i) contact extends from formal roles to a personal basis (it certainly did).[62] While no one of these factors itself explains what happened in World

War II, together they can suggest the processes that worked to create such a difficult situation for women.

The reactions of the general public were not as hostile as those of servicemen, but they were still mostly negative. As one embittered woman soldier complained, "the only time a Spar was really considered a Coast Guardsman was on a crowded bus with one vacant seat." Women soldiers longed for the days when they were inconspicuous and resented the fact that when one woman soldier got out of line, suddenly all women soldiers were drunkards or prostitutes. If one woman said she hated the service, suddenly "all women hate the service." Some families just could not picture their sweet, darling daughter in a warrior's uniform. The comments in surveys as to why women should not be in a women's reserve ranged from "Women are more help in industry, defense work, farming" and "they are better off at home" to "it would mean too close contact with soldiers or too hard a life."[63]

In order to counteract the potential enlistees' fear of resentment by male soldiers and civilians, the Army drafted a new recruitment strategy. Help her overcome her specific fears and objections, recruiters were told. The answer to the concern that "men don't think it a good idea" might be:

> Of course, a few men still don't, but you'd be surprised how fast the situation is changing. At first, the boys couldn't imagine what life in uniform could be like for a woman. But now most of them have met attractive Wacs and are beginning to see how they live and what they do on the Army posts. They note that the Wacs are happy and busy, that they like their work, and are having a lot of fun while doing a splendid job. Now the Wacs are as much a part of the social life at any Army post as the boys.[64]

If the recruiter could determine the status of a particular man who must be won over for the woman to enlist, a more specific strategy was suggested. If he was a civilian:

> Well, you understand why, when you look at it from his angle. Just between us two, it's a matter of personal principle with a man; he wants to carry the full load himself. Even though he has been deferred because of age, health, or job, he is really self-conscious about not being in uniform, though he may not mention it. He realizes that the job you'd do in the WAC is really a *woman's*

job . . . and that the only reason men have been doing it in the past was that there were no Wacs to do those jobs then. Just wait till he sees you when you come home on your first leave. He'll be so proud he'll show you off to the whole town.[65]

If the objector was in uniform:

He's afraid that being in service will change you. He wants the same sweet girl waiting for him when the war is over. What he doesn't know is that you will not only stay just as feminine, but that your charm and appreciation of his problems will increase. Our biggest job, as women, will come after the war when we have to help men become adjusted to the peace. How can we do this well, if we don't understand a little of what these men are going through? After this war Wacs will make very good wives of the men who are in service. They will know Army terms, lingo, and have experiences to share with their husbands. They will understand their husbands better. By being a Wac, you can help him do the job now, hasten the war's end, and prepare yourself to help him even more when the war is over.[66]

These recruiters emphasized that women's work was women's work, whether in the military or on the homefront. High-ranking officials agreed with this view. As Rear Admiral Ross T. McIntire, surgeon general of the United States Navy, explained in an open letter to the young women of America, "In the hospital corps you can fill a man's job and still do a woman's work."[67] In sum, women soldiers were to perform stereotyped female tasks such as clerical work so that the men could get down to the business of war, the fighting. While some fathers, husbands, and boyfriends bought the this-is-woman's-work argument, many did not, or were still worried about the immorality rumors. Hostility to women joining the services remained high throughout the war.

Early in 1945, the Wacs suffered a blow to their morale from which they never recovered. The crisis began with the announcement that large numbers of civilians would be sent abroad as soon as the war ended. These women were to perform clerical and administrative tasks similar to enlisted Wacs and were to wear WAC uniforms, but they would not be subject to military discipline or supervision and would be better paid and have officers' privileges. They could earn up to $745 a month, while an enlisted Wac in the same office would make a maximum of $138. Any pride that Wacs had developed in their image and in their uniform was destroyed. The general public would not be able to distinguish these civilians from the Wacs and would blame the Wacs for any misbehavior on the part of these undisciplined, unsupervised civilian workers.[68]

Just as insulting, the high command gave Wacs working in the same office the least desirable, most taxing jobs in order to keep morale high among the new civilian women. The Wacs felt betrayed. The sacrifices they had made in the name of patriotism now seemed ridiculous as the military began to favor civilian women. Army leaders blamed Congress and the lack of a draft, but their arguments did not mollify the Wacs. The Army even arranged that when Wacs accumulated enough points for discharge, they could obtain one of the overseas civilian jobs. Of more than 8,000 Wacs stationed in Europe, only 126 accepted the Army's offer. The others would not listen to the military's inducements to reenlist and went home.[69]

"The Wacs got plenty out of their service," concluded one veteran; we "came home with an awareness and determination that is the result of travel and foreign service." They found that their experience gave them a broader outlook on life, an understanding of complex organizations, self-discipline, and the skills to cope with any problem or crisis. "I certainly would do it again," a corporal decided, "but I am not so certain the Wacs should be continued in peacetime." Still resenting the superior treatment accorded civilians, and still wounded by the slander, most servicewomen felt the women's units should be disbanded. "Women cannot be regimented," another decided, "and with the war over there is no need for it." A lieutenant who interviewed a thousand Wacs who served in Europe reported that most agreed that "nothing could send them back to their own homes and kitchens as fast as life in the Army." She discovered that the most important postwar plans of the majority of women in the WAC "included just what all women want—their own homes and families. Wacs, like everyone else, are dreaming of peace and security."[70]

Unfortunately for the women veterans, their problems were not over when they returned home. The women's reserves had no control over the reception the ex-soldiers would receive. Army psychiatrists were especially worried that women veterans would require a greater period of readjustment than the men: "Even more than men, these women have become unsuited to their former civilian environment because the change in their pattern of life was more radical . . . Most of them have matured, have broader interests and a new and finer sense of values."[71] The women found the vulgar jokes and stories on Wac morals had preceded them into civilian life. Many just never mentioned their military careers. Plans of the ex-Wacs varied considerably: 29 percent wanted to be housewives, 40 percent wanted to work full-time, 8 percent wanted to go into business for themselves, 8 percent wanted to go to school. Only 6 percent stayed in the service for the postwar transition period.[72]

The women ex-soldiers who wanted to work full-time could not expect to be treated as veterans. Many potential employers, including some government agencies, claimed that they had never heard that the women's reserves had become a regular part of the military and that women veterans deserved the same treatment as male veterans. This failure to recognize women veterans could not always be considered accidental. The Veterans of Foreign Wars, for example, adopted new by-laws after the war to ban women from membership.[73]

By 1946 only a handful of volunteers remained in uniform. Their fate and the fate of the women's reserves would not be decided until 1948. The generals and admirals urged Congress to create peacetime women's reserves, with a small number of women soldiers, no more than 2 percent of the total military, to serve as a nucleus in case of future wars. Months and months had been lost in World War II simply establishing these reserves. The arguments convinced Congress, and in 1948 President Truman signed a bill guaranteeing women a place in both the regular services and the reserves.[74]

In reviewing the official WAC history, General George Marshall was disturbed by its tone, which suggested the WAC had been a failure. He admitted that "there was a great reluctance of army officers generally, particularly those in high control, to the interjection of a female organization." He recalled the difficult time he had securing Budget Bureau approval, and noted the "bitter opposition" from southern congressmen who, as his wife put it, "would kiss your hand and give you a corsage but they be damned if they would let you have any rank in the government, particularly in the military." Indeed, Marshall had selected Oveta Culp Hobby as WAC director in part because of her impeccable credentials among southern politicians. Furthermore, he had to contend with jealousy on the part of the Army Nurse Corps. For Marshall, the bottom line was that the WAC "triumphed over these difficulties." Indeed the General had fought a brilliant war in committee, and had triumphed. But he never realized that once the women were in uniform their problems had just begun.[75]

What if instead of inducting women into the services, the military had made more extensive use of civilian women, disregarding the feminist argument that women had to contribute directly to victory if they were to be respected in wartime or postwar America? Outside the high command, the hostility of the male soldier never subsided and worked against any good that women soldiers could do for the war effort. The men simply would not allow women to leave their private sphere. If the women had been civilians, then the time devoted to creating new rules and regulations could have been better spent, women could have dated men of their own choosing, regardless of rank or hints of promotion, pregnancy would not have been an escape, and the male soldiers would not have felt as threatened by civilian women.

Yet the generals and admirals did not trust civilians, especially in times of war. As Admiral Jacobs explained to Senator David Walsh during the initial debates on whether or not to establish a women's reserves in the Navy: "It is considered necessary that they be members of the Naval Reserve because of—1. The nature of their duties; 2. The necessity for their being available at any time or place; 3. Discipline, and 4. Permanency of personnel."[76]

The high command expected to issue an order—soldiers must accept women in the public sphere—and create a harmonious and cohesive armed forces. The women's services never had a chance either to develop a unique role or to become fully integrated. The generals and admirals did not realize the need for a stronger structure for their women's units. It never occurred to them that women needed a mission, mentors, and a share of power. They also badly misjudged their power over the men and the level of resentment that developed. The structure of the situation was decisive, as the very different outcome experienced by nurses demonstrates. Despite the generals' and admirals' best efforts, threats, and rewards, the military remained this man's army.

2.
Victory for the Angels of Mercy
Nurses Break Through

*The emotion-charged capping ceremony at
the Johns Hopkins Hospital Nursing School,
May 1943.*

The **WAC and WAVES** had been given an impossible mission: they not only had to raise a force immediately and voluntarily from a group that had no military traditions, but also had to overcome intense hostility from their male comrades. The situation was highly unfavorable: the women had no clear purpose except to help send men to the battlefront; duties overlapped with civilian employees and enlisted male coworkers, causing confusion and tension; and the leadership cadre was unprestigious, inexperienced, and had little control over women, none over men. Although the military high command strongly endorsed their work, there were no centers of influence in the civilian world, either male or female, that were committed to the success of the women's services, and no civilian institutions that provided preliminary training for recruits or suitable positions for veterans. Wacs, Waves, Spars, and women Marines were war orphans whom no one loved.

The situation faced by Army and Navy nurses was exactly the opposite. Nursing had a highly favorable image, shaped by the extraordinary stature of historic figures such as Florence Nightingale, Edith Cavell, and Clara Barton, and made real by the obviously selfless devotion of scores of thousands of active nurses around the country. Young women aspired to become nurses, a career Americans felt was suitable to the presumed innate skills and impulses of women. Best of all, nursing experience was considered an excellent preparation for marriage. A famous heritage of wartime nursing roles already existed, and had been institutionalized since the first decade of the century in the Army and Navy nurses' corps. Furthermore, thousands of nursing schools were in operation, and nurses with military experience had the option of careers in schools and hospitals that drew upon military training. Finally, with 98 percent of the nurses women and the tradition of (male) doctors exerting final authority in medical matters well established, no one expected any job conflicts would emerge between men and women over nurses' roles.

Beneath the surface there were problems, however. Nursing was an attractive field for young black women, but the highly segregated structure of hospitals, training schools, and nurses' associations blocked their movement into the field. A more subtle conflict simmered between the trained registered nurses (RNs), who had diplomas, white caps, and a middle-class outlook, and the growing number of practical nurses and nurse's aides, who were poorly trained older women from working-class backgrounds who needed jobs and wanted to help sick people. The conflict was not so much over money—for all civilian nurses received low pay throughout the 1930s and 1940s—but over prestige, work roles, power, and control over the boundaries of nursing service. The RNs were particularly worried that hospital administrators (all male physicians) would replace them with the less technically trained auxiliaries.

At the most basic level, the tension within nursing revolved around the question of what it meant to be a nurse. How could the disparate dimensions of the field be integrated? Nursing enjoyed a great humanitarian tradition and clearly attracted so many women because of its goal of helping sick people. On the other hand, the remarkable advances in medical science and technology and in the organizing, financing, and delivery of patient care had wrought radical transformations since the days of Nightingale and Barton. Nursing was poised to become a technological field that required extensive training, far more than was usually available. Should nurses be technicians or humanitarians? If both, then what about the auxiliaries, who qualified for the latter but not the former? And was nursing a lifetime career, or just a way station on the route to marriage? If a career, where were the perquisites, promotions, and pensions? If a prelude to marriage, then what role was there for married nurses, if any, and how could a cadre of expert technicians be fostered for just a short while? The underlying debate focused on the term "professional." Nursing leaders wanted to promote professionalism and the technical dimension of nursing. They wanted to define sharply the boundaries of the emerging profession (through control over schooling, licensing, and the auxiliaries). They wanted to clarify the relationship of nurses to hospitals and doctors, and to society in general.

The debate might have gone on for decades save for the war. (Suddenly women had a unique skill desperately needed by armies in the field) Not only did the physical condition of the soldiers and sailors depend on medical care, but even more important their morale depended upon it. The institutional mechanisms, in both civilian and military realms, were in place. The women were ready to serve, and the leaders of nursing were ready to make their field a real profession.

Nursing expanded rapidly in the twentieth century, in tandem with the growth of hospitals. The first three nursing schools opened in 1873, when there were only 1,278 hospitals in the country. By 1935 there were 6,200 hospitals, of which 2,500 had nursing schools. By 1940, the number of students reached 85,000, and 280,000 women (and a few thousand men) were active graduate nurses.[1] The war would accelerate this growth and greatly expand the number of trainees.

(Primary devotion to "tender, loving care" of the sick patient was the image that brought women to the field in the first place, and it still does.) Nursing leaders, however, realized during the war that quite a different role was necessary for a profession: the nurse had to be a well-trained, efficient specialist, conversant with the latest technology and devoted to a cooperative health care endeavor.[2] The different roles were not logically contradictory; the nurse-as-technician would use tender, loving care as one of many therapeutic techniques.[3] However, the hospital training schools had a vested interest in nurses-as-healers for they were more interested in getting the free services of students than in providing expensive technical training. To overcome this obstacle, the profession had to socialize student nurses in an academic atmosphere and develop advanced research skills. The long battle to shift training out of the hospitals and into universities began in the 1940s and was finally successful in the 1960s.[4]

The new technical-bureaucratic role was strongest among the Army and Navy nurses. They had more college education than their sisters who worked on the home front, and, of course, the military always emphasized the importance of bureaucratic rules and forms. The chief complaint soldiers and seamen had about the medical care they received was that it was too impersonal. Doctors and civilian leaders also began to complain about the excessively technical training of nurses and suggested that they were losing their nurturant bedside manner.[5] Among nurses, tension developed between the younger, better trained, more scientific "professionalizers" and the older "traditionalizers." The latter were more willing to hold hands and empty bedpans and resented the superior skills and attitudes of the new women.[6]

Balancing a nursing career with marriage was a major problem before the war. The great majority of nurses practiced for a few years and then married. Most women looked upon nurses' training as excellent preparation for marriage and motherhood, rather than as a career in its own right.[7] Wives could continue part-time work as private duty nurses, but they were prohibited from holding most full-time regular jobs. Before the war many woman opted for a nursing career and no marriage. As late as 1943 there were 41,000 single nurses over the age of forty, mostly in hospital or public health work.[8] Barriers to married nurses fell rapidly during the war—even the Army and Navy reluctantly surrendered—so that by the 1950s the majority of nurses were married, and the unmarried career nurse became much less typical.

During the war the relationship of nurses to the government took center stage. Casualty projections totaling in the millions led the military to build, equip, and staff hundreds of large hospitals at home and overseas, and to funnel about a tenth of all soldiers into the medical corps. The planners set quotas of up to 70,000 nurses and expected them to play a vital role in carrying out the promise that American soldiers would have the finest medical care in the world. No one trembled at the thought of women nurses—tens of thousands had proven themselves in the First World War. Soldiers who envisioned the day they might be wounded had good reason to want these women in the military. (About 300,000 of the Army's 500,000 wounded were in fact aided by female nurses.[9]

The recruitment of nurses was handled, as it had been for decades, in extraordinary fashion. Neither the government nor the nurses themselves would handle the job. The nurses' organizations were too weak, and the government had delegated responsibility to a private organization with quasi-official status, the Red Cross. The Red Cross did its job well. Before Pearl Harbor it signed up 40,000 nurses as a "first reserve," eligible and willing to volunteer.

In contrast to their doubts about the Waves, Wacs, Spars, and women Marines, Americans seemed unanimous about the wisdom of having *some* women in the military, the nurses. Despite the urgent need for nurses on the home front, civilians were highly supportive of their serving in government. Representative Frances P. Bolton told a national radio audience that "Nursing is the number one service for women." Most important of all, the women wanted to serve. "There has been a larger number of volunteers from nursing than from any other American profession," boasted the *American Journal of Nursing* in pointing out that 43 percent of the active registered nurses in the country had volunteered. "Has it not always been women's work to bind up the wounds of the world?" asked Bolton. This profession, she continued, "prepares you to meet the shock of the devastation man has wrought in God's world and fits you to take your part, your women's part, of re-creation in the world that we must build upon the ashes of that which has been destroyed."[10]

The nurses who enlisted were, in general, young, single women with only a few years of experience since their graduation from hospital nursing schools; 40 percent had attended college. The more senior women stayed at home handling supervisory and training needs. The median age of Army nurses in 1945 was 28.5 years, about the same as male officers, a year older than enlisted Wacs, two years older than enlisted men, and three years older than Navy nurses. About 40 percent of the Army nurses were aged thirty or older, the same as male officers but rather more than Wacs (29 percent), enlisted men (24 percent), or Navy nurses (22 percent).

The family backgrounds of military nurses are not yet known, but they probably resembled those of the profession at large. Nurses represented a truncated cross section of the class structure, with the very wealthy and the very poor underrepresented. Small towns and rural origins were overrepresented, as were Catholic families.[11]

Only 2 percent of all registered nurses in the country were black, for very few nursing schools were integrated and the southern black community was too poor to afford adequate hospitals or training schools. The Army enlisted about five hundred black nurses, keeping them in segregated units to serve black troops. Some were detailed to prisoner-of-war camps, an action strongly protested by the black community. The White House forced the Navy to accept black nurses in 1945; all four blacks who enlisted served in integrated units.[12]

The departure from civilian medicine of so many nurses and doctors at a time when rising incomes produced a surge in demand for medical care made leaders aware that the country faced a severe long-term crisis. Representative Bolton, working closely with nursing organizations, found the remedy in federal aid to nursing students. The Cadet Nurse Corps, operating between 1943 and 1948, spent $161 million to send 125,000 nurses through school.[13] The program paid students an attractive stipend and helped upgrade the 1,100 schools involved, both black and white nursing schools. Enrollments soared 50 percent or more in most schools. The Cadets were not obligated to join the military upon graduation, but were to serve for the duration in a specified list of either civilian or military establishments. The war ended, however, before most were graduated.[14]

Late in 1944, as battle casualties mounted to a thousand a day, the Army decided to raise its quota of nurses from 40,000 to 60,000 then 70,000. With most eligible nurses already in the military, and the Cadets not yet ready, the Red Cross was unable to meet the increased demand. In January 1945 the President called for a draft of nurses. Leaders of the national nursing associations were willing to go along only if the draft were extended to all women, filling the deficits in the WAC and critical civilian jobs as well.[15] An overwhelming majority of Americans polled in February 1945. supported the drafting of nurses.[16] Events proved the Army had overestimated its casualties; no nursing shortage actually developed and the draft bill was quietly dropped.

The strategy for the treatment of casualties was primary reliance on male corpsmen and pharmacy mates working near the front lines or aboard ship. The basic policy was to keep the nurses away from dangerous areas. The capture of nurses in the Philippines at the beginning of the war was unexpected and was not repeated. The corpsmen—male draftees who outnumbered the nurses eight to one—

also handled most of the routine bedside care, as well as ancillary tasks that in civilian hospitals were done by nurse's aides, practical nurses, or male orderlies.[17]

The primary role of military nurses, besides specialized surgical and technical work and treatment of especially difficult cases, was the training and supervision of the enlisted corpsmen and pharmacy mates. The nurses were assigned these duties, not out of feminism on the part of the surgeons general, but because they had appropriate training and formal certification.

Practical nurses could volunteer as enlisted Wacs or Waves, and might be used as substitutes for corpsmen, but they were not admitted into the nurses' corps. Many of these women, enticed by the prospect of continuing their training or learning the skills of a medical aide or technician, soon discovered that enlisted women were outranked by nurses and corpsmen and often found themselves being used as charwomen.[18]

Women physicians fared little better. At the beginning of the war, they could serve as civilian contract surgeons or be commissioned as Wacs or Waves to care for other service women or servicemen's dependent women and children. The American Medical Women's Association (AMWA) advised its members not to take such second-class positions and campaigned to have women commissioned in the medical corps as doctors. April 16, 1943, President Roosevelt signed legislation enabling women to enter the Army and Navy medical corps. The total number of women doctors was very small and only a handful served throughout the war. A by-product of the AMWA's lobbying efforts and resulting legislation was that more women were admitted to medical school beginning in 1943 and more women graduated from medical schools in the postwar period. Before 1943 women candidates had been flatly denied entrance to medical schools charged with supplying doctors to the military. Now that women could be members of the medical corps, they were admitted to most schools. The Harvard Medical School discovered that by 1943 its choices were limited to women with college degrees and outstanding medical school aptitude test scores and seventeen-year-old men who applied during their first year of college. It discarded its historic prohibition of women.[19]

The role of nurses in the highly bureaucratized, hierarchical military was greatly affected by rank. At the opening of the war, Army and Navy nurses had "relative rank," that is, the pay and perquisites of officers but not the full command authority. In both services the nurses were given full officers' status in 1944, in recognition of their de facto command roles. The system, in theory, maintained male supremacy, for the medical services were almost always under the command of male officer-physicians who never doubted the continuity of civilian doctor-nurse relationships.[20] In practice, however, the military system represented a spectacular role reversal quite remarkable in the annals of male-female relationships. Tens of thousands of women were formally and practically in charge of hundreds of thousands of men, none of whom could reasonably aspire to equal status for the duration. Imagine a great new wartime industry—aircraft manufacture, for example—in which all the plant supervisors were men, all the foremen were women, and all the workers were men!

The nurses had no experience in commanding men. Asked if they had as much authority over corpsmen as they needed, 83 percent said yes; 72 percent felt the doctors backed them properly in their exercise of authority over corpsmen and patients. The nurses learned early how to handle their job: "On her tour of duty from 3 P.M. through 10 P.M. she is supervising the boys. They sometimes grouse about taking orders from girls, but only from a masculine sense of dignity. Although a nurse can have a negligent corpsman 'masted'— called up for official bawling out—it practically never happens."[21] The nurses overwhelmingly felt their relationship with both doctors and corpsmen was "very satisfactory."[22] How the corpsmen felt is not difficult to determine. "Some nurses lord it over enlisted men as if they were animals," one veteran complained. "No man likes to be bossed around by a woman," another added.[23]

In memoirs nurses occasionally report experiencing an early hostility that gave way to a cooperative lets-get-the-job-done attitude, with the corpsmen respectful of their superior skills. Yet another dimension in the relationship between servicemen and nurses besides authority and skill was always present: sex. The Army prohibited fraternization between officers and enlisted personnel; the Navy allowed it. In practice the nurses, scarce and highly sought after, were monopolized by the male officers, and the enlistees resented it bitterly. The consensus among them seems to have been, "Any trouble we had with nurses was not so much their fault as the fault of the system. It was always rank, rank, rank. It made some of the nurses high-hat, and even with the others it was a bad thing they had to keep their distance from the enlisted men." As one veteran summed it up, "Not permitting nurses and enlisted men to be seen together certainly is not American!"[24]

There was a darker side to the reaction: men began inventing and spreading rumors about the sexual immorality of the nurses. A prominent California author noted that veterans "say they are now called 'geisha' girls, because the social life of certain nurses, through their pull with the gold braids, has kept them from performing the duties for which they are being paid." A Chicago magazine editor reported that the nasty rumors have been "given some credence, since servicemen themselves have contributed to such stories."[25] A Cadet nurse in St. Louis explained to Eleanor Roosevelt that the chief reason so few graduating Cadets were enlisting was the rumor campaign:

> Everywhere one turns—on trains, streetcars, at social gatherings or the USO—men of our armed forces debase the very organization that protects and heals them in their afflictions. If one asks their opinion about joining, they answer emphatically "No!" and really don't mind going to great lengths to discourage any likely candidate . . . Civilian doctors aren't much better. In this respect the Army is by far the worse of the two. Occasionally one does find a Navy man who gives a favorable comment about nurses (that is probably why I plan to go into the Navy in July).[26]

Veterans divided equally in their opinions as to whether the chief contribution of nurses to victory was professional skill or morale building. The legitimate role of morale building was the guarantee that excellent medical treatment would be available. But as one nurse noted, "It is hard to convince the average male officer that our main duty lies with the sick, not the well."[27]

Pregnant nurses overseas were immediately shipped home. Of 1,000 Army nurses in the Southwest Pacific theater, 70 became pregnant. Of the 20,000 who served in the European theater during the war, 1,100 were evacuated for pregnancy, of whom one in six was unmarried. All told, under 1 percent of the overseas nurses experienced an extramarital pregnancy. The insignificance of the pregnancy rate is underscored by the facts that the Army made marriage difficult, and, at the same time, pregnancy was a ticket home.[28] Why then the malicious gossip? It was a reaction to the sexual-social strains imposed upon enlisted men by the military system, joined, in some cases, with a firm belief that no women, not even nurses, belonged in uniform.

On the home front nursing services grew critically short. The Cadet program proved essential to the survival of many hospitals—and patients—as the students substituted for the missing graduate nurses. Hospitals without nursing schools, usually very small ones, as well as large hospitals greatly expanded their use of practical nurses and nurse's aides. Retired RNs were coaxed back to duty with patriotic appeals. Half of the hospital administrators surveyed in 1945 believed the war made nursing worse because of the shortages of graduate nurses, the tendency to use students as "workhorses," and the growing "independence" of nurses.[29]

The fears of RNs that they might be permanently replaced by lower paid, less qualified personnel were heightened by the successful effort of the Red Cross to recruit 100,000 unpaid volunteers to work as nurse's aides. The Red Cross made hospital work seem both glamorous and patriotic; it appealed to middle- and upper-class housewives who thought rolling surgical dressings was useless makework. If a volunteer took a paid hospital job—an important development the Red Cross had not anticipated—she had to resign her status and turn in her Red Cross uniform. The practical nurses and aides proved their worth in wartime. While the volunteers fell away after the war, the hospitals kept their much-enlarged paid staff and used them to undercut the pay scales registered nurses thought they deserved.[30]

The postwar career opportunities for the nurse veteran were mixed. The demand for nurses was soaring, and most veterans wanted to continue their careers. Taking advantage of veterans' benefits, many acquired advanced training with an eye toward technical specialization. Upon returning to civilian life, however, they were shocked to discover that they were offered only poorly paid, low-status positions involving menial work of the sort corpsmen had done. Furthermore, autocratic civilian hospital administrators gave nurses less authority than the military had, offered few channels for promotion or advancement, and refused to provide social security or other retirement benefits. The nurses who had not gone to war, aware they had worked harder for less pay than the military nurses, disparaged the value of military experience. Marriage—and escape—was a quick solution for many veterans; by early 1947, 22 percent had married and a total of 38 percent had left the profession.[31]

The long-term results of the war were far more positive. The nursing associations, once weak and leaderless, devoted themselves to reconceptualizing what nursing was all about and how it should be organized. Professionalism was the new goal. The military experience had demonstrated that technical skills, bureaucratic structure, and administrative leadership were more important in providing patient care than a nurturant bedside attitude. Even though married women predominated among postwar nurses, many nurses gave up their careers when they married. Some nurse/wives with no children chose not to work. A 1947 survey asked nurses why they were no longer active in the profession. An overwhelming majority, 77 percent, stated that they were now married and that they no longer needed to work. In this sample, 11 percent said that they had left temporarily for personal reasons but intended to return to nursing at a later date.

Low wages and marital obligations were the biggest obstacles to increasing the number of nurses in the postwar period, even though married women predominated among postwar nurses. The average nurse earned about $1 an hour or $175 a month in 1946. About one nurse in eight lived in hospital quarters. Private duty nurses earned the lowest salary, $153 a month. Nurse educators averaged the highest, $207. Institutional, public health, and office nurses ranked in between. Many retired nurses said that better pay and working conditions would enable them to hire help for their homes and return to nursing. One married woman with children explained that the expenses of working and paying to have her family and home cared for about equaled or exceeded her earnings as a nurse. "It costs me from 20 cents to $2.20 plus nine hours of my time (8 on duty and 1 hour en route) to help relieve the nursing shortage."[32]

The autonomy of nursing could best be secured by strong licensing laws and the maintenance of sharp boundaries between RNs and auxiliaries. The American Nurses' Association (ANA) emerged from the war as the premier organization. It then became racially integrated, and the National Association of Colored Graduate Nurses subsequently disbanded.[33] The Red Cross lost its powerful role as supplier of military nurses and nurse's aides. The other two major wartime coordinating agencies, the National Nursing Council and the Procurement and Assignment Service of the War Manpower Commission, both disbanded. The close spirit of cooperation among nursing spokeswomen in wartime and, indeed, the presence of so many strong women provided a leadership tradition that would prove permanent.[34]

Nurses still had their antagonists. The Budget Bureau, annoyed by the limited proportion of Cadets who enlisted (about 40 percent), tried to slash the budget of the Cadet Nurse Corps in late 1944. Strong opposition persuaded the President to overrule his staff.[35] Late New Deal and Fair Deal proposals by Senators Elbert Thomas and Claude Pepper and other liberals for massive health care programs, while supported by most nurses, were destroyed by the American Medical Association. Hospital administrators, unwilling to grant veteran nurses either status or salary comparable to what they received in service, organized to present their own views forcefully. The Taft-Hartley Act of 1947 exempted hospitals from the National Labor Relations Act. The National Organization of Hospital Schools of Nursing fought against the accreditation proposals of the nurses, and against their dream of moving all nursing education into universities. Although the Pentagon, approving the role of its nurses, raised the status of the three nurses' corps, the number of military nurses never reached one-sixth of the wartime peak, even during the Korean and Vietnam wars.[36]

Spurred by the veterans, nurses debated the value of unionization as a mechanism to strengthen their postwar position. In order to stymie outside union organizers, the ANA in 1946 dedicated itself to improving the working conditions of nurses and authorized collective bargaining procedures.[37] The professionalization of nursing did not happen instantly. It took decades for the awakening of the young wartime nurses to work its effects, and for the organization built in the 1940s to develop its full strength. That the war was the great watershed in their history few nurses would doubt.

The contrast between the success of the nurses and the failure of the Wacs, Waves, Spars, and women Marines could not have been more striking. Nurses were seen as heroines, achieving distinction while maintaining a feminine image. The media image of the nurse as heroine was dramatically displayed in two factually accurate films about the one hundred Army and Navy nurses who served during the Japanese invasion of the Philippines. In *So Proudly We Hail* (1943) and *Cry Havoc* (1943), as the men were being defeated the women were victorious. The inherent feminism of the situation was underscored in *Cry Havoc,* where men served only as helpless cases for the women to give care.[38]

In sharp contrast, Wacs, Waves, Spars, and women Marines were viewed as performing male jobs that would make them unfeminine, even though they were actually employed in traditional female jobs. What the general public never grasped, and still does not, was that the vast majority of military jobs were noncombat. Somehow military equaled warrior and all jobs were viewed as warrior work.

The nurses could exercise control over their skills, limit and regulate their numbers, create a professional image, and appear to preserve their femininity all the while. On the other hand, the nonnursing women's reserves had a negative public image. They possessed no distinct skills or training and never made substantive gains in leadership positions within the military. Nurses professionalized in spite of the doctors, not because of them; they gained control over their profession. The Wacs, Waves, Spars, and women Marines did not.

3.
Volunteer, Worker, or Housewife?
The Choices Women Made

Red Cross volunteers folding bandages at Bayway Community Center, Elizabeth, New Jersey, April 1944.

Women in uniform anchored the public end of the spectrum in the war, demonstrating by their regimentation their sacrifice of traditional female roles. Yet 99 percent of American women led more private lives during the war. To call them "civilians" is a stylistic necessity that obscures the enormous variety of their life-styles, economic circumstances, and sacrifices for the patriotic cause. Each had to strike a personal balance between the public and the private, and the choices ran the full range of possible responses. Volunteer work and paid war jobs were what the government asked, with patriotism, prestige, and high pay the lures. The civilians had their own priorities, however, and the government, unwilling to go to the extreme of drafting women, had to accept their decisions.

The basic decision involved the choice of some combination of activity in volunteer organizations, paid labor force participation, or unpaid work in the home. Younger women sometimes stayed in school, and disabled or institutionalized women usually had little or no choice. Unwanted unemployment had virtually disappeared in the country by 1942 or 1943. The options available were restricted by numerous factors, especially the relative availability of employment opportunities of different types in rural versus urban areas; the implied or expressed needs and wishes of other family members; differing skills, resources, and tastes; and community norms regarding the boundaries of race, class, and gender. The data available to the historian are not detailed enough to explore all the interactions among the various factors, but it is possible to outline the ways the patterns of choice varied across time and across lines of age, race, region, and class.

Volunteer activity in officially approved war programs absorbed the leisure energies of about one-fourth of the women. Participation varied by life-cycle stage, class, and race. Housewives in their thirties and forties were the most active, as were established residents in their communities. Mothers of young children, older women, workers, and newcomers had less time, energy, and opportunity to contribute. Women with white-collar husbands and those with some college experience were two to four times as likely to volunteer as women from less privileged backgrounds. Blacks were largely excluded, as were virtually all Hispanic women. Despite rhetoric in Washington about the need for participation from a full spectrum of the American people, it did not happen that way.[1]

Working-class women did not differ from middle-class in their eagerness to volunteer, despite their lesser familiarity with the issues and less supportive attitude toward aggressive military actions. However, they had more children to tend, fewer household conveniences to ease their chores, and less access to automobiles. They were also more often full-time workers with little leisure, fatigued in the evening and preoccupied on the weekend with housework and catching up on sleep.[2]

Middle-class women not only had more time available, they also had much more experience with organized social activities outside the home. Except possibly for some Office of Price Administration (OPA) projects, nearly all war-related activities at the community level were set up or run through established clubs and networks of local influentials. The country club crowd did not run everything, though grumbling to that effect was common. Middle-class women had learned in high school and college the skills necessary to work effectively, and networks of friends drew each other into favorite activities. Working-class women felt uncomfortable with loosely structured assignments, and were ill at ease in the company of women with tailored clothes, fancy manners, and cosmopolitan outlooks. Nearly all community groups were already structured along class, religious, and racial lines. Since local political and civic leaders handed out most of the assignments, the clubs and church auxiliaries in which working-class women were active were generally ignored.[3]

Volunteer activities divided sharply along traditional gender lines. Asked what sort of assignments they might be interested in, 64 percent of civilian men mentioned air raid, fire control, and similar tasks, compared to 7 percent of the women; on the other hand, 60 percent of the women, and only 6 percent of the men, thought in terms of nursing, sewing, first aid, nutrition, child care, and entertainment of soldiers. In practice, the segregation was not quite so sharp. Thus, 20 percent of New York City's 400,000 air raid wardens were women; usually they staffed the telephone banks. In some states the women's division of the state defense council was so active in starting projects before men got around to them that the men decided they were women's work and probably not important.[4]

The Office of Price Administration established a nationwide volunteer service to help administer prices, rents, and rationing. The paperwork involved in the routine distribution of coupons was largely handled by volunteers, especially schoolteachers. However, decisions on requests for extra rations were made by local boards, which were nine-tenths male. When the OPA issued the "General Max" across-the-board consumer price freeze in April 1942, it set up watchdog panels to ensure that the country's 2 million retailers stayed in line. The generally upper-status Republican volunteer pool was reluctant, at best, to assume the role of snooper. OPA Deputy Administrator John Kenneth Galbraith, an advocate of paid inspectors, publicly declared that "no Gestapo of volunteer housewives" was wanted. The price panels proved ineffective save for help in explaining the complexities of the system to neighborhood grocers and shopkeepers.[5]

The volunteer activities women chose often included a strong private component. Home nursing instruction, first aid, and short courses in nutrition attracted millions of women who readily grasped their utility around the home. Bond purchases were important as tokens of support for the national effort, but even more so as mechanisms to rebuild family savings that had been ravished by a dozen years of depression. Victory gardens were especially popular, even in large cities where vacant lots had to be used. One-fourth of the urban population, and a larger portion of rural folk grew millions of bushels of tomatoes, potatoes, and fruit in 1944, cutting their cash food bill while easing the shortages of rationed goods. New enemies had to be conquered: one housewife reported that "meetings are being held here and there to discuss what to do with the rabbits that threaten the tender greens, the consensus being to eat them." Home canning stretched the garden products over the year; many small towns set up communal canning operations with a share-your-pressure-cooker theme.[6]

Succor for the men and women in uniform was the major responsibility of the United Services Organization (USO) and the Red Cross. The USO, created in 1941 by the major religious welfare groups, relied largely upon women volunteers to staff recreational centers serving bases, large cities, and transportation points. The USO clubs near bases also served as informal meeting places for service wives. USO affiliates recruited young women, after careful screening, to serve as hostesses and dance partners. (They did not have to be young, one soldier noted. "Anyone six to sixty-six" would be fine.) In Indianapolis, regiments of Cadettes and Liberty Belles were organized by women's clubs. A Cadette had to be single, college educated, able to submit excellent references, and prepared to complete a "preinduction training course." She had to dress according to regulation (no sweaters, saddle shoes, or bobby sox); after a trial period she received her pin and spent at least eight hours "on duty" each month. Two regiments of 345 black Indianapolis Cadettes contributed 50,000 hours of duty in the segregated USO posts. In Boston, the Coordinating Council of Colored Organizations for National Defense protested at the policy of a USO club that allowed black hostesses only if they refused to dance with white servicemen.[7]

The American National Red Cross, although superficially similar to the USO, took a much different approach to volunteers. Before World War I, Mabel Thorp Boardman had seized control from Clara Barton and created an upper-class, paternalistic organization with a strong link to high society. In 1916, a committee of men displaced Boardman and rebuilt the Red Cross as an elite corps of professional social workers. Miss Boardman's volunteers were allowed to maintain high visibility at the local level—though without any power—because the Red Cross depended upon them to raise funds and to defuse any criticism. During World War II, the Red Cross expanded rapidly along the lines of the self-image it maintained: a quasi-governmental agency prepared to handle the emergency welfare needs of the nation. The problem was what to do with the hundreds of thousands of women who volunteered to help. The professional staff distrusted them and felt they were not needed. Yet the links to the upper strata in every community in the land had to be maintained.

The compromise was a series of programs peripheral to the main business of the Red Cross that would absorb over one and a half billion volunteer hours and keep the funds flowing. First aid, water safety, home nursing, nutrition classes, canteen services, accident prevention, and the Junior Red Cross kept millions of volunteers active at a cost of only a third of the $190 million annual budget. The most socially useful program, set up by Mrs. Walter Lippmann, involved training clubwomen to serve without pay as nurse's aides in civilian hospitals. The most spectacular waste of volunteer time was the Production Corps, which attracted 4 or 5 million women. Their job was to hand-knit millions of garments for soldiers and to roll billions of surgical dressings. The Red Cross vehemently denied that machines could do the job—arguing first that not enough factories could make dressings, then that the Army had specifically asked for their help, and finally that, though the machinery existed, a labor shortage prevented its utilization.[8]

The voluntary participation of black women was low throughout the war. The OPA made a deliberate effort to attract blacks, with scant success; fifty-nine out of every sixty local boards were lily white, and fewer than one-fourth of 1 percent of the agency's half million volunteers were black. The largest organizations of black women, the Baptist and Methodist church auxiliaries, concentrated on religious matters such as missionary work, although their male ministers were often deeply involved in political affairs. Among the black middle class, the Alpha Kappa Alpha sorority was the most active, combining war service with demands for racial equality in its Double V campaign for victory abroad (over Nazism) and at home (over racism). The National Council of Negro Women, a coalition of a hundred organizations led by civil rights activist and educator Mary McLeod Bethune, stressed racial solidarity, voter registration, and a "hold your job" appeal to women who had broken through racial barriers. The Illinois Association of Colored Women focused on defeating job restrictions and racial covenants in housing, in addition to the more usual USO activities.[9]

The thoroughgoing segregation in American society, together with the peripheral status of blacks, their small middle class, and the active racism of enough whites to veto their participation, strengthened the call of black leaders for the Double V campaign. For the most part, high-status whites who controlled volunteer activities ignored the black community entirely. A noted exception was the American Women's Voluntary Services, founded in January 1940. Not only did the headquarters in New York integrate, but many individual units included a "variety of racial and nationality groups" as well. More typical, however, was the Red Cross announcement of a policy of segregating blood from black donors, which brought the quasi-official extension of segregation to a new and highly emotional program. The Red Cross could shrug off the complaints of blacks and even their widespread boycott of both the blood drive and community programs because it did not depend financially upon poor minorities. However, to validate its primary mission of serving all American service personnel, the Red Cross had to provide services for black troops. Furthermore, the White House was watching closely. Eleanor Roosevelt, the most visible Red Cross volunteer, vigorously opposed racial discrimination. The President appointed his closest aide, Harry Hopkins, to the national board and his former law partner to head the entire agency.

A high-level board meeting held in 1942 with two dozen prominent blacks included leaders of the National Council of Negro Women, Alpha Kappa Alpha, and the National Association of Negro Nurses. The meeting helped reduce tensions somewhat. Although the Red Cross refused to change its blood policy, it did accede to demands that blacks be hired to run facilities for black soldiers, that blacks be appointed to national and local staffs and steering committees, and that more vigorous efforts be made to recruit black nurses. The Red Cross sought out social workers, YMCA leaders, and alumnae of black colleges to meet the needs of overseas black troops. By the end of the war, 6 percent of the overseas staff was black (compared to 8 percent of the soldiers). However, only at remote Fort Huachuca, Arizona, and Tuskegee Army Air Base Station Hospital did the Red Cross open black-staffed centers in the states. A mere handful of local boards added blacks, and except for maids and janitors, only a few dozen of the 40,000 paid staff in the states were black.

Apart from first aid and water safety, few Red Cross volunteer programs anywhere served the black community.[10]

In terms of net contribution to the war effort, volunteer activities may have been negative. They absorbed energies that would have been more effective in the production of war materials. Volunteerism was an obsolete policy in a professionalized, industrialized warfare state, as the British and Soviets fully realized. However, by concentrating their work on projects of obvious direct benefit to servicemen and their own families, American women found an outlet for patriotism that strengthened their private domain, even if it had little impact on the winning of the war.

The real contributions of volunteer work to the patriotic cause were to raise participants' morale, to demonstrate that the rich were doing their share, and to heighten the sense of awareness throughout the community that the nation was involved in a total war. The British and Soviets hardly needed to remind their people that the conflict was a matter of survival. By contrast, for most Americans the fighting was distant, the dangers remote. Propaganda campaigns alone had little effect, but by tying the war to the local and the personal with air raid wardens, first aid classes, USO clubs, and, yes, bandage-rolling sessions, the volunteers encouraged factory workers to be speedier at the machines, soldiers to be more resolute, and administrators to be more ingenious. The public opinion polls, which Roosevelt and the political elite followed so closely, were thermometers for morale; the volunteer effort itself was the furnace.

The importance of psychology was reflected in the government's fear of rumors. Posters everywhere warned that spies were lurking behind every wall—careless talk would kill an American boy. "Wanted For Murder!" was the dramatic caption of a stark poster showing an innocent-looking woman who had spoken one word too many. Not only was the news heavily censored, the military also meticulously scissored away at correspondence from soldiers and sailors abroad. There were no enemy spies, as the government well knew; even after the entire German and Japanese fleets had been sunk, the censorship continued. The purpose of the propaganda and the censorship was to clamp as tight a lid as possible on rumors that might lead to discouragement, frustration, strikes, or anything that would cut back military production. Active middle-class clubwomen, being curious

and gregarious, were the prime carriers of rumors. Their full participation in volunteer work helped to neutralize negativism and to
build up instead an image of a united, energetic nation fully committed to winning the war.[11]

The American strategy for defeating Germany and Japan depended upon maximum output of war material and food, with just
enough civilian goods available to maintain homefront morale. The
secret weapon was womanpower. Between 1940 and 1944, the number of employed women leaped from 12.0 million to 18.2 million,
then fell back to 15.8 million in 1947. These women were especially
important in the durable manufacturing sector, where few traditionally had been employed. In steel, machinery, shipbuilding, aircraft,
and auto factories, 1.7 million women were at work in 1944, in
stunning contrast to a mere 230,000 five years before. In 1947, after
the emergency, those industries had jobs for only 580,000 women.[12]

The enormous publicity attending Rosie the Riveter prompted
questions at the time about the long-term implications of new job
roles for women. Would they quit after the war? Would they squeeze
out more "deserving" male breadwinners? Would family life be adversely affected? Historians casting about for the roots of the feminist
movement in the 1970s likewise pondered the phenomenon. Did it
set a "time bomb" of rising expectations that would later explode?
Did the war emergency temporarily lower barriers to women's self-
realization, only to have them raised again after the war? Our concern is with the women workers themselves, who they were, why
they took jobs, why they quit, what their war and postwar labor
force participation revealed about their values.

One misconception must be cleared away immediately. Very few
of the women were strangers to paid employment. Even during the
dark depression years, nearly all women leaving school searched for,
and eventually obtained, a job. Of urban women born in 1915, 91
percent had entered the work force by 1938 (compared to 96 percent
of the men). Some farm youth may not have had paychecks to show
for their work on the family farm, but they too knew what it was to
labor. Paid employment before marriage had long been the norm in
America, though nearly all working women quit their jobs when they
married. Thus, as the war boom began, there were millions of

housewives who at one time, usually between school and marriage, had some paid labor force experience. Millions of other women attending high school or college or currently unemployed were also potential recruits for the wartime labor force.[13]

When the civilian economy had to expand from 48 million employees in 1940 to 54 million in 1944, the government viewed all of these women as possible war workers. At the same time, 12 million men joined the armed forces, so an additional 18 million people had to be recruited to the labor force. Nearly 8 million came from the ranks of the unemployed, the remainder from population growth, those leaving school, and women and older men not in the labor force in 1940. The increase among working women twenty-five to sixty-four years old between 1940 and 1945 was 4.0 million, of which 1.3 million was attributable to population growth and 2.7 million represented "new" workers.[14]

Redistributing priorities as Americans prepared for war proved as problematic and taxing as the numerical increase in employment which took place in the early 1940s. Durable goods manufacturing more than doubled its employment, from 4.2 million in 1940 to 8.7 million in 1944, led by the expansion of aircraft and shipbuilding employment from 275,000 in 1940 to 2.5 million in 1943. Ordinance industries employed from ten to forty times as many workers in 1943 as 1939. The only major white-collar sector to expand notably was federal civilian employment, which rose from 1.0 million in 1940 to a peak of 3.8 million in the summer of 1945.[15]

National attention focused on Rosie the Riveter, on the women employed in the vital munitions, aircraft, shipbuilding, and related industries that supplied the Allied armies. In March 1944, 2,690,000 women were thus employed, chiefly as unskilled or semiskilled factory workers. One in six women workers in 1944 was in the war sector, compared to only 4 percent of the smaller war industry in 1940. One-fourth of the 1944 munitions workers had been employed in the war sector in 1941, 8 percent came from civilian goods factories, 18 percent came from other jobs in trade, domestic service, personal service, and clerical trades, while 49 percent had been outside the labor force, chiefly as housewives (31 percent) or students (16 percent). Indeed, Rosie and her sisters represented a wide range and complex set of origins.[16]

Rosie's glamour should not distract us from a complete view of the jobs women held during the war, however. In 1940, 26 percent of all workers were women, including 36 percent of white-collar employees and 26 percent of blue-collar workers. By 1945, women comprised 36 percent of civilian workers, a 10 percent gain. The greatest increases came in sales, clerical, factory operative, and farm jobs (see table 1; all tables are at the back of the book).[17]

The war boom had a radical impact on white household workers. Traditionally, it had been one of the major employment opportunities for women, accounting for 27 percent of all jobs in 1910 and about 20 percent in the 1920s and 1930s. In Chicago in 1941–1942, most white domestics received free room and board, plus $8 or $10 in cash every week. The arrangement was particularly attractive to singles and separated women, who otherwise would not have had a home, but the work was dreary and long, the loneliness severe, and the lack of retirement benefits a risk.[18]

The million white domestics declined sharply to only 670,000 during the war, as the lure of a good paycheck, social security benefits, and a more formal relationship with employers proved strong. Nine out of ten continued into postwar jobs, and very few were willing to return to housework. Rich families still had help, but by 1950 nine out of ten household workers lived out and had broken at least partially from the suffocating intimacy of the past.[19]

The war boom allowed black women to improve their status, though only small gains were scored in the battle against racial discrimination. Traditionally, black women had much higher labor force participation rates than whites, primarily because black wives and mothers had to work to keep their families going. However, four out of five were confined to very low-wage jobs as laborers in the cotton fields or in the kitchens of the southern white middle class (see table 2). These jobs were exempt from minimum wage, social security, or protective legislation.

On the eve of the war, 10 to 15 percent of workers on federal relief programs such as the Works Progress Administration (WPA), Civilian Conservation Corps (CCC), and National Youth Administration (NYA) were black—numbers equivalent to their proportion of the population but far below their need. In the WPA, few women were hired to begin with (five of six were men), and black women faced special barriers. The WPA sewing project, for example, was 93 percent white. State and local relief was especially vital in the cities, particularly northern and border cities where a majority of the black families were on relief in the late 1930s. In the rural South, where relief programs were grossly inadequate to begin with, only the most severely deprived black families were allowed access. The termination of cutback of welfare programs during the war affected urban blacks most; fortunately, the war boom opened jobs in the cities. In the rural South, the solution was mass exodus. The proportion of blacks on farms plunged from 39 percent in 1930 and 35 percent in 1940 to 21 percent in 1950 and a mere 2 percent in 1970.[20]

The employment profile of black women during the 1940s shows large gains in service work outside homes (such as cleaning, serving, and cooking in hotels and restaurants) and in factory work. The all-white policies of the southern textile and tobacco factories that employed large numbers of white women would not be broken until the 1960s. Instead, black women took hard, dirty jobs in commercial laundries and foundries and also in munitions plants operating under federal contracts and apparel factories in states with good fair employment laws like New York. The few black women who secured supervisory or crafts jobs were downgraded at the end of the war.[21]

The gains made in clerical jobs were mostly in the federal government. While the Post Office, Treasury, Justice, and other old-line departments remained 98 percent white, the War and Navy departments and the new emergency agencies welcomed blacks. In 1938, 90,000 (or 10 percent) of federal employees were black, of whom only 10 percent held white-collar jobs. By 1944, 274,000 blacks held federal jobs, of which 60 percent were clerical or administrative. In social work the numbers of black women reached majority levels in Cook County (Chicago); in other large welfare offices a similar pattern emerged. Throughout the South, school boards, anxious to maintain segregated schools in the face of growing legal challenges, yielded to legal pressure from the NAACP by dramatically increasing the pay of black schoolteachers, hoping to reach parity before the Supreme Court challenged their separate-but-equal fiction. The average salaries of black teachers jumped from 51 to 85 percent of the white scale in the rural South between 1940 and 1949, and from 60 percent to 93 percent in the urban South.[22]

In the private sector, the barrier against black women in clerical or sales jobs proved nearly unbreachable. The Urban League tried to place a few carefully selected women in highly visible jobs as department store clerks and telephone operators. The Bell companies in St. Louis, Newark, and New York hired their first black operators in 1944. In 1946, the Urban League counted fifty black saleswomen in New York and Boston department stores, and about the same number of clerks. Nationwide, 0.9 percent of the women employees of general merchandise stores were black in 1940, 2.7 percent in 1950, and 4.0 percent in 1960. In retail food stores, the corresponding proportions were 2.2 percent, 4.0 percent, and 3.8 percent, and in drug stores, 2.1 percent, 4.6 percent, and 4.5 percent. Not until the 1970s would black women achieve more than token representation in private sector white-collar jobs.[23]

The number of black domestics actually increased slightly during the war, as they recovered some of the positions abandoned by whites. In war boom centers like Washington, D.C., they could earn double what maids were paid before the war. Some did move into war jobs. One Atlanta woman had made $460 a year before the war as a family maid. She was paid $1,820 as a drill press operator in 1943, and $2,477 in 1944. Her neighbor, a maid who was paid $312 a year, became an anodyzer at an airplane factory and earned $1,664 in 1943. The arrival of military allotment checks allowed many part-time maids to quit work. Those who continued working with private families in Atlanta earned 25 percent more in 1944 than before the war—not enough to cover inflation, however. Black maids and cooks in commercial establishments, laundry employees, and clerks saw pay increases of 50 to 55 percent. The pay for those working in factories doubled.[24]

The wide gap between employment opportunities for black and white women reflected numerous factors—the concentration of most blacks in the rural South, their restricted educational opportunities, the hostility of white women who did not want to work alongside them, and, above all, the nearly universal white consensus that strict segregation was necessary and inevitable.

The employment opportunity differences between white women and white men were also large, but the only parallel to the racial case was the slightly less universal consensus that sex segregation in the job market should be complete. The geographical locations of white men and women, of course, were nearly the same, and women had a slight edge in educational achievement. There were two important behavioral differences that were reflected in the work patterns of men and women: first, women constantly and voluntarily fluctuated in and out of the labor market, whereas men remained once they entered. Second, a man continued to rise to better jobs and higher wage rates, whereas a woman's first job was often her highest in terms of money and advancement. How much these behavior patterns caused sex segregation in jobs and how much they were caused by the segregation is difficult to tell.

If definitions of broad occupational groupings showing proportions that were women are made much finer (for example, "stenographer" instead of just "clerical," or "police officer" instead of "other service" in table 1), the degree of segregation would appear much higher than is apparent in the broader categories.[25] There simply were few jobs in 1940 anywhere in society in which men and women competed on reasonably equal terms. Instead, jobs were implicitly classified either as "men's" or "women's" work. During the war women increased their share of jobs in many areas, especially in the clerical, sales, and factory operative categories, but, except in the sales field, the wartime gains were quickly offset by 1947. Despite all the attention Rosie received, she rarely became a foreman, craftsman, or skilled factory worker. In any case, she could not hold her gains.

The wartime increase in employment was the result of complex flows into and out of the labor force. The flow patterns can be simplified by taking two snapshots of all women born before 1930, the first showing what they were doing in late 1941, the second showing what the same individuals were doing in March 1944 (see figures 3 and 4 and table 3). The Census Bureau did not follow individuals over time, but in a special survey in March 1944, it did ask women to recall their status at the time of Pearl Harbor. The largest group of women, 30 million strong, were at home in 1941 with no paid employment; most were housewives. How did they respond to the wartime situation? Seven out of eight were still at home in 1944. The other 3.7 million were working, usually in a blue-collar factory or service job (see figure 5 and table 4).

At the time of Pearl Harbor nearly 6 million women were in white-

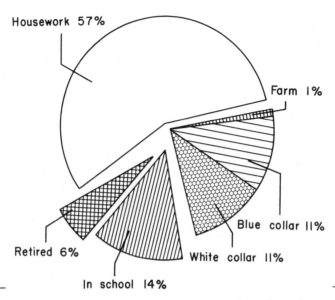

Housework 57%

Farm 1%

Blue collar 11%

Retired 6%

White collar 11%

In school 14%

Figure 3. Occupational status of women at Pearl Harbor. Source: Mary Elizabeth Pidgeon, Changes in Women's Employment During the War, Women's Bureau Special Bulletin 20 (Washington, D.C., 1944), passim.

collar jobs. A million of them had become full-time homemakers by 1944, for the most part as newlyweds trying to begin a family. More than three-fourths (78 percent) were still in white-collar work, though many had changed employers or titles. Relatively few (about 206,000, or 3.5 percent) accepted blue-collar employment. In sharp contrast, men were much more likely to cross class lines. Salesmen of durable goods that were no longer produced, like automobiles and appliances, were forced to shift. One-fourth of the 2 million men in sales or clerical jobs at the time of Pearl Harbor had shifted to factory jobs by 1944, many with the awareness that work in a "critical industry" provided both good pay and good protection from the draft.[26]

Another 6 million women were doing blue-collar work in 1941. Their behavior resembled that of their white-collar sisters. A million had become homemakers by 1944, while three-fourths (74 percent) were still in factory or service jobs. Many had parlayed their experience into high-paying munitions jobs. Relatively few (266,000, or 4.5 percent) had taken clerical or sales positions. College and high

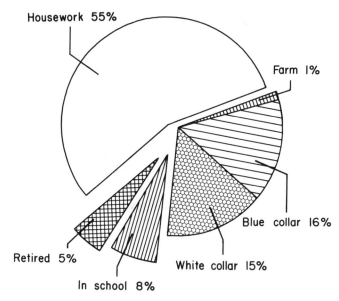

Housework 55%

Farm 1%

Blue collar 16%

White collar 15%

In school 8%

Retired 5%

Figure 4. Occupational status of women in 1944. Source: Mary Elizabeth Pidgeon, Changes in Women's Employment During the War, *Women's Bureau Special Bulletin 20 (Washington, D.C., 1944), passim.*

school claimed 4.5 million in 1941. By 1944 half of this group had taken jobs, usually in clerical or sales work; one in nine was a full-time housewife.

Another way of looking at the movements is to ask 1944 housewives and workers what they had been doing at the time of Pearl Harbor. Of the 36 million women at home or school in 1944, some 7 percent had been at work in 1941, and even more had worked off and on during the interval. On the other hand, the 14 million women employed in March 1944 were a heterogeneous group (see table 5). Ten million had been at work in 1941 (some of whom had dropped out for a while but then returned); 2 million had been in school in 1941. They were normal entrants into the labor force, though some had dropped out of school sooner than planned to take jobs. Another 4 million were homemakers in 1941. These women may have been employed sometime in the past, but they needed retraining and readjustment to handle their new jobs. Their employers had to readjust as well, for such a large proportion of newly hired persons meant

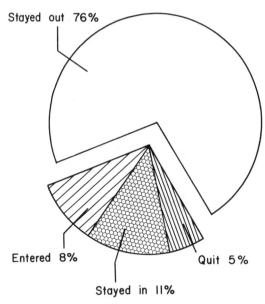

Figure 5. Labor force movement of wives with husbands present, 1941–1944. Source: Mary Elizabeth Pidgeon, Changes in Women's Employment During the War, *Women's Bureau Special Bulletin 20 (Washington, D.C., 1944), p. 29.*

that cadres of older, experienced women workers were often too small to provide the necessary on-the-job training.

Some 2 million women employed in December 1941 had returned to their homes by 1944, thereby canceling most of the impact made by the 3.7 million homemakers who moved the opposite way (see table 3). This large reverse flow hints at the cross-currents that affected individual choices between homemaking and paid employment.

These labor force participation rates include both married and single women. While most single women already worked, the war did accelerate the trend toward working wives. In 1940, only 15 percent of wives whose husbands were present were in the labor force, compared to 19 percent during the war, and a postwar average of 22 percent. Thus we can conclude that the war experience produced a 7-point upward shift in the labor force participation of wives—an increase of 2 million individuals.

The overwhelming majority of wives did not, at any one time, hold full-time jobs. Of the 28,510,000 wives whose husbands were at home in 1944, 76 percent were homemakers both then and at Pearl Harbor. (If these women held jobs they popped into and out of the labor force so erratically that they defied any recording system.) Eleven percent of the wives were working at both dates, 5 percent had quit, and 8 percent had entered the labor force. How these patterns compared with peacetime is problematical—probably a few more entered, a few more stayed, and fewer quit, but the difference could not have been very large.

Wives of servicemen were much more mobile than other women (see figure 6). Only a minority (43 percent) were outside the labor force both at Pearl Harbor and in 1944. One in four were employed at both times, and one in five entered the labor force. About one in ten quit their jobs in the interval to return home. In terms of employment, the condition of service wives may be compared to wives whose husbands were absent in 1940 and after the war; in each case, half of the wives were in the labor force. In March 1944, 51 percent

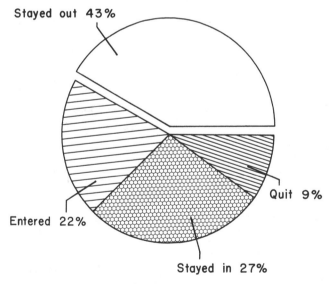

Figure 6. Labor force movement of service wives, 1941–1944. Source: Mary Elizabeth Pidgeon, Changes in Women's Employment During the War, *Women's Bureau Special Bulletin 20 (Washington, D.C., 1944), p. 29.*

of the soldiers' wives were employed—probably one-fourth as year-round workers, with one-half moving into and out of the labor market. Their employment rates would have been even higher, but many were living near their husbands at remote military posts that had very few civilian jobs (see table 6).[27]

The shift in the labor force participation rates was least for mothers of children under six (a rise from 9 percent to 12 percent), and greatest for older wives without children to care for (31 percent postwar; 1940 and wartime data unavailable.) When mothers left the house for paid employment, many American commentators raised an alarm; they feared that it would destroy the nuclear family or, at least, trigger a rise in juvenile delinquency. At any one time during the war, however, nine out of ten mothers with children under six were *not* in the labor force. By contrast, in 1981, 50 percent of all women with children under six participated.

Relatively few mothers took jobs; but turn the question around, how many working women had children to care for? A Woman's Bureau Survey of major defense centers toward the close of the war showed that 20 percent of all working women, or 32 percent of women who were not single, had children under fourteen. The 1940 census indicated that 21 percent of nonsingle working women had children under eighteen, and this rose to 31 percent in 1948. The government's program of encouraging day-care centers was ostensibly focused on the needs of these working women with children. Actually, the motivation of Washington was to lure mothers who were not employed—the vast majority—into taking war jobs on the promise their children would be well cared for.[28]

The number of women employed at any one time, and their labor force participation rates, are averages that obscure two of the major characteristics of women workers—fractionality and discontinuity. A large proportion of women worked part time (fewer than thirty-five hours per week), especially those in retail stores, restaurants, and domestic service. In addition, women, especially wives and mothers, moved into and out of the labor force on a month-by-month basis. Thus, between August and September 1944, 1.5 million homemakers took jobs, while another 1.0 million women quit jobs for full-time housework. Consequently, the number of women employed at some time during the year was 30 to 40 percent higher than the average number employed. Finally, even full-time, year-round work-ing women often quit the labor force for years at a time, again chiefly to become full-time homemakers. Thus, of the 1.4 million women who first opened social security accounts in 1938, only 14 percent worked every year through 1948. Another 29 percent worked con-tinuously for two to ten years then quit; the remaining 57 percent worked intermittent patterns of varying lengths. As a result, women averaged a short stay on jobs, and comparatively few built long-term careers.[29]

The high turnover of women workers also meant that the number of women with work experience at any one time was significantly higher than those currently employed. Thus, 48 percent of all women worked at one time or another in 1944, including 53 percent of urban women, even though the average in any one week was 37 percent. By the end of 1942, two-thirds of all women aged twenty to twenty-nine had accumulated social security credits—that is, they had worked for a while since 1937. Even this underestimates the true labor force experience, since women in teaching, domestic service, government, and farming were not covered by social security. Among women aged fifteen to thirty-four in 1940, 85 percent worked at one time or another before 1960 and 56 percent had social security work expe-rience by the end of 1942, before large-scale war employment of women began.[30]

We can conclude that while the war certainly caused an increase in the average number of women employed, it did not mark a drastic break with traditional working patterns or sex roles. Wives continued to switch into and out of paid employment, only going into the job market a little more often than before the war. There was no evidence of increased careerism and no indication that women's primary in-terest in home affairs was lessened. An analogy with college students is apt: they fluctuate in and out of the job market, usually on a part-time basis, without lessening their primary collegiate interests. If jobs become more accessible or especially well paying, or if their campus activities become less interesting, their labor force partici-pation may increase. But in no sense can the number of student workers be used as an index of their devotion to (or liberation from) college life. Historians who use women's labor force participation rates as an index of their liberation are likely to discover, as did

William Chafe, "a strange paradox." "Women's [job] sphere had been significantly expanded," he wrote, "but most Americans continued to subscribe to the belief that women were (and should remain) primarily homemakers."[31]

Soaring marriage and birth rates also reflected women's preferences for homemaker and motherly roles. The rate of marriages per 1,000 single women had averaged 69 in the 1930s (down from 81 in the 1920s). For the entire 1940s decade, rates jumped to 92. In part, the phenomenon represented marriages long delayed by the depression. By the end of the 1940s, however, proportionately more women were married than at any other time in the century. In 1940, 48 percent of all women fourteen to thirty-four years old were married, rising sharply to 59 percent in 1946 and 62 percent in 1950. The proportion of women aged twenty to twenty-four who were single fell from 47 percent in 1940 to 39 percent in 1946 and 32 percent in 1950. The median age at marriage, which had eased down from 21.9 years in 1900 to 21.5 in 1940, dropped sharply to 20.3 in the immediate postwar era.[32]

Family responsibility, therefore, was the major reason most women did not work. The housework requirements of food preparation, cleaning, and personal care of family members was culturally defined—by the women themselves—as the responsibility of women. Husbands, furthermore, pressured wives not to work. Wealthy women who could afford to hire servants for some or even all household duties rarely took jobs. They found outlets for their energy in social and cultural affairs and in volunteer work. If household duties were lessened because of the presence of other women (mothers, grown daughters, in-laws and so on), or because of the absence of children or husbands, women were more available for outside jobs, but they still were reluctant to take them.

The market demand for their labor was the other side of the coin. In rural areas, paying jobs were scarce and often hard to reach (very few women drove automobiles). Throughout the depression years, jobs of any sort were not easy to obtain. The chief cause of the upsurge in women's employment during the war was, of course, the shortage of men. Even so, wages for women had to rise rapidly to attract enough to take jobs. But long-term forces were also at work.

The increasing complexity of the economy steadily enlarged the number of white-collar clerical and sales jobs, and the rapidly growing number of women with a high school education provided a labor pool ideally suited for this work.[33]

Careerism, patriotism, or a sense of adventure rarely were cited by women in factory or service jobs, though most did enjoy the work. When they worked it was because their family needed the cash—the husband might be unemployed, ill, retired, or absent, or the savings depleted by the depression, or the needs of dependents especially great in a society where welfare services were still imperfect.[34]

Business and professional women, while relegated to the lower tiers of employment opportunities, also cited the need for money to support dependents. Volunteer service—or perhaps joining the military—absorbed most of the patriotic impulses of middle-class women. Careerism was a factor, but traditionally it had involved foregoing either marriage or children. The reason the combination of marriage plus a career grew more attractive during the 1940s was that adventurous young, well-educated women who wanted a career more and more insisted on being married. Of the college alumnae over fifty in 1947, 35 percent had never married; of those in their thirties, only 22 percent were still single. Of all the alumnae, 42 percent were housewives in 1947, 19 percent were working wives, 31 percent were single career women (the remainder were graduate students, unemployed, or retired). The younger women were especially eager to combine marriage with a career, usually with an interlude for rearing children.[35]

To some women the private sphere was unattractive and they sought jobs as an escape. Those who took jobs to avoid the boredom of housework soon discovered that they still had to do the cooking and cleaning and that the most readily available paid jobs could be just as boring and tiring. Some, about 4 or 5 percent of the mothers, worked to escape their children. They were the primary clients of day-care centers and foster home programs. Other working women were establishing their independence from their husbands, often as a prelude to divorce or separation. Taking psychological refuge in a job was hardly unknown to men of course, but no one ever asked a man to explain why it was that he wanted to work. Whatever their reasons for re-entering the paid labor force, women enjoyed the new experience and their new workmates. Asked point blank, four out of five war workers liked their jobs, including 84 percent of those without children and 70 percent of those with children.[36]

Why then did millions of women quit jobs during and after wartime to return to the home? An eagerness to become mothers was the main reason, but not the only one. Were women forced out of the labor market at the end of the war? Yes and no. In heavy industry, many women were pushed out. However, the number of women employed in light manufacturing, services, and the white-collar sector did not decline. To move from overall labor market forces to the specific motivations of individuals requires direct testimony. In 1951 the Census Bureau asked a sample of the 4,244,000 women who worked during the war but not afterwards what their chief reason was for quitting. Half (2,130,000) pointed to family responsibilities, notably, for 1,388,000, babies born during or shortly after the war. One in eight (569,000) cited age, illness, or disability. Lack of a suitable job pushed back one woman in twenty (238,000). Return to school or a move to a rural area were the explanations for 11 percent of the women (479,000). Only 2 percent (85,000) cited poor working conditions or lack of day-care facilities. One woman in six (743,000) said her husband objected to her work. In addition, another 418,000 women worked during the war and shortly after but had quit by 1951 because of their husbands' objections. Thus, of all the women who worked at some time during the war (an unknown number but probably at least 20 million), 1,161,000, or about 5 percent, quit because of their husbands' opposition. The husbands' wishes played a larger role than these figures would suggest, for in 1944, 71 percent of married war workers said their husbands wanted them to quit at the war's end.[37]

The structure of the consensus that wives should not work when their husbands could support them can be explored through an October 1945 Roper poll of a cross-section of the nation's adults. Sixty percent of the people argued against women working, and a mere 24 percent favored it, with the rest qualified or unsure. The net negative response was, therefore, -36 points. Only one group was favorable—blacks at a slim $+5$. The degree of opposition varied, however. Those relatively more favorable were the college-educated

(− 17), professionals and managers (− 19), employed women (− 21), southerners (− 23), singles (− 25), the rich (− 26), the young (− 30), and women (− 32). The strongest opposition came from residents of the Plains states (− 48), poor whites (− 46), middle-income whites (− 44), people with some high school but no college experience (− 43), the unemployed (− 43), the old (− 41), and men (− 41). Thus, support for the new role of working wife came from the younger, better-educated, more affluent Americans for whom individualistic talent and achievement were more salient than traditional roles, plus the women who actually worked and, especially, the racial minority that had long known the necessity of wives working.[38]

The social consensus thus held that women's family roles ought to be more important than their work roles. But what did the women who had to make the choice think? To probe into the feelings of women who left jobs to become mothers, in-depth interviews must be studied, not just nationwide statistics. In 1951-1952, a team of psychologists interviewed 379 women who represented a cross-section of all women in the Boston area who became mothers in 1946. When they discovered they were pregnant, 68 percent of the women were unequivocally pleased, 24 percent had mixed feelings, 7 percent were displeased. Negative feelings were rare among first-time mothers; the displeasure usually involved a second or third child who was not planned so soon. Working women were *more* pleased than those who were not working. Asked how they felt about giving up their outside jobs, 8 percent said it had been a reluctant sacrifice; 16 percent left with mixed feelings—they were glad to have a family but had enjoyed their work; 41 percent said it was no sacrifice at all, for they did not particularly like their job; 35 percent said it was the opposite of sacrifice, for they were eager to give up outside work and start raising a family. Well-educated women who were more involved in their work were also more eager to become mothers. They had enjoyed interesting jobs before and now welcomed the new challenges of motherhood. Less-educated working-class women's attitudes toward work were unrelated to their acceptance of pregnancy; work was one thing, motherhood another, and they did not see a connection. In all, the women were nearly unanimous in feeling that motherhood, not paid employment, was their primary career. Only 6 percent were dissatisfied with their life, 8 percent had mixed feelings, and 86 percent welcomed the mother role, especially that of child nurture. They were less enthusiastic about housework, feeling that they were perfectly justified in turning over cleaning and other chores to hired help if they could afford it. They were not about to give up child care. Furthermore, they distinguished between outside interests, which were desirable and even necessary, and outside employment, which interfered with their true career.[39]

During the depression, economic hardship exacerbated tensions inside many families. In the late 1930s, 85 marriages in 10,000 were broken by divorce each year. The rate would have been higher if there had not been legal obstacles in many states and, especially, a shortage of employment opportunities by which divorced women could support themselves and their children. Many unhappy couples of necessity had to stay together. During the war, many hasty marriages took place, often involving soldiers who soon were separated from brides they hardly knew. However, a soldier could refuse divorce actions, dependency benefits were attractive to women, and the pressure of patriotism undercut demand for divorce. The return of prosperity alleviated much of the financial distress that had troubled families. The number of estranged couples (measured by husbands living alone) dropped. On the other hand, new job opportunities gave women contemplating divorce a much better prospect for supporting themselves, and prosperity also increased the potential for alimony. The product of these countervailing factors was an increase in the divorce rate to an annual average of 114 per 10,000 marriages during 1941–1945.

Nearly all the divorces during the war, and many of them in the late 1940s, involved couples who had married before the war. Hasty service marriages were undone only when the veterans returned. In 1946 and 1947, the annual rate surged to 158 per 10,000. Continued postwar prosperity helped stabilize marriages after 1947, as did the increasing numbers of babies. The divorce rate fell to 104 in the late 1940s, declining to 95 in the early 1950s. Both men and women were quick to remarry, so the number of divorcees in the population never grew large, and the norm of companionate relationships grew even stronger.

In long-range terms, the likelihood that a marriage would terminate in divorce was steadily increasing. One in six couples married in 1915–1919 eventually divorced (see figure 7). One-fourth of the couples married in the late 1930s eventually divorced, and the rate was only slightly higher for marriages that occurred in 1940–1944. A small drop occurred after the war, but the trend continued to increase regularly. One-third of the marriages that took place in the early 1960s will probably end in divorce. Thus, the war period marked no discontinuity, though it did alter the tempo and the immediate causes involved in the breakup of marriages.[40]

War-related divorces typically involved young couples who had not been acquainted very long and who had only a poor opportunity to know each other before the husband was shipped out. Immaturity was a basic factor, often leading to infidelity. In most divorces where adultery was involved, the husband was the guilty party; in war divorces, however, the wife, who had more opportunities, was more often involved in affairs than the husband. Divorce was signaled when the veteran refused to return to his bride. Unlike the many

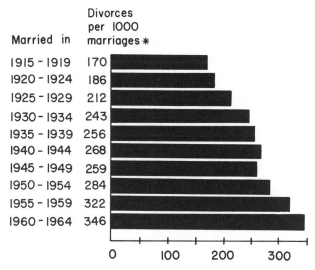

Married in	Divorces per 1000 marriages *	
1915 – 1919	170	
1920 – 1924	186	
1925 – 1929	212	
1930 – 1934	243	
1935 – 1939	256	
1940 – 1944	268	
1945 – 1949	259	
1950 – 1954	284	
1955 – 1959	322	
1960 – 1964	346	

*Probability that a marriage would ever end in divorce.

Figure 7. Lifetime chance of divorce by year of marriage, 1915–1964. Source: Samuel H. Preston and John McDonald, "The Incidence of Divorce Within Cohorts of American Marriages Contracted Since the Civil War." Demography, 16 (1979), 10–11.

divorces that produce bitterness, recrimination, and years of guilt feelings, the war divorces involved shallow relationships and did not seem to have a lasting impact on either party.

Social norms during the era condemned divorces generally, yet family and friends usually approved when a woman sought divorce, especially when heavy drinking, physical abuse, or infidelity had ruined the marriage. But approval had to be weighed against the economic hardships involved. Most divorces involved working-class couples, who had little wealth in the best of times. A wife seldom received property from a divorce settlement, but the courts normally awarded her custody of the children and small child-support payments. However, half the former husbands did not bother to pay what little was due. About half the women took full-time jobs, and most were aided by their families or welfare agencies. Nearly all the women remarried within a few years. Nine out of ten women said that divorce had made their lives happier; almost none thought it had been a mistake.[41]

Widespread wartime family disruption, which most women constantly feared, never materialized (see table 7). To be sure, temporary disruptions occurred when the husband moved to another city to take a war job. Yet this pattern was more than neutralized by the decline in the proportion of husbands who deserted their families. Military service created another, and more serious, disruption. Nearly 16 million Americans served during the war years, and no one knew how many would come back safe and sound. In fact, 27 percent were in combat, 300,000 died (not all in combat), and 500,000 were seriously disabled.[42] What proportions of women had close relatives in the service is not known exactly. The most informative survey that has turned up—hardly a national sample—covered employees at a major defense factory in Chicago. Seven out of eight of the women had a relative in service, usually a cousin or brother. One in six had a husband or fiancé at war[43] (see table 8).

Wives with husbands at war constituted a much smaller proportion of the population than commonly supposed. Hollywood used the theme of separation of lovers countless times for dramatic effect without much regard for statistical accuracy. A census survey in March 1944 showed that 2,580,000 wives had husbands in service, or 8.0 percent of all wives. Younger wives, of course, were more affected; 40 percent of wives under twenty had a husband in service, compared to only 11 percent of wives aged twenty to forty-four and 0.4 percent of older wives.[44] Draft calls continued, however, and increasingly affected husbands and fathers. By war's end, 41 percent of the soldiers were husbands, and 21 percent were fathers. That implies about 5 million service wives at peak, or one wife in seven. (Since there was a turnover in the military, the peak was probably a little under 5 million wives in the summer of 1945.) By war's end, half the soldier-husbands were fathers. Not all the wives had to worry about their husbands being involved in combat. Twenty-nine percent of the husbands stayed in the states during the entire war; as late as D day, half the Army was still stationed at home. The average duration of service was thirty-three months; the average overseas stay was sixteen months before V-J day, plus long additional months during the slow demobilization process. Furthermore, most of the men who served overseas never saw combat. Only one-fourth of the married soldiers, in fact, saw combat; two-thirds of the front-line units were composed of younger, single men. Indeed, of all the soldiers, only 10 percent were both married and saw combat, and only 5 percent were fathers who saw combat.[45]

Regardless of his or her marital status, each soldier always had a mother. Some mothers had died, however, and others had several children at war. We can estimate that about half the women aged forty-five to seventy-five in 1945, or about 8 million women, had sons or daughters in the service. All communities honored their blue star and gold star mothers. One black widow in Albemarle County, Virginia, sent nine sons to war, while eight other families there claimed five or six.[46]

The most important demographic change of the 1940s was a sudden, unexpected increase in fertility, which gave the United States a uniquely high birth rate among modern societies for about twenty years. From 1927 through 1939, the annual number of births varied between 2.1 and 2.3 million, and the birth rate per 1,000 population dropped from 20.5 to 17.9. The turnaround came in 1940, coincidental with economic recovery (and with the draft, which at first exempted men who were *already* fathers; men who first became fathers during the war sometimes received informal exemptions).

By 1943 the number of births climbed to 2.9 million. The departure of several million husbands overseas lowered the total to 2.7 million in 1945. With demobilization the numbers climbed rapidly, reaching 3.6 million in 1950 (a rate of 24 per 1,000), peaking at 4.3 million in 1957 (a rate of 26 per 1,000). Since infant mortality declined steadily, from 6.5 percent of all births in 1930, to 4.7 percent in 1940, 2.9 percent in 1950, and 2.0 percent in 1970, the number of surviving children climbed even faster than the birth rate.[47]

With the increasing number of children per woman (see figure 8), the task of caring for small children reversed its downward slide during the war and by 1960 returned to nineteenth-century levels. An equally dramatic fall in child-care responsibilities began in the 1960s and continues downward today. To the extent that women's roles in society at large were limited by their child-care responsibilities, it is clear that the "baby-boom" era from 1940 to 1960 was strikingly different from previous and later periods. In this regard, World War II and its aftermath marked a sharp discontinuity in history.

During the war, the historic gap between urban and rural fertility narrowed dramatically. Throughout the twentieth century, and prob-

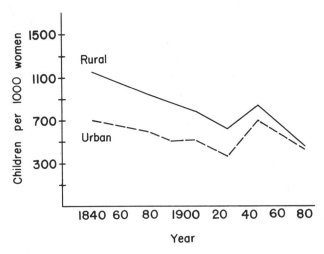

Figure 8. Fertility of rural and urban women, 1840–1980. Source: Bureau of the Census, Historical Statistics of the United States *(Washington, D.C., 1975), p. 15;* Statistical Abstract of the United States, 1980 *(Washington, D.C., 1980), p. 29.* Statistical Abstract, 1946, *p. 27.*

ably all earlier times, urban fertility rates were far below rural and farm rates. In the 1940s a sudden reversal of trends occurred: urban fertility jumped 44 percent (1943–1947 average versus 1930–1940 average), while rural nonfarm rates climbed 23 percent and farm rates inched up by merely 8 percent (see figure 9). Were fecund women moving from farms to cities? Did urban life suddenly acquire new attractions for raising families? Housing and medical opportunities improved faster for farm women than for urban women, as did income. Yet their fertility increased only slightly, while dramatic changes were taking place in the towns, cities, and suburbs.

Money constituted one simple advantage enjoyed by urban dwellers. Although they had less in-kind income (such as homegrown food), and although prices were probably higher in large cities, urban residents had a much wider range of job opportunities, especially for women, and the jobs paid more (see table 9). The lure of bright lights can be glimpsed there, providing an explanation for the cityward migratory flow of the postdepression years. Cities, however, had always been richer than rural areas, in terms of cash income and job opportunities, and the pattern cannot completely explain why

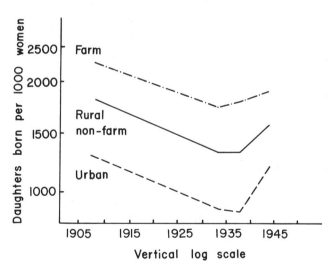

Figure 9. Gross reproduction rates, 1905–1947. Source: Bureau of the Census, Statistical Abstract of the United States, 1949 (Washington, D.C., 1949), p. 25.

urban women suddenly increased their fertility faster than their rural sisters in the 1940s.

Two forces produced the fertility increases in the 1940s: more women married, and wives, especially younger ones, had more babies. This compound effect was most pronounced among the best-educated women (see table 10).Before 1940, the more education a woman had, the fewer children she would bear. College women, in particular, married later and had smaller families. In the 1940s and 1950s, the differential partially closed. Women at all educational levels produced more children, but college women, especially the younger ones, set the records for the largest proportional increases. Once the influence of education is measured, the remaining effects of race, husband's occupation, family income, and urban-rural residence on the birth rate increases proves quite small. Thus, the best-educated women in America led the baby boom, and education served as the dominant factor influencing this tremendous increase. The better-educated women more frequently lived in cities, hence the urban birth rates rose fastest.[48]

The profile of the baby boom differs sharply from the old days of high fertility. In the 1940s women planned their families more and began to limit their size. Birth-control information became widely available, more so after the military began distributing prophylactics to millions of men.[49] Women in the 1940s had first, second, and third children in large numbers, but the rate of fourth births held steady, and the rates for fifth and up declined.[50] Very large families (six or more children) were no longer desired, and the era of unrestricted fertility had ended. However, the ideal size of family increased from two to three children during the 1940s. Fifty percent of women twenty to thirty-four in 1943 considered no more than two children to be ideal; by 1948 the proportion was down to 33 percent, and by 1955 to only 17 percent. Looked at another way, the proportion of young women who considered four or five children to be ideal climbed from 21 percent in 1943 to 30 percent in 1948 and 49 percent in 1955.[51]

Both the pattern of actual births and the reports of ideal family size demonstrate a strong trend toward natalism—that is, motherhood became an even stronger ideal and reality for American women. One interpretation is the economic hypothesis that relates the baby boom to the long-term economic recovery after 1940, in particular the favorable economic opportunities available to young people, including not only higher wages but greater access to home ownership.[52] Home ownership trends did change sharply after 1940. From 1890 to 1940 the proportion of families in owned dwellings held quite steady at about 45 percent. By 1950, the proportion had jumped to 55 percent; it leveled off at 62 percent in 1960. Younger families (head aged twenty-five to thirty-four) increased their ownership rate from 22 percent in 1940 to 35 percent in 1950 and 44 percent in 1960. After a fifteen-year hiatus of little residential construction, the housing industry began to boom in 1945. New houses were easy to obtain on long-term, low-cost mortgages. Furthermore, they were larger, better-built, and in more desirable neighborhoods than previously.[53] Yet the baby boom began in shared houses, rented rooms, Quonset huts, and trailers—that is, during the worst of the housing shortage. Furthermore, the housing situation had never been better in the late 1950s and early 1960s, when fertility began its sharp fall. It seems reasonable to attribute natalism to deep value shifts, with the blossoming of suburbia as an effect, rather than a cause, of those values.

Incomes of young people did improve dramatically during the war years. In 1941, only 60 percent of men aged twenty to twenty-four earned any income; by 1948, the proportion was 91 percent, climbing to 94 percent by 1956. On average, men employed in 1948 made 28 percent more money, after inflation, than those employed in 1941. Since young women also held jobs and earned money, marriage and children proved more feasible financially in 1948 than in 1941. In 1941, most couples said that the cost of children was the main reason they limited their family size. The costs did not decline, but income went up, thereby overcoming a major obstacle.[54] Paradoxically, improving financial opportunities for youth *and* falling fertility both characterized most of the twentieth-century American experience. Furthermore, per capita real spendable income (adjusting for inflation and taxes) rose only slightly between 1944 and 1958, the halcyon years of the baby boom. [55] We can conclude that income changes assisted in the birth of the baby boom but cannot claim paternity.

The soaring marriage and birth rates during the war, accomplished without benefit of propaganda campaigns, strongly suggest that young women wanted more than anything else to be wives and mothers. Indeed, women readily admitted these familial preferences to con-

temporary public opinion pollsters. The disruptions of war, particularly the absence of millions of highly eligible grooms combined
with the unprecedented opportunity to earn and save money for later
marriages, probably kept the number of marriages from going up
even faster. It certainly postponed for millions the day when couples
could set up full-time housekeeping. However, with unprecedented
prosperity, the opportunity for a husband not in the armed forces
to support a family was greater than ever before.[56]

Government manpower experts concerned with staffing the war
factories realized their uphill battle: "Women must be induced to
change their customary life pattern of school, a few years of work,
marriage and children. Some must remain in jobs, others must go
to work." Hence a vast propaganda campaign directed by the government in cooperation with all the media tried to induce women to
change their life-cycle preferences.[57]

The dismal record of recruiting campaigners reflected the constant
failures of mobilization drives. In Akron, Ohio, for example, the
government interviewed 87,000 housewives, of whom 18,700 indicated a general interest in taking a job, yet only 630 women actually
accepted jobs when offered. In Milwaukee, Buffalo, Syracuse, Detroit, and New England mill towns the same pattern prevailed; homemakers could not be talked into changing their plans. It seems likely
that objective conditions such as the absence of men and availability
of high-paying jobs had far more impact than the propaganda. The
personal decisions women made during the war did not reflect the
temporary value changes promoted by the government to serve the
public exigencies of the times.[58]

Public opinion, of both men and women, remained firm on the
point that society would be better off if mothers remained with their
small children. The orientation of American society toward the welfare of children is striking. Juvenile delinquency, though often no
more than boisterous youth loose on the street after curfew, seemed
more of a threat than a shortage of bombers and tanks. A social
worker pointed out that, "Churches are against employment of women
with young children more strongly than ever before because of what
is happening to home life and children." A Catholic priest warned
that, if mothers "neglect their children to go into industry . . . we
may definitely lose any peace that the war can win." A housewife,
noting the concerns with juvenile delinquency in her area, reported

that sentiment there had hardened: "Many people feel actual scorn for a woman who has young children but works." Adolescents, another woman added, "need a woman in the home even more than small children whose needs are mainly physical."[59]

The government's propaganda campaign for women to work came under fire from social commentators and newspaper editors, but most important was the resistance of mothers themselves. A 1943 Roper survey showed that 67 percent of single women aged twenty to thirty-four would consider taking a war job, compared to only 27 percent of married women.[60]

Government officials determined to get more hands in the factories proposed a solution to the dilemma of reluctant mothers: public day-care nurseries established with federal funds. A great deal of delay and confusion ensued, but by 1943 tens of thousands of new nursery schools opened around the country. Despite the projections showing there ought to be a heavy demand, only half the capacity was used, often by mothers who did *not* have jobs. The vast majority of working mothers preferred to leave their children with family, neighbors, or friends. In Fort Wayne, Indiana, in 1943, 11 percent of public school children came from families whose mothers were working, but exactly fourteen of these children (not 14 percent) were enrolled in after-school centers.[61] Of 740,000 women employed in ten major war centers in March 1944, only 1 percent made use of public or private day care.[62] Even with day-care centers or nearby baby-sitters, mothers continued to demonstrate the greatest amounts of resistance to taking war jobs.

Single women and older mothers whose children were grown often did take jobs. The participation rate of women aged thirty-five to sixty-four increased from 25 percent in 1940 to 36 percent in 1945, then slipped slightly to 31 percent in 1947. The median age of women workers climbed faster than the age of all women, from thirty-two years in 1940 to thirty-four in 1945 to thirty-seven in 1950. Thus, more older women wanted to work. The median income of all women in 1945, allowing for inflation, was 38 percent higher than the median earnings of the smaller number of women who worked in 1939.[63]

In 1940, 27.4 percent of all women aged fourteen and above were in the labor force. By 1944, the rate had jumped to 35.0 percent. In 1947, after the postwar reconversion, the rate dropped to 29.8 percent—lower than the wartime peak, but higher than prewar. During the 1950s the rate crept slowly upwards, matching the wartime peak around 1960. The participation rates varied sharply by marital status: single women always were highest, married lowest, with widows and divorcees in between. Between 1940 and 1944, the participation rate of each group increased, but not at the same pace. Between 1944 and 1947, the rates for each group fell (see table 11).

The *change* in the overall rate can be decomposed statistically into three factors: one factor reflecting the rate of married women, one for unmarried, and a third reflecting the changing sizes of the groups (see figure 10). Of the sharp gain between 1940 and 1944, 72 percent can be credited to the changing behavior of wives, 36 percent to the changing behavior of single women, widows, and divorcees, and a *negative* 14 percent to the changes in marital status. That is, most of the increase in women at work was due to wives taking jobs more often than before, about a third was due to unmarried women working more, and the changes in the propensity of these different groups to take jobs was partly (14 percent) offset by the shrinkage in the size of the single group and the growth of the married group (working single women married and quit their jobs). If the shift in marital

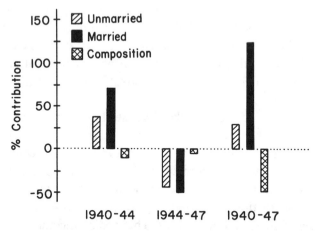

Figure 10. Components of change in labor force participation rates, 1940–1947. Source: Bureau of the Census, Statistical Abstract of the United States, 1949 *(Washington, D.C., 1949), pp. 292–293, 296; Richard Jensen, "Crunching Numbers by Hand: Statistical Programs for the Texas Instruments 55 Pocket Calculator,"* Newberry Papers in Family and Community History, *Chicago, 1981, p. 21.10.*

status had not taken place during the war, there would have been an additional quarter million women at work in 1944.

Between 1944 and 1947, the shrinkage in labor force participation affected both marital groups. Many single women went back to school; many wives went back to homemaking. The proportion single continued to drop and the proportion married rose. Just as in 1940–1944, this shift involved working single women who married and quit their jobs. This time, however, the compositional effect moved with the overall trend, not against it, and caused 13 percent of the drop in labor force participation. If the 1944–1947 shift toward marriage had not happened, an additional hundred thousand women would have been in the labor force in 1947.

Looking at shifts over the entire seven-year period, the components take on remarkable values. The overall change in participation was a modest 2.4 points—from 27.4 percent in 1940 to 29.8 percent in 1947. The rising participation of single women accounted for a third (32 percent) of the 2.4 point shift, and that of widows and divorcees for a seventh (14 percent). However, the rise in the rate of the large group of wives from 16.7 percent in 1940 to 21.4 percent in 1947 accounted for 121 percent of the 2.4 point shift. The compositional factor offset two-thirds (68 percent) of upward effects generated by each marital group. If the 1940–1947 shift toward marriage had not occurred, an additional million women would have been at work in 1947. On the other hand, if married women had not found work more in 1947 than in 1940, 1.3 million fewer women would have been at work in the latter year.

Counterfactual hypotheses aside, the two most important forces at work throughout the period were the changing behavior of wives and the countervailing process of the marriage and baby boom. Women were going two ways at once: more wanted jobs, and more wanted marriage and children. How to balance these conflicting demands was a problem faced by millions of women—a problem compounded by changes in the workplace, in pay scales, in internal family relationships, and in the values of the American people.

In summary, demographic conditions or life-cycle patterns dramatically changed in the 1940s: women remained or reentered the labor force in record proportions, and they generated soaring marriage and fertility rates. Did deep societal values change? Yes: Americans emphasized more strongly the primacy of family and children in their lives during the war than in previous eras. True, more mothers returned to the workplace after raising, or sometimes simply beginning, a family. Yet vacillations characterized the work patterns of most women. As a consequence, government campaigns to provide incentives for women to work often failed miserably. While nine out of ten women worked sometime during their lives, only one in ten even thought in terms of both marriage and a career. When this small percentage of the female population was then forced to choose, the great majority again was prepared to sacrifice all career ambitions in favor of marriage.[64]

The decision to take a paid job involved consideration, not only of private family needs and patriotic impulses, but also of the reaction of the community at large, and in particular of male co-workers. Whether they welcomed or rejected women in new job roles shaped the psychological atmosphere that made work either a happy or an unpleasant experience. In traditionally female roles such as teachers, clerks, salespersons, and textile factory employees, community and male resistance did not materialize. Yet it did develop on the part of both male employers and co-workers when women began to move into traditionally male jobs. In some industries, notably, railroads, lumber, mining, construction, and protective services (police, fire, military), and in virtually all industries at the level of corporate officials, foremen, and skilled craftsmen, men held over 95 percent of the jobs during the war. The issue of mixing the sexes occurred primarily in semiskilled and unskilled blue-collar jobs, especially factory work.

Employer reluctance was high at the beginning of the war but soon crumbled as it became clear that, with only minor changes in operating style, a large pool of labor could be tapped. The resistance of the blue-collar men was deeper and more sustained. In part, the resistance was based on fear that cheap female labor would either eliminate jobs for men or lower their pay and status and, in part, on a fixed mentality that clung to the belief that woman's place should be in the home.[65]

Thus, even when authorities successfully recruited women to replace men off at war and women accepted such wartime employment, the problems had just begun.

4.
Making Way for Rosie
Changes in the Workplace

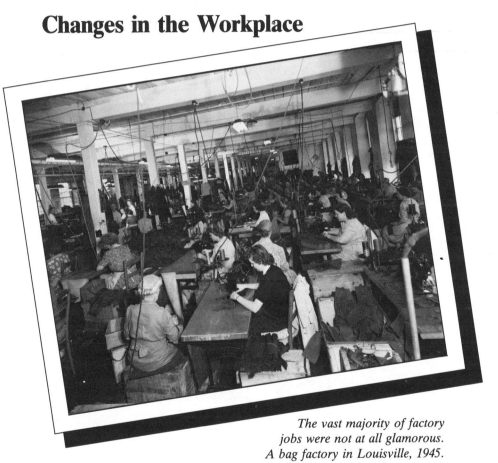

The vast majority of factory jobs were not at all glamorous. A bag factory in Louisville, 1945.

The expansion of the female labor force from 12 million in 1940 to 18 million in 1945 involved more than quantitative growth. It forced changes in the roles of women as workers as perceived by management, by the women themselves, and by their male co-workers. In some situations, it also involved an engineering adjustment to the particular needs of women.

For the majority of employed women, the war brought no revolution. Conditions were more hectic, and wages were higher, but the work of waitresses, maids, and production employees in civilian goods factories that had traditionally hired large numbers of women (food processing, tobacco, textiles, garments) did not undergo much transformation. In the white-collar realm, however, important changes did occur in roles—that is, in the commonly accepted standards of what was proper behavior for women. In particular, the belief began to crumble that one breadwinner was enough in a family—that wives with employed husbands should not work. In the blue-collar realm, especially in munitions factories, concerns more likely involved the role of women workers taking traditionally male jobs, and the changes that would have to be made in working conditions originally designed for men.

In occupations where women had long been accepted, the major adjustment management had to make was a sharp increase in wages to retain their workforce. In New York, for example, women's weekly wages in apparel and textile factories shot up 61 and 75 percent, respectively, between 1939 and 1943. Beauty shops never got war contracts, but beauticians' wages rose 28 percent. The pay of domestic servants in New York City, formerly the worst paid workers, doubled. They were offered as much as waitresses or sales clerks by 1943, but frequently quit for jobs that offered more status and freedom.[1]

In the white-collar sector, the major impact of the war came in the lowering of certain barriers for advancement. World War II was fought with typewriters and telephones as much as bombers and bazookas. High schools, furthermore, were graduating women in record numbers, awarding 6 million diplomas in the 1940s. The decade was, therefore, propitious for a permanent increase in white-collar women. Between 1940 and 1950, the number of women in white-collar jobs jumped 65 percent, while the number of other women workers increased by only 27 percent. (The corresponding increases for men were 39 percent and 14 percent.)[2]

Entry into white-collar jobs was the easiest part. Advancement of status, in terms of public and self-esteem, salaries, decisionmaking power, and careerism, required assets that gave men as a group the advantage. Assets of white-collar work included permanence in the paid labor force, the existence of upward mobility ladders, group self-control over educational and other entry requirements, and recognition of the inherent importance of the work. Women in clerical and sales jobs rarely possessed such assets, although professionals, particularly nurses, teachers, librarians, and social workers, had the potential to acquire them. One major group of women, nurses, both recognized the problem and was in a position to turn the exigencies of wartime to its advantage. Indeed, as we have seen, the war years had a more profound, favorable, and permanent impact upon nurses than upon any other group of working women. Women dominated no other professional or semiprofessional field.[3]

The war opened with a national shortage of 50,000 teachers. Low wages, uncertain tenure, the lure of defense jobs, and the needs of the armed forces accounted for the mass exodus of teachers. Rural areas, typically paying the lowest wages, were hardest hit. Although the average national teacher's salary was $1,441 in 1940, in rural areas teachers made only half as much.[4] Workers in many factories could make four times the salary of rural teachers and twice that of city teachers. High school dropouts often found war jobs that paid more than their old teachers received. Male teachers, furthermore, were not in draft-exempt jobs; many quit their teaching jobs to take defense positions. Idaho school boards were forced to use 500 new liberal arts graduates, 350 out-of-staters, and 325 former teachers to open their schools in September 1942. Nationwide in school year 1942–1943, 192,500 teaching positions became vacant. Approximately 37,600 experienced teachers transferred from other school systems, and many jobs were filled by new or retired teachers. Half of the new teachers had received substandard training and had been issued emergency certificates. By June 1943, 15,100 positions still remained unfilled.[5]

School boards across the country had rules against married women teaching. As the war progressed and the shortage of qualified teachers reached critical proportions, many boards actively recruited married women and either winked at or suspended their restrictive rules. After the war, most states dropped their former bans, thus allowing the emergence of a new career for married women. Though high school students also quit in record numbers during the war, proportionally more teachers quit than students, and the faculty shortage continued throughout the war period and into the postwar world.[6]

In contrast with the teaching and nursing professions women held only 11 percent of all proprietary and managerial positions in 1940. They usually owned small retail businesses, served as department store buyers, operated boardinghouses, or held minor administrative posts that often included clerical duties. They were effectively barred from the higher reaches of industrial management.[7]

War had an immediate and devastating impact on many of the nation's 2,250,000 small proprietors: their businesses collapsed. Speciality shops such as ladies' ready-to-wear garment shops, automobile dealerships, and washing machine distributors were hardest hit. In New York state alone, over 100,000 small businesses folded.[8] World War I had promoted many home-operated businesses such as the making of Army and Navy uniforms. Yet the Fair Labor Standards Act, passed between the wars, had reduced to nothing home work in knitwear, including uniforms.[9] War, then, had a direct effect on women proprietors and managers. For many, war meant closing shops, entering a new field, or waiting out the hostilities. Those who did not wish to start all over again worked in offices or became active in volunteer work. Unfortunately, we do not have enough information on the small businesswomen to know how many changed businesses, how many quit permanently, and how many quit just for the duration.

Lawyers were in high demand during the war, and women with law degrees quickly obtained good jobs, especially with the federal government. Openings ranged from fields such as consumer and social services to the Department of Justice and Surgeon General's office. Some, but less, headway was made by women lawyers in state and local government, with geographical differences apparent. In the South and Midwest, the new openings were in the public service area. In contrast, in the other regions, more lawyers found positions with private firms, but very few ever became partners.[10]

Over 3 million women and 4 million men held clerical or sales positions in 1940. Five million clerical workers, equally divided between men and women, were at work in 1941. Employment of women nearly doubled during the war and they soon outnumbered men. Clerical, typing, and secretarial positions became a feminine domain. Male clerical workers were employed only under special conditions, as on the factory floor or freight depots, or where the job had additional technical qualifications, as in a lumber yard. Although most corporations had no restrictions on married women, one in three, including most of the very large firms, discharged pregnant women, usually as soon as the condition became known. The same firms were slightly more lenient with their blue-collar women, who were less likely to be dismissed for pregnancy and when on leave could more often retain their seniority. The corporations enforced a dress code: three out of five prohibited clerical workers from wearing slacks.[11]

The need for clerk-typists expanded throughout the war as the federal government and armed forces continued to grow. As one wit warned, "There is a bottomless pit in Washington, D.C., which swallows little girls who can hit typewriters."[12] On the eve of Pearl Harbor, over 85,000 typists and stenographers held jobs in government defense agencies. It seemed that in the nation's capital any woman eighteen years old, in moderately good health, and without a criminal record could get a clerk/typist position, starting at $120 a month.[13] By 1944, over 6,600 vacancies remained unfilled for stenographers and typists in the Washington area. Part of the problem was that the young women recruited became homesick or could not find adequate housing arrangements. In addition, many had poor typing skills, which resulted in inadequate work and low morale. The Navy, which prided itself on never hiring anyone until she was "trained," found itself hiring untrained women and sending them to special clerical schools at government expense.[14] Washington officials were desperate for more employees. A 1944 manual for hiring officials instructed:

> Every effort should be made to place applicants with a history of mental disease if . . . they will be able to perform satisfactorily, without hazard to themselves or others . . . Applicants who have a history of mental instability are not to be instructed to report to Washington, D.C., for employment, inasmuch as they might have more difficulty in adjusting to conditions in Washington during wartime than would an individual with a perfectly stable nervous system.[15]

Despite the racism that had eliminated black candidates since the Wilson era, many black women were recruited for federal clerical positions. Between 1940 and 1942, black clerks quadrupled in number, but still comprised only 2 percent of all clerks. When blacks were hired in large numbers, such as in Washington area bureaus, they were often segregated. It was even harder for black women to get promotions than white women. One survey followed blacks and whites with initially similar efficiency ratings. When promotions were passed out, the whites were promoted six times more often than blacks.[16]

The paperwork of war accelerated the creation of new clerical and secretarial positions throughout the country. These low-level, low-salaried positions were even less likely than factory jobs to lead to advancement for women. A comparison of the weekly salaries of men and women in New York factories and offices from 1940 to 1944 reveals that both sexes could almost double their money by taking skilled or semiskilled positions in factories. While office pay did creep upward during the war, the $28 a week that a New York receptionist was paid in 1943, or the $26 earned by a bookkeeping machine operator, was far less than the $40 to $60 a week earned by a factory worker with no more skill and much less education.[17]

Few articles, newspaper stories, films, or radio shows featured secretaries, whereas Rosie the Riveter was everywhere. "Emphasis has been so placed on war industry, farming, and fighting," complained a college alumnae spokeswoman, "that by public inference [clerical] jobs are not considered essential to the war effort; their former prestige has been transferred to the assembly-line worker."[18] Few manuals were written in the war period to instruct a supervisor on how to handle clerical workers. Perhaps part of the reason was that women were not novelties in the office. The war only amplified an existing trend that actually grew faster in the postwar era.

If money, glamour, and opportunity for advancement were not the main inducements for women taking clerical jobs, what were they? Job security was one key factor. Blue-collar jobs paid good wages, but only for the duration, as women rightly feared. After the war, white-collar salaries went up faster than blue-collar wages. Clerical work was more "feminine," permitted attractive clothes, encouraged good grooming, was clean, emphasized intellectual and interpersonal skills, was physically less tiring, rarely involved night hours, was located in a prestigious skyscraper or Main Street building instead of a grimy industrial district, and involved regular contact with well-educated, well-paid colleagues who tried to be polite to one another. A secretary, furthermore, could pride herself on an individual relationship with her boss; she was not just one of the gang. All of these advantages can be summed up in a word: clerical jobs were "classy."[19]

With enormous amounts of money in the hands of wartime consumers, retail sales shot up. Retail employment rose 43 percent between 1939 and 1944, but saleswomen accounted for 92 percent of the gain, as their numbers doubled. Young men were drafted, or took factory jobs that paid 48 percent more on the average. Women could earn more in factories, too, but relatively few women crossed the white/blue-collar line. Most new saleswomen had been housewives or students before the war. The most striking gains came in food stores, where a mere 16 percent of the paid employees before the war had been women; by 1944, 36 percent were women. Supermarket managers realized that they needed to replace the departing men with "those who would not normally be employed at all, women, older men, negroes, and those handicapped by physical defects." With suitable training, new equipment such as hand trucks, and some men to do the heavy lifting, the new women surprised the managers by doing quite well. They even became "butcherettes," invading the fringes of a jealously guarded skilled craft. The managers agreed that a young married woman was the best to hire, for "she is less likely to be flirtatious than her younger sister."[20]

Could the saleswomen hold their gains when the veterans marched home? They had proved their worth to the managers, and seldom had unions to compete with. Turnover was heavy, as many quit for marriage. Conversely, housewives found a part-time job at the supermarket, dry goods store, or restaurant quite attractive, despite the low pay, because of the flexibility of hours and the pleasure of meeting people. The number of saleswomen did not decline between 1944 and 1946, even though the number of salesmen increased by a third. The women held on to salary gains, too. A full-time saleswoman was paid 52 percent of what salesmen made in 1944, and 55 percent in 1946. During the war, saleswomen earned 35 percent less than their sisters in the factory, but by 1946, the gap had shrunk to 25 percent.[21]

Women were about as likely to be found in higher management as in the posh, paneled private clubs where moguls consorted at lunchtime. When the war began, middle management in corporate America was equally free of women. Only 6 percent of the entries in a 1939 national who's who of women were in business, and with very few exceptions they ran their own little establishments (tearooms, millinery shops, secretarial schools), were partners with their husbands, or were managing small family-owned operations. The war provided the first major breakthrough for women, as many an executive secretary unexpectedly found herself promoted when her boss exchanged his pin stripes for an ensign's stripe.[22]

The basic impediments to women's advancement up the corporate ladder into lower and middle management were lack of training, career instability, the stereotypes held by senior management, and restrictions against married workers. The high schools and colleges enrolled very few women in technical or managerial curricula; those alumnae interested in careers rarely entered the corporate world. The "business schools" that many women attended taught shorthand, typing, and feminine charm. When insurance companies and other corporations did offer in-house educational programs, few women enrolled, and they soon dropped out. The emerging career patterns in corporations assumed a longevity and a continuity of employment that few women met. Senior managers, accurately gauging the average pattern among women, hastily concluded that *all* women lacked the skills and ambition to succeed. Many women in both blue- and white-collar work, and even some in management, feared they would lose status if their supervisor was a woman.[23]

Formal corporate rules and explicit governmental policy effectively blocked married women from access to supervisory positions. In the 1930s, 84 percent of the nation's insurance companies, 65 percent of the banks, and 63 percent of public utilities had restrictive rules preventing married women from holding *any* jobs. Furthermore, 77 percent of the nation's city school systems refused to hire married teachers, and 63 percent routinely fired a teacher if they discovered she had married. Fear of unemployment among "breadwinners" underlay such restrictions on wives, as well as unsuccessful but widespread attempts to pass state laws prohibiting employment of wives in government. Careerist single women tended to favor such legislation, as did housewives.[24]

The vicious circle was at work. With so little opportunity, few women prepared for supervisory jobs; with few role models and no support networks, those who did get promoted lacked the knack of dealing with subordinates. Even in teaching, where the supply of talented, ambitious careerists was large, men controlled nine out of ten senior administrative positions.

During the war years, many women made their move. The tight labor market and the departure of so many men into service forced the abandonment of formal restrictions. The hope of combining career and marriage emboldened women to hold on to the ladder of advancement, while their demonstrated skills forced executives to reappraise the old stereotypes. The rapid growth of personnel and research departments, as well as other staff positions, provided opportunities for upward movement for women who would not be trusted for line positions with responsibility for production. The recruitment of women into previously all-male factories necessitated hiring women as personnel officers, supervisors, and matrons. Retail establishments with a female clientele, especially food and department stores, hired women in large numbers and upgraded their more experienced people. From a third to a half of department store buyers were women, though old traditions still kept them from dealing with "big ticket" items, or even with shoes.

The most revolutionary change came in banking. Not only was the industry all-white, but above the secretarial level it had been nearly all-male. The banks had to hire women as cashiers, tellers, and even as loan officers during the war. Afterward the senior management wanted to replace the women, but the feminine revolution had so lowered the pay scale that not enough college men could be found to train for the jobs. By 1950, half of all bank employees in large cities were women, as were 15 percent of middle management and 1 percent of the senior officers.[25]

The wartime breakthrough in middle management was a first step, but it was inadequate to break the vicious circle. Women students would continue to avoid technical and managerial curricula for decades to come. The process of networking was fostered by the 150,000-member National Federation of Business and Professional Women, 14 percent of whose members held managerial jobs by the end of the decade. But most members were still secretaries or teachers, or operated their own little stores; furthermore, the Federation was based in small towns and provided little assistance for career women in large cities, who remained very much on their own.[26]

Breakthroughs in the white-collar sphere involved adjustments in sex roles that seemed more dramatic at the time than they do in retrospect. In the 1980s, people think it natural—even stereotypical—that grocery clerks and bank tellers are women; it is hard to realize that the first women ever to be hired at some supermarkets and banks are still on the job. Stereotypes based upon misperceptions eventually become passe and are soon forgotten. Stereotypes based on actual fact——like the physical differences between men and women —or upon deeply held values regarding masculinity and feminity, did not vanish so easily, no matter how harmful they may have been to women or to the nation's military effort.

In the blue-collar world, particularly in heavy industry, the changes in attitudes required by the war were significantly greater and had to be accompanied by a reorganization of manual work processes originally designed for men. From the point of view of the national emergency, the employment of women in factory work was a ne-

LIBRARY ST. MARY'S COLLEGE

cessity; from the point of view of many women, it was a welcome opportunity. But two questions arose: Could women do the work? Would men let them do it? American management was not free to hire whomever it wanted for a job. The labor market was segmented in several different ways. For our analysis, the most important segmentation was by sex.[27] That is, there were two labor markets, one for men and one for women, and practically every job was stereotyped by custom as male or female. Only in a few job categories— for example, quality inspector—did men and women often compete for the same jobs in the same plants.[28] With the enormous expansion of factory jobs during the war, and the departure of millions of prime workers for the armed forces, the traditional dual labor market became a serious obstacle to full employment. Not only did the custom of assigning certain jobs to men and others to women become a problem; even more difficult was the eradication of stereotypes that had grown up to justify the dual markets.

Male employers and employees alike showed little enthusiasm for the advent of large numbers of women in factory work. Among a thousand manufacturing firms in the state of New York in September 1941, half had never considered hiring women. Another survey of 623 key defense plants immediately after Pearl Harbor revealed that, despite the growing labor shortage, only 27 of them used women. Companies producing for the war effort typically had "cost-plus" contracts; they would be reimbursed automatically for all their expenses, plus a profit fee. The idea was damn the expense, full speed ahead. Normally, of course, a company that could cut expenses would increase its profits; it was just the opposite in the war. The biggest profits, and the most acclaim, went to companies that could hire as many people as fast as possible and crank out the war material. To hire women when men were still available slowed production down because of the need to provide training in the basics of industrial processes. Hence women were not hired until the supply of men ran out.[29]

In the early months of the war, the process of converting factories from civilian to war production involved shutdowns and layoffs until new equipment could be installed. Men displaced from their regular jobs during the conversion showed the most reluctance to approve women in factories. One-half of these laid-off men, as compared with only one-fourth of all other men, argued that men should be hired first. Unemployed men and their wives also showed strong resistance to hiring women workers. A high correlation existed between men's awareness of the manpower shortage and their willingness to endorse a womanpower campaign.[30]

Factory work was acceptable to some women, but not to most. Education, class, and racial background strongly influenced their attitudes. In 1943, only one woman in eight in the prime employment years (ages twenty to thirty-five) thought in terms of factory jobs when considering their ideal work plans. Factory work was acceptable to those with only an elementary education (37 percent interested), in sharp contrast to its rejection by better-educated women (only 2 percent interested). The heavy doses of government-inspired media propaganda on the joys of manual labor obviously did not carry much credibility. A third of the women would *consider* factory work in peacetime if it paid well. The main variation again was by education: two-thirds of the elementary school group would consider it, one-third of those with high school experience, and only one in eight of those who had tasted college. Three out of four of the blacks would take factory work—but most factories would not take them.[31]

Management and foremen gradually admitted women into the factory world on a trial basis. Factory policies rarely were set by top corporate executives. Plant managers, typically college-educated engineers, made the decisions, and they used engineering criteria to evaluate the results. Many were soon delighted; as one aircraft manager explained, "when we started hiring women last September we thought we could use 500. The firm soon hired another 1,000, then 2,000, and then 4,000 women."[32] The year of greatest change was 1943. Women increased 77 percent at Ford plants and 139 percent in General Motors plants. The female proportion of the work force varied greatly from plant to plant; in 1943 rates of 5 to 20 percent were typical in former auto plants (producing tanks, army trucks, and airplane engines) Detroit's Briggs Manufacturing Co. moved from 570 women in 1942 to 4,393 in 1943, a change from 2 percent female to 38 percent. At the nearby Briggs Aircraft Plant, the numbers jumped from 300 to 6,656, a change from 2 percent to 51 percent.[33]

While white women were finding factory jobs plentiful in 1943, black women were not. By April 1943, the vast majority of automotive plants had hired no black women workers, even if they had hired sizeable numbers of white women and black men. Corporate flagship plants, often under federal pressure, had a few black women who mainly served as janitoresses or restroom matrons.[34]

Most firms had maximum age limits for employees, but they soon learned in the manpower crisis that the over-forty women could do the job. For example, by 1943 virtually all former auto factories had lifted traditional restrictions against older workers. Two of the three holdouts reported that it was still difficult but not impossible for women over forty-five to be hired for production jobs. Only the Chevrolet Grey Iron Foundry refused to consider hiring older women. At Elmira, New York, one machine shop employed 200 older workers. Morale was high and no replacements were needed. Airfield officials discovered that older women were adept at jobs that allowed them to sit. Older workers tended to be more sincere, dependable, and especially qualified as inspectors and leaders. As the war progressed, more and more employers claimed, "their age doesn't matter at all. If we think they can do the work here, we don't care how old they are."[35]

Forty-four-year-old Marguerite Hoffman heard that the age barriers were down but was still worried that she would not be hired at Douglas Aircraft. She was soon delighted to learn she had passed the physical; they offered her a job the same day. Physically handicapped women also found a spot in defense factories. A New Jersey industrialist discovered, "there are many jobs which they can do. In our plant we have several paralysis victims who cannot walk far or well but whose finger dexterity on assembling is excellent. We also have a blind girl who is doing a splendid job of gauging automatic screw machine parts." Nevertheless, the fact that some factories lowered traditional barriers against the old and the handicapped should not obscure the fact that American society gave first preference to youth and health. (Too young was another matter: seventeen-year-old high school graduate Betty Boggs was hired at Doaks Aircraft but was not allowed to work more than a seven-hour shift until she reached her eighteenth birthday.)[36]

Soon managers hired women in most of the unskilled and semi-skilled job classifications. Indeed, many foremen in aircraft plants discovered that these new workers could master almost all aircraft jobs. Inexperienced workers were selected for most jobs almost at random. Sometimes employers assigned women to jobs on the basis of height, weight, or body build; such decisions were often ill-advised. A woman personnel officer of Consolidated Aircraft admitted, "When we first hired women for the factory we thought that what we needed were big strong girls . . . We soon learned that we were wrong. A lot of these little 90 pounders can outwork the big girls on the tomboy jobs . . . the husky ones, oddly enough, do best on the machines or at the assembly tables, where they can sit as they work."[37] At Lockheed, preparations were underway by July of 1941 to determine which jobs women could handle should they be needed to replace drafted men workers. A woman working in the medical department was asked to try a series of jobs. Lockheed managers figured if one woman could handle the work, then other women could.

At the semiskilled and skilled levels, companies preferred, whenever possible, to train women for inspecting jobs and men for machine operator positions. As the war continued and more men were drafted, the need for semiskilled and skilled women workers grew pressing. The consensus of efficiency experts, reached decades before, persisted during the war: women could excel at jobs requiring a high degree of dexterity, manipulative skill, and speed; those involving patience, attention to detail, and ability to perform well at repetitive tasks; and those that required working to close tolerances, such as inspection jobs that used gauges and micrometers.[38]

By 1943, a woman could hold almost any factory position, but some sort of de facto segregation usually existed. For example, one New Jersey plant had women drive all the trucks, a second had men driving all trucks, a third had women doing all the X-ray work, the fourth had men doing that. Typically half or two-thirds of the women in a plant would be concentrated in a handful of job classifications. A few jobs seldom if ever fell to women. In the shipyards, for example, only men undertook the heavy and dirty tasks of ship and tank cleaning, or high risk operations such as sandblasting. Sometimes entire industries, such as construction and mining, remained virtually all-male throughout the war.[39] Historians Ruth Milkman and Karen Skold have systematically documented for the shipbuilding, automotive, and electrical manufacturing industry that the war increased, not decreased, sex segregation in the workplace. New patterns of segregation were added to established patterns; women worked in either female-dominated sections or female-dominated job classifications.[40]

When men had been promoted as far as possible and skilled jobs still remained unfilled, factory managers began upgrading women workers. These efforts met with hostility or overt resistance. Even highly educated engineers could prove hypersensitive. Her male colleagues were astonished and angry when the first woman engineer at Lockheed swore like a man. She explained to a counselor, "That's the only way I can get their attention. If I say we ought to do it this way, they don't hear me; and if I say, 'God damn . . .' then they pay attention."[41] Apprenticeship programs often required set-up work and lifting of heavy materials, which women workers had to skip. Women who jumped to skilled positions without undergoing the lengthy apprenticeship aroused sharp antagonism on the part of men who had. Furthermore, men viewed these "ninety-day wonders" with skepticism and feared for their own job security and seniority.[42] Yet even at wartime peak, women held only 4.4 percent of the skilled jobs in American industry.

In the early twentieth century, industry had responded to the availability of unskilled immigrants by simplifying job operations, often using efficiency experts to plan the process. During the depression, however, industry tried to keep as many of their skilled workers as possible, and so adjusted work processes to their talents. During the war with skilled manpower in extremely short supply, and with the new women employees largely unskilled, a reverse process took place. Jobs were again "Taylorized"—that is, broken down into discrete operations so that the unskilled or semiskilled could do most of the work without much strength, training, experience or familiarity with a range of tools. The technique was perfected at the shipyards, where women were quickly taught basic welding skills, with more complex operations left to a cadre of male craftsmen. With the return of the veterans after the war, many of whom had developed mechanical skills, the process of upgrading the skill level resumed. It proved more efficient to employ skilled workers (invariably men) than to split the work with unskilled workers who needed training.[43]

Plant officials had to calculate the optimum number of hours of overtime for the highest degree of output per woman hour of work.

Studies showed an increase in absenteeism and a decrease in efficiency with the lengthening of hours. The percentage of hours lost per hundred hours ranged from 8.7 percent for a forty-hour week, to 9.6 percent for a forty-eight-hour week, to 12.4 percent for forty-five- to fifty-four-hour weeks, up to 14.6 percent for a fifty- to sixty-hour week. Furthermore, many women refused to take jobs that required excessively long weeks.

Overlong work schedules, despite the overtime pay, took an extra toll on women juggling two jobs—home and factory. One-third of the factory women averaged under seven hours of sleep regularly. "I get to bed at 1 A.M. Then about five o'clock the paperboys [her sons] would start throwing the papers and calling and waking me up. If I got three hours sleep for years and years, all the time I worked on swing shift, I was doing wonderful." Those working nine or ten hours often had to survive on under six hours of sleep. For some, overtime pay was the only way to make ends meet. However, most women, when weighing fatigue versus overtime pay, preferred not to lengthen their work day or work week. Women ranked overall health and family responsibilities as top consideration in choosing not to work overtime. "I would rather have Saturday free even though I lose the extra overtime money. I get very tired." Another added, "No time to do housework, no time to be with family. It is too much. You don't want overtime. Eight hours of that is enough." A Women's Bureau survey of women in wartime industries showed that two-fifths of all working women and three-fourths of all the mothers carried the major load of housework on top of factory work. These double jobs caused double burdens. One worker explained, "no kidding, I'm so tired sometimes I don't know whether I'm coming or going." Moreover, for many women the home responsibilities were more burdensome than the factory work. A woman worker exclaimed, "work's fine . . . but what drives me crazy now is my home and kid . . . What a mess!" The local laundry or dry cleaners, often closed or overburdened, could supply little relief for working women. "I done everything. I'd walk to the store [she hitchhiked whenever possible]. I'd do my washing, do my ironing and any cooking or baking or anything. I done that all before I went to work [about 2:30 P.M.]." Obviously, many women yearned for the day when they would have only one full-time job. Two-thirds preferred an eight-hour day and 40 percent preferred forty hours a week.[44]

Married women who did wish to work on Sundays for overtime pay were rewarded with frowns and grumbling from their neighbors. A Sunday school teacher "jumped down our throats for working on Sunday," and told the overtime workers that it was "against God and against the church, against everything to work on Sunday." Interestingly, the teacher's husband worked on Sunday but apparently was not subject to such hell and damnation lectures. Only married women who were not the primary breadwinner sinned by working on the Sabbath.[45]

Most factories adopted a six-day, forty-eight-hour week for all employees, and operated two or three shifts. Women objected that odd hours interfered with their family responsibilities, or, for single women, with their recreation and social life. Women in small towns complained particularly about the lack of recreation for those who worked the second and third shifts. In larger towns, twenty-four-hour entertainment spots opened up to accommodate these night owls. Married women, on the other hand, sometimes preferred evening and night shifts, especially if their husband worked a day shift and could care for the children. Shopping proved easier during the day, since many stores closed before women workers finished the first shift.[46]

Small plants could hire women informally; giant operations required complex procedures and coordinated media campaigns. Disaster resulted when media campaigns to entice women workers ran ahead of the screening and hiring processes, for the applicants might become frustrated and never return. In most cases, propaganda and hiring offices coordinated their work and signed up new workers quickly. "There was just one form you had to fill out. I think they gave you some small physical, and otherwise it wasn't much more than that." One filled out the form and they said, "Okay, you start next Monday." On the other hand, an applicant at Douglas Aircraft had to supply copies of her birth and marriage certificates, which required sending for them, before she could start work. Applicants at Lockheed also found a more complicated and slower hiring process, including a dexterity test, an IQ test, and a trial day in a "mass production line" at the Los Angeles office, plus two days at the main plant. Even three days was a relatively quick process; the munitions factories clearly wanted to hire.[47]

Why did women who had decided to work choose the giant war plants? "I was partly motivated by patriotism, [but] not entirely," explained Freda Campbell. "I thought, well, this would be a good time to get out and get something else." Campbell vividly remembered the campaigns to entice women to the factories. For her the time just seemed right. "Most of them needed the money. If they didn't need it, at least they could sure use it." Another worker moved from Seattle to Los Angeles to be close to her father who had enlisted. She applied at Doaks Aircraft. "It was something to do, because I didn't know anyone and I didn't see any way of ever getting acquainted." Josephine Houston applied at North American Aviation because a friend asked her to go with her. "Let's apply, because they train you." Houston, mother of eight children, knew that black women seldom had such an opportunity to earn a decent wage. Ironically, "I got hired and she didn't, because her [blood] pressure was up."[48]

First impressions were vivid, exciting, often frightening. Flora Chavez remembers, "It was like going into a cave or something." These plants were "dingy, messy looking places." Norma Cantrell agreed. "It was like you were walking into a big, huge cavernous barn; high, white. Dead white from the lights." Other workers also remember the lights: they "were different, you know and I had to get my glasses changed for different types of light . . . it was—the lights and everything—really something new. It's a new beginning in life."[49]

Women who had not worked in a factory before often had no preferences for jobs and were assigned to unskilled positions. Marie Baker, a tube bender, was given a typical training experience for such unskilled positions. "I took ten minutes to learn." But, she added, "I didn't really like it, but it was a job . . . [at the time] I was so excited about a job that I didn't really care." Clella Juanita Bowman agreed. "I just decided that whatever they put me on, I'd do," and "I'd do the best I could." Such spirit did not keep new workers from worrying a bit about exactly what their job entailed. On learning she was to become a detailed tube assembler, one fretted, "Oh, that's in plumbing." She feared that it would be dirty work, perhaps cleaning the toilets on the plane.[50]

Some women were taught their jobs by a co-worker on the line. While at first nervous around the machines, one finally started asking, "Well, tell me how this thing works . . . then it gets to be fun."

Others were shown movies twice a week for several months on how to operate various machines. At some point trainees were told, "Okay, time's up; transfer now," and they were sent to their respective departments. Even those unsure of themselves during the first weeks on the job soon gained some confidence. "I felt that I could go ahead with it, and then it was just routine from then on." Many of the unskilled and semiskilled workers would then talk about their work as "easy" or "monotonous" or "child's play . . . I got very bored." After two reviews, one at the end of six weeks, another at the end of three months, "you worked permanently unless you did something awful."[51]

Women with work background were told, "We'll put you on . . . inspection." Some preferred inspection, " 'cause I could sit down." Such workers could not see how others could prefer riveting, which "just shakes the daylights out of you." Many highly talented women were hired during the war years. However, "some of them— I tell you. I just wondered just where in the world they came from."[52]

New workers had to learn to pace themselves in terms of industrial time. They had to punch in and out and take breaks at a specified time and of a specified length. They were supposed to do what the foreman said and be a team member. Such a routine was a new experience for most former homemakers. "The bell would ring and we'd all quit and have coffee or juice, whatever, and then we'd all come back to work again . . . The whole works would just stop and then we'd all start up again." One woman had to learn not to get to work too early. "I think we weren't supposed to clock in before ten minutes of, otherwise, it would look like you needed to be paid overtime." Others had to learn to pace themselves and not out-produce the rest of the department. Subtle and not so subtle pressure was applied to those who forgot to keep pace. "What the hell's the rush?" was followed by, "The war is going to go on. Don't worry about it, we'll win the war." One overachiever had a sign pasted on her back: "Genius Working."[53]

For some women the factory environment remained an unpleasant work experience. "The work was hard. It was hot. It was dirty. It was noisy . . . And the sweat! We used to go to the water coolers for salt tablets every hour." But others discovered their talent for mechanical work and loved the job. They felt a sense of accomplishment that extended beyond patriotism and paycheck. "I'd be the only one that would be doing it so I just felt like I really had something." "You knew why you were tired. You knew that it was a healthy tired and that you produced something that made you feel this way." "I think it showed me that a woman could work in different jobs other than say an office which you ordinarily expect a woman to be in," and "I think it just really opened up . . . another field of thought, another viewpoint on life in general."[54]

As women entered the factories in large and ever-increasing numbers, companies hurried to recheck their safety plans. "They made darn sure that we wore that hat and you had to wear those safety goggles and they wouldn't let you get away with very much." Still, safety inspectors from federal and state agencies saw many problems on their tours. Videll Drake was asked by her supervisor in front of a safety inspector, "Vi, didn't I give you a respirator?" Drake answered, "No, I don't know. What is a respirator?" Another complained, "That grease spinning around in the air always seemed real heavy and there was no ventilation to speak of." As a result, workers were "hot in the summertime and cold as the dickens in the wintertime." Other complaints included, "Windows do not open, no fans," and "Floors rough, uneven, broken and patched in spots," and "Rats as big as cats run around the workroom and roaches crawl up the walls." "I think there was a degreaser tank over there, and I'm surprised no one fell in it. I was scared of that thing." Longer hours, a tendency to overcrowd facilities, and pressures for increased production added to these hazards. Furthermore, fatigue lowered a person's resistance to occupational poisons and infectious disease, increased the risk of accidents, and lowered overall morale. A daughter was so upset when her mother was injured that she quit to learn to be a nurse. "Mom, I'm not going to work at that factory any longer. Here you got hurt and you may be crippled the rest of your life."[55]

Women workers did experience special as well as general hazards. They were more susceptible to dermatitis than men, and pregnant women were vulnerable to a number of industrial chemicals. Norma Cantrell developed a skin disease at Vega Aircraft in 1942 that began on her arms and hands and spread to behind her ears and neck. "Working in the sweat and metal shavings—your hair would slip down and you'd try to get it up—your hands [were] filthy with chemical and little bits of metal." She finally quit her job.[56] Although efficiency experts demonstrated that women tired faster than men, they concluded that women recovered from fatigue faster than men, if given a few short breaks. No one doubted men were stronger than women, especially in lifting and carrying weights. On average, a 150-pound man was two and a half times as strong as a 100-pound woman and one and a half times as strong as a woman his own weight. State laws had long recognized this bological fact by limiting the amount women workers could lift; however, these laws set the same limit for *all* women regardless of individual weight or strength. The average limit was thirty-five pounds, and it could range from twenty-five to fifty pounds. Even where lifting was an incidental part of a job, women might be prevented from holding that job by the quite arbitrary state laws.[57]

Women had fewer accidents but lost more work days than men.[58] That is, they had fewer minor accidents but took off more time to treat them, or used such opportunities to spend time at home catching up on other responsibilities. To be fair to the men who often performed the most dangerous and hazardous tasks, it was necessary to compare accident rates for men and women employed at similar jobs. On general assembly line work, women had fewer accidents. Yet as welders, women had three accidents to every two for men. Accidents could happen even when a woman was not engaged in especially dangerous work. In one plant, a co-worker accidentally knocked a ten-pound steel plate onto one woman's foot. "Lay down!" they told her, "blood is coming out of your foot." In addition, women were more prone to certain types of injuries. For example, women had twice the rate of back strains as men. The National Safety Congress of 1944 noted that "in manufacturing plants in which most work is repetitive and does not require much moving about in congested areas and no heavy lifting . . . women are as safe or safer workers than men."[59]

Much to the dismay of employers, women often ignored rules about proper clothing, hair covering, and safety shoes. In fact, 9 percent of the injuries in shipyards occurred as a direct consequence of women's failure to wear safe attire.[60] Sometimes the women were not told immediately to wear safety gear. "I hadn't been on the job an awfully long time, 'til they had me get safety glasses. But I didn't have them the first day. Indeed, the management journals and safety congress proceedings were filled with loud complaints about management's inability to force its women workers to be safety conscious. Managers often debated whether to require uniforms. Even more vexing was the problem of getting women to wear caps or hair nets. "It's hard to make youngsters tie up their glamour bobs," sighed one manager. At the 1943 National Safety Congress, the vast majority of employers reported hair-covering problems. Managers tried to persuade women that their personal appearance while at work would not suffer, and that it certainly would stand less chance of being damaged for other occasions. A young worker grumbled about the snoods all workers with long hair had to wear. "I used to think I looked dopey in that, and I hated to wear it." One manager claimed success with a hard-line approach toward wearing a cap: "The first time this is neglected—they are OUT!" Another insisted that his approach was better. His company had been so successful in appealing to women's vanity to protect their looks that they wore their caps on the street and at the picture shows. Similarly, a new worker was impressed when she discovered that "most of the women were wearing these fancy snoods," and she immediately purchased one. Another wore a pink hat that matched her pink pants. The hat was a present from the husband of one of her co-workers. Soon everyone in the department wanted such a hat, so the husband went into the hatmaking business. Since one got a "ticket" if caught with one's hair not under a hat, such incentives to wear hats could significantly reduce the number of tickets issued in a department.[61]

Movie star Veronica Lake cut off her long gorgeous hair as part of a publicity campaign to urge women to wear sensible hairdos during the war. Unfortunately, a short-haired Veronica had little box office appeal; her career was a casualty of excessive Hollywood patriotism. One worker grew so tired of the foreman fussing after her about her loose hair that "she pulled the hat off of her head and she pulled her hair off and just handed it right to him and said, 'Now if this thing will get caught in the drill, here you take it.' " Few women wore wigs in the 1940s, and the poor foreman, completely taken aback, "gave up on the hat."[62]

Unfortunately, the only way some women learned the hazards of not wearing a hat was by seeing an accident. Dozens of women were scalped as they caught their hair in drills and lathes. "She got careless and she put it [a twelve-inch drill bit] behind her head . . . The drill was still going and she had long hair and she didn't happen to have anything on her head for protection . . . We had a heck of a time getting that drill out of her hair."[63]

Dresses were inconvenient and even dangerous in many factories, so women switched to overalls or slacks—doubtless reinforcing male opinion that sex roles were changing fast. Workers had mixed reactions about wearing slacks at work. "I had never worn them. I was a lot heavier then . . . And I felt very self-conscious in them." In contrast, another worker liked being singled out: "It made me look like I was different and I was working someplace and nobody else was and people would look at me." The new costumes proved convenient: "After we got used to wearing slacks, we'd take cold if we changed back to dresses, so I quit buying any dresses." While many felt strange wearing slacks at first, "I won't get out of them now and I'm not even working in the plant." Some, however, never changed. "I never did like pants. To this very day, I don't like pants."[64]

One way or another, most shops found a working compromise on the uniform and hair-covering issues. The shortage of safety shoes proved an intractable problem, however; not enough were ever made in sizes small enough to fit all women workers. Those lucky enough to find safety shoes in their size complained that the arch supports were just too heavy. The "foot problem" remained a serious impediment throughout the war.[65]

The characteristics of the new workers required factories to redesign many tasks. As one foreman explained, "The real difference between men and women is in the ability to lift and carry. But we all know that jobs can be broken down so that some of the heavy work is eliminated or that mechanical devices can be employed." Since a woman's hands are shorter and proportioned differently (thumbs shorter, index fingers longer), some shops redesigned the work desks and the tools for women. One Chicago plant with 85 percent women employees redesigned a cutting machine so that a hand lever that formerly took a man two hands to operate could be operated with two fingers by a woman. At Vultee Aircraft special jigs were added. Small changes, like providing a ladder for women at a place where a man might jump, also helped the transition. The advent of women also forced many factories to make long overdue safety adjustments. The improvements benefited all workers, men and women. As one foreman explained, "by making machines simpler for women and designing them for women as far as we possibly can, we make it safer for all workers and gain more in production." Charlotte Carr, assistant deputy chairman of the War Manpower Commission, reported that many foremen confessed to her that "these are machines we always knew we ought to guard, and now we are guarding them." Male workers used to the environment often ignored safety practices with the fatalistic attitude that if a hammer was going to drop on their heads they could not stop it. Others smoked around inflammable materials. "It was against the law, but they did." It seems likely that the arrival of the sensitive, safety conscious women raised the level of safety practices, if not the consciousness, of men.[66]

A woman worker's morale depended upon the quality of her surroundings. As one expert explained "women are much more concerned than are men about the general neatness and cleanliness of their surroundings, especially of the washrooms." Some factories such as steel mills had never provided rest rooms for anybody; management now installed them for women. Employers discovered that women workers liked to fix up their rest rooms, adding curtains, wallpaper, plants, and cots. The immediate effect amazed many employers, who discovered, "Morale is low if the plant is dirty and the washroom dingy."[67]

The entry of women into formerly all-male preserves raised issues of courtesy and morality. Women workers were often joked about or subjected to constant whistling. In one Detroit plane factory, the foreman had to move women because the men were wasting so much time "whistling and ogling." Flora Chavez explained the strategy at Lockheed. "The best thing was, we just banded together and gave them a hard time, too, by grouping together . . . They couldn't get just one." Another was more explicit. "Oh, when a fellow whistles at me, I whistle right back at him. He doesn't know what to do next." One group of women devised a more elaborate solution. They held indignation meetings and then "every time a handsome young buck came through the door, we whistled and shouted. 'Look at Tarzan, isn't he wonderful, oh, handsome!' " As a rule, the more women in a department, the less whistling. While most men did not insult the new women workers, they did not necessarily accept them any more than the whistlers did. As one housewife commented, "the men don't like 'em there." Although women in factory work never suffered the slanders that women in the military did, the harassment they received was a clear signal that the men did not want them there.[68]

In some plants, however, the introduction of women workers produced positive results. A representative from Vega Aircraft concluded, "mixing women workers with men has stepped up both morale and output." In part, competition between the sexes was responsible. As one woman inspector at Douglas Aircraft said, it "keeps men on their toes keeping up with us."[69]

As everyone expected (or feared), the arrival of women raised questions of sexual behavior. The FBI called upon the women's director at Lockheed to track down the woman recruiting playmates for a nearby army camp. One plant admitted to firing fifty "prostitutes," and another instituted careful screening procedures and opened separate entrances for men and women to avoid large groups of mixed sexes congregating before and after work. Yet, the men and women did meet, and some plants even bragged that, "If they're not wives when they are hired, they soon will be." One newlywed at Consolidated Aircraft explained, "around San Diego, the saying is, 'if you want to find a husband, get a job at Consolidated.' That is how I found mine." Some did not settle for one husband. The FBI came to Lockheed to talk to a woman who had married "ten men and was collecting their allotment checks. She'd marry them just before they'd ship out."[70]

Married men and women both expressed concern over mixing the sexes. Jealous husbands did not want their wives to work alongside other men; housewives wondered if their husbands might be flirting at the plant. "There is a feeling that family relationships are threatened and that the women are exposed to unnecessary temptations," noted a social worker. One worker "saw two women fighting one time over a man and one woman had got a husband. And I never saw a fight that was any worse, more fierce, than what those two women was." Yet a 1944 survey at Stewart Warner's Chicago plant showed that workers thought they could handle the new environment. "In your experience, is the moral atmosphere where you work such that you could tell parents that their daughters will find war production plants good places in which to work?" Yes, replied 78 percent of the machine operators, 78 percent of the clerical help, and 70 percent of the inspectors.[71] In short, infidelity was rare in the work place, but when it was discovered it captured headlines and public interest, and troubled the wives at home.

Homosexual relationships were rare. "There was one couple that were pointed out as lesbians, but that was the only ones that I ever saw." Another worker was asked by her co-workers if she had seen two women kissing over in a corner. She went back to look, "Yeah, they were kissing. But they never got rid of them. They just separated them to another building." One woman received an education when she encountered two female co-workers at a beach. "Hey, you guys act like you're married or something." The couple replied by handing her a copy of Radclyffe Hall's novel of homosexual marriage, *The Well of Loneliness.*[72]

Factories were seldom cold, mechanical, impersonal places; interpersonal relationships were an integral part of the work experience. These relationships were with male and female supervisors and with male and female co-workers. Foremen set the tone in each department. "Some of them they'd work you to death and others, they just dilly-dallied around and wouldn't do much and come in any old time they wanted to come in." Foremen could set a bad example and create low morale. One foreman would call women at home at night and "sit on the phone for an hour talking." Some leadmen "used to make some of the women cry over riding them on the job or just giving them a hard time." Others served as a big brother to the women and soon the other men would "put their arm around your shoulder, they let you know that they liked you, you could be friends, you could talk." Other women simply said, "Hi! and kept on going" and "never got any static" from the men.[73]

Friendships between women helped build high morale. "Everybody was a foreigner, then, so to speak, from another state." They would eat in the cafeteria and "we'd all laugh and joke together and we all stayed close." "There was one girl . . . that would always show me pictures of her son in the Navy," trying to play matchmaker. Many felt something special between the workers. "There was just a bond . . . Even now, some of us [who] worked there a long time—one woman got us started on a Lockheed Friendship Club—we meet three or four times a year." Most women, however, did not spend time outside of work with other workers. "We didn't mingle much that way, and just as soon as the day was over, we'd sign out and away we'd go." For many, it was simply a matter of the pressure of other duties. Time after work was spent washing, cleaning, and shopping. Attending church was often the only social life.[74]

The few minority women who worked in large factories were seldom segregated. California factories vigorously opposed racism. One southern woman who moved to Los Angeles and worked at North American Aviation found her first assignment was working with a black woman. She refused to work with the woman, "so they fired her. They told her they couldn't have that. She had to work wherever she was assigned," and had to work with every employee, "whether she was black, white, green, brown." One or two such firings and a unit had no more problems. In the Midwest, however, tensions were high. Hate strikes against the introduction of black workers shut down Detroit's huge Packard bomber engine plant, and similar incidents caused trouble in Evansville, Indiana, and at other points. In the Northeast, state officials working with civil rights agencies carefully planned the introduction of blacks into factories. The whites were assured that they were qualified and needed. White women were especially concerned about sharing rest rooms with people they had heard were dirty and diseased. The recommended policy was to begin with white-collar workers, since it would "minimize fears of loss of status on the part of white industrial workers" and managers would encounter "less resistance."[75]

Tensions in Baltimore exploded in a seven-day hate strike terminated only by seizure of the plants by the U.S. Army. Trouble began when white women objected to sharing toilet facilities with the first black women assigned to their department at Point Breeze Works, a Western Electric Company plant. Twenty-two white women staged a walkout and demanded separate facilities, but the company denied the request. The white women returned to work, but soon a petition began circulating among white employees throughout the plant until over 1,500 signatures had been collected. The Point Breeze

Employee's Association, an independent union that held bargaining rights, called for a strike vote. The results were 1,800 to strike and 1,144 not to strike. Many government agencies tried to mediate the grievance, including the Regional and National War Labor Boards, the Fair Employment Practice Commission, the U.S. Conciliation Service, the War Department, and the White House. The workers walked out on December 13th. A week later the U.S. Army took possession of all five strike-bound plants, but most whites remained on strike because the rest rooms were not segregated. In March of 1944, the Army turned the plants back to Western Electric. Fearing a city-wide race riot, black and government civil rights leaders capitulated. Management installed new segregated lockers and rest rooms "in a manner directed toward harmonious relationship of those involved."[76] Racial tensions in the workplace, not supported by the community, could be overcome by vigorous action such as in California and New York. But not even the power of the federal government could control hatreds deeply rooted in the community at large.

The biggest difference between male and female workers was not in their physical ability but in their attitude toward work. Men and women revealed different interests, needs, and problems. One careful observer decided that men were interested primarily in those things related to economic security and advancement, such as pay scales, seniority, life insurance, pensions, and employment. Women, on the other hand, appeared to be interested in such issues as thrift, welfare, overtime, rest periods, fatigue, social contacts, and injuries. Supervisors discovered that women workers were more likely to admit mistakes and ask for help. They responded well to praise and poorly to the brusque and profane criticism usually given to men. Women underwent greater physical changes than men as the exercise of new muscles caused soreness and excessive fatigue led to menstrual irregularity. Special exercises and careful coaching kept new women workers from becoming discouraged and suffering the psychological complaints that were as debilitating as physiological ones. Women were more likely than men to become unhappy in the early days of employment if they did not make what they considered proper progress almost immediately in learning a job. Apparently, "women learn more slowly than men, because they learn meticulously." Another foreman suggested, "Men may like a job but not like their supervisors or co-workers, but this is not true of women."[77]

Special handbooks on how to handle women workers soon found a place on the personnel manager's shelf. One book counseled supervisors to "treat the women war workers as you would treat your mother or daughter or sister." Another warned that women must have a "damn good foreman." But the most revealing suggestion of all, pointing out the basic similarities between all novices, was a handbook warning that "women *must* be supervised as men *should* be."[78]

Quite naturally, managers chose their older, experienced workers, inevitably men, to train as supervisors. Traditionally, a person became a supervisor after years of training and observation. During the war, everything speeded up, which often led to fast promotion and low quality supervision. One labor editor noted that "quite a number of personnel directors in plants are mere greeenhorns, without previous experience and little ability." If required to handle all problems involving women, male supervisors proved at a major disadvantage. They found it awkward and embarrassing to tell a woman that her sweater was too tight, or to determine if she were feigning monthly illness or abusing her rest room privileges.[79]

In theory, a woman supervisor needed the same qualifications as a man. She needed training in the company style, management skills, and work requirements, an acquaintance with unions, and the ability to deal with the community at large. Women college graduates seldom became supervisors because they refused to start with bench work and then later move up to supervisory positions. One expert thought that older women would be a good source of leadership material for supervisory or administrative jobs. "Many of them have had executive experience in club work or as teachers before they married, or have done some other work which fits them for leadership in industry." However, they lacked a sense of industrial discipline and an understanding of the norms and rhythms of the factory, and most women workers also lacked the advanced technical experience that foremen needed. Only in industries traditionally dominated by women, such as textiles and clothing manufacture, were a large number of women employed as supervisors. Indeed, the 1940 census listed 410,000 men employed as managers and officials in manufacturing and only 18,000 women.[80]

Women were often denied supervisory positions because an over-whelming number of both men and women claimed they preferred male supervisors. One Vultee personnel officer was distressed because she could find neither women foremen nor women workers who preferred to be supervised by women. Men felt a loss of status working for women; the women themselves did not seem to believe that other women commanded either the technical or the human relations skills needed for leadership.[81] One company experimenting with women as supervisors reported one bad experience after another. They concluded, "when they are good, they are very, very good, but when they are bad, they are awful." Consequently, some managers adopted the attitude, "We know women don't usually make good supervisors so we really don't expect you to succeed." With such a lack of encouragement, with no role models, and with senior supervisors failing to take a junior woman aside for coaching as they often did a man, women supervisors were not likely to succeed.[82]

Managers and workers alike listed more specific reasons why women supervisors failed: they are "too fussy, particular and prying," "too skeptical of their women employees," "too emotional." Women "take things too personally," are "too dictatorial." Moreover, women "over-supervise"; they cannot distinguish "between loyalty to the aims of the organization and loyalty to themselves. They like constant expressions of loyalty to themselves and may become offended if these are omitted." They are "too defensive" and tend "to compensate by masculine demeanor." Women supervisors should "not expect extra consideration," since "men criticize each other mercilessly." Hence women "can't command the loyalty or respect of their peers." In addition, some women workers claimed that "working for a woman is not exciting enough. We like to have some men around."[83] Whether or not the criticisms were fair, they represented a deep-seated hostility toward women supervisors by both men and women that remains with us today.

Most large plants did hire women as counselors or housemothers. They were expected to "control" women from too frequent visits to the rest room, and to act as advisers to the new "girls" who had a host of personal problems. These "matrons," often older women, also kept the women's wash rooms, rest areas, and cafeterias clean.[84]

The highest level of women supervisors were the personnel officers, often selected from the nursing staff, foreladies of the sorting department, and office workers with appropriate backgrounds. These women served as go-betweens. Yet not all employers with large numbers of women workers had women personnel officers. For example, five shipyards averaging 700 to 3,200 women workers had not one woman personnel worker on their staff. An even more prestigious and rarer position was the personnel director who played a role in screening women workers, positioning them, and watching their progress. Some factories that would not have a woman foreman would still hire a woman as personnel director, but their authority only extended to other women. Even women supervisors with wide-ranging functions worked under the direction of male supervisors or foremen.[85]

Male supervisors at first could not imagine why the company should hire counselors or advisers for one sex. At Lockheed the new coordinator of women's activities, Susan Laughlin, had been ignored by her supervisor until one day when an urgent message came. "A girl had come in in a bare midriff, and all the men were hitting themselves with hammers. Then he realized I could be of some help." Occasionally men sought advice from women counselors regarding their wives or girlfriends. But the majority of men "were still pretty macho and thought they could handle their own things. As did the . . . men supervisors." One woman who was "losing too much weight" asked her foreman to be reassigned. When he said no, she went to her woman counselor and was reassigned.[86]

Women counselors and supervisors often acted as mentors and promoted networking among women workers. One such woman supervisor "was kind of a friend of mine that belonged to the union. She'd give me a lot of points on things, you know." Veteran women workers also served as mentors.[87]

A primary goal for supervisors was to cut absenteeism, a major threat to production goals. Absenteeism grew worse as the war progressed. Four distinct causes of absenteeism were involved: psychological maladjustment, workplace conditions, logistical problems, and family needs. Most of the recently hired workers in war industries were new workers, unaccustomed to the discipline, tight schedules, and high pay. Since managers were reluctant to fire scarce workers, and since the pay for four days' work was already high, it was easy to take Friday off without jeopardy. Absenteeism was highest in noisy, dirty shops, and those where morale was poor. The night shift was always unpopular. Logistical problems such as transportation and housing shortages were especially troublesome in boom towns. The main cause of absenteeism for women, however, was family need. The double job of worker and housewife—indeed the triple job, with mother added—meant that employment often interfered with more important responsibilities. Shopping and laundry had to be done and the house had to be cleaned and children cared for. "No mother is going to work when her child is ill, and few wives will work when their husbands are ill," one woman noted. Absenteeism rose sharply in the summer, when school was out. When family duties became too pressing, women quit their jobs for a while. If family arrangements failed, three out of four mothers preferred to stay home to care for their children rather than turn them over to a day nursery. When she was ill or fatigued herself, a woman stayed home to rest and catch up on her chores. It is surprising that absenteeism rates for women war workers were not much higher than they were.[88]

Factory conditions influenced turnover rates just as they did absenteeism. A survey of workers who had quit their steelmaking jobs in Bethlehem-Fairfield and South Portland showed that 78 percent of these disgruntled workers listed "in-plant" conditions (management, general working conditions, and earnings) as the primary reasons for leaving. Army supply depots began to develop social recreational programs for workers after they discovered "we lost good workers because they got so bored living in the little nearby community with nothing to do after their working hours." A study of fifty-six Baltimore establishments over a sixty-day period showed 28,000 turnovers. The three main reasons given by both men and women for leaving these jobs were unsatisfactory housing, low wages, and inability to perform the assigned tasks.[89]

Women workers had additional reasons. Pregnancy often meant a woman had to quit her job. A survey of a hundred midwestern factories turned up only a handful of plants with leave policies. Supervisors tended to blame the women for pregnancies. When an unmarried pregnant worker tried to obtain leave at Douglas Aviation without anyone knowing about it, her counselor went to a supervisor.

"Oh Cookie, you and your women!" he chided. "Yes, you and your men who get them pregnant!" she shot back. The Ford Motor Company had an iron-clad policy: when a woman's pregnancy was discovered she was laid off for a year. In Michigan workers laid off because of pregnancy were disqualified for unemployment compensation. They also lost their seniority at Ford. Consequently, they concealed their pregnancies and continued to do work too heavy for them, with miscarriages, abortions, or births on the factory floor the inevitable results.[90]

Working mothers soon found their lives overly complicated and had to rank their priorities. As a social worker explained, "some here regard their jobs as temporary, and when difficulties arise, they resign." Special problems plagued the wives of servicemen, who often "took leave at the drop of a hat when their husbands got leave, or quit their jobs to follow their husbands to a new camp." The general problems were summarized by a labor editor who cautioned, "remember women are subject to all the disadvantages of a group of workers relatively new and used largely as a fill-in or marginal labor supply."[91]

The relative quality of work and output of men and women workers proved as difficult to gauge as their absentee and turnover rates. In some plants such as shipyards, work done by women compared favorably to that done by men, especially when women had received similar training. In aircraft plants, one engineer explained "there are more than a million and one separate and distinct parts in one of our bombers, not counting rivets, and most of them are so light in weight that women can assemble and test them as easily as men. Better in some cases." In some plants, women consistently outproduced men on the same jobs. An aircraft expert concluded, "Women are better than men for jobs calling for finger work. They will stick on a tedious assembly line long after the men quit." Reports from shipyards showed that women were better engineer's helpers. Foundries reported that women were better than men at making the small cores. As one industrialist summarized, "women excel at tasks requiring sharp eyes, suppleness of wrist, delicate touch, repetitive motion and exactness."[92]

Women could not, however, outproduce men at all tasks. One aircraft spokesman concluded, "Women can do from 22 to 25 percent of the work in this plant as efficiently as men." When evaluating older workers, managers had to weigh the lower rate versus the high degree of steadiness of these workers. At least one plant concluded that while older women showed some "diminution" in production, this was "counter-balanced by their increases in stability and judgment."[93]

Speed and quality of workmanship were not necessarily related. Apparently women took pride in good workmanship even if it meant a slower work pace. Women "did more careful work in inspecting operations in manufacturing of cutters for gear shapers involving careful measuring." Women in Vultee plants "exhibit less tendency to pass over minor errors in their work." Some women also seemed to take their job more seriously than men, especially if their husbands, fiancés, or brothers were fighting overseas. In one shipyard the "best worker," a woman, explained, "we know it must be done just right else the motor of the ship might fail and the men aboard would be at the mercy of a German submarine." She returned to work with "frowning attention."[94]

Thus, plant officials rated women equal to or better than men on some tasks and equal to or inferior to men on others. Three-fifths of the managers of 146 factories surveyed believed women workers in general produced the same amount or more than men; a fourth believed that the women produced less than the men. It is notable that only 15 percent answered that it depended on the job.[95]

Male owners, foremen, and co-workers confused traditional stereotypes with women's actual performance. Men assumed that because women took a job on a temporary basis—whether to supplement the family income or to help the war effort—she would not be able to handle the job well or take her work very seriously. They helped the process along by word, deed, and insult. They refused to spend time training women for better positions or supervisory roles; they resented adjustments companies made even when they actually benefited all workers; they maintained that women had much higher absentee and turnover rates; and they argued endlessly that women just could not do the work as well as men. The point was that some of the men—certainly the majority of the articulate ones—did not want women in the plant. The truth or falsity of the statements was far less influential than the ferocity with which they were held.

Most factory work consisted of unskilled or semiskilled jobs that did not require long training or special expertise or aptitudes. Women learned quickly and often stuck to their tasks more rigorously than did men. Therefore, while women did constantly switch back and forth and into and out of the labor market, when they took a job they were serious about their work and often excelled. Management learned the worth of women workers through these experiences, and as time went on kept bidding up women's wages to reflect this fact.

Given their equal performance record in the areas of unskilled and semiskilled war production work, and the strong social norm that called for equal pay for equal work, it would follow that women received the same pay as men. They did not. In 1944, women in manufacturing averaged $31.21 per week and men $54.65. The raw total includes a component of sex discrimination, but it also compounds a number of objective differences between men and women, including experience (women had less), rank (far more men were in skilled classifications), industry (more women in low-wage textiles and apparel), and hours worked (less overtime for women). The relative weights of all these factors cannot readily be determined from the data now available. To analyze wage discrimination, however, we can compare the hourly wages of unskilled men and women in the same labor market (see figure 11) and we can compare starting hourly wages for unskilled workers in defense plants (see table 12).

Just before the war, wages for unskilled men were improving faster than those for women, as heavy industry finally recovered, so the ratio line was falling. When the supply of unemployed men ran out in 1942, industry started bidding for women; when the draft began removing young men from the factories in 1943 and 1944, the wages that had to be paid to attract women continued moving up relative to men. Interestingly, the upward relative trend continued after the war, suggesting that factories which had overcome traditional stereotypes about the unsuitability of women were trying to keep women just as they were leaving the labor force. Women were forced out of certain traditionally male jobs in 1945, yet in terms of industry as a whole, their numbers and their relative wages kept going up. In newly opened war plants, women started at the same rate of pay as men, or only slightly lower. Likewise, in older plants where women took over jobs formerly assigned to men, the pay

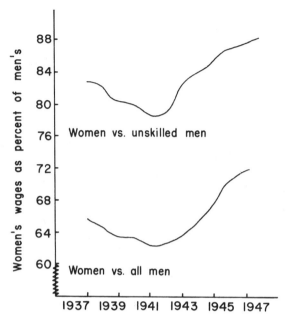

Figure 11. Hourly factory wages: women compared to unskilled men and all men, 1937–1948. Source: Bureau of the Census, Historical Statistics of the United States *(Washington, D.C., 1975), p. 172.*

differentials were zero or small. The sharpest discrepancy in wages came in factories that had traditionally hired women for rigidly defined "women's jobs," which paid twenty to thirty cents an hour less than roughly comparable jobs assigned to men.

The male supervisors and plant directors sought engineering solutions to human relations and personnel problems. When it worked their praise was quick: "You're not a woman, you're just a worker."[96] But some human relations problems proved intractable because wages were more than payment for so much machine work. They were the standard of worth that employees used to compare each other and, more specifically, that men used to measure themselves against women. The deeper tensions between men and women on the factory floor involving relative pay, job security, and self-image demand a thorough exploration of Rosie's relation with the men of the factory and unions.

5.
Sisterhood versus the Brotherhoods
The War for the Unions

*The friendly unions allowed women
to become members but not leaders.
Sheffield, Alabama, June 1942.*

While management was finding ways to come to terms with women workers, the nation's labor unions floundered in facing the challenge of accepting and integrating women into the workplace. Vigorous leadership and strong support during the New Deal had rebuilt the union movement, but the leadership and the overwhelmingly male rank and file were not prepared for the drastically changed situation of wartime. The number of union members had doubled from 3.5 million in 1930 to 7.3 million in 1940; during the war, the numbers leaped to 12.6 million. By 1944, one-fourth were women—3.5 million members—with most in the aircraft, shipbuilding, rubber, machinery, textile, clothing, ordinance, and radio industries.[1] With victory over the corporations so newly achieved and fears of postwar depression rampant, the unions had good reason to feel insecure. This insecurity was heightened when millions of women became members because women had little heritage of labor militancy, had historically worked for less money, and were now seeking to keep or to gain jobs traditionally held by men.

Labor unions in the 1940s can be divided into two types: those barring or trying to bar women members and those allowing them. The types varied by industry but not by AFL or CIO affiliations; in California in 1941, for example, 11 percent of the AFL and 11 percent of the CIO members were women.[2] During the war, all but the most recalcitrant unions (construction, railroads, mining) accepted women. After the war, however, the unions traditionally closed to women

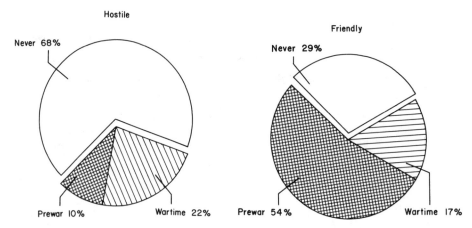

Figure 12. Acceptance of women in locals of hostile and friendly unions. Source: Department of Industrial Relations, Division of Labor Statistics and Law Enforcement, Union Labor in California (San Francisco, 1942–1947), passim.

soon managed to shed their female members, while those unions open to women in the prewar era kept theirs, and added more.

The situation in California graphically displays the split attitudes of unions toward women.[3] In 1940 the unions in certain industries such as construction, aircraft, automobiles, transportation, furniture and lumber, utilities, and postal were "hostile" to women members. Only one local in ten had even a token woman member. (See table 13 for the industry breakdown showing the proportion of locals that had any women members.) In the aggregate women comprised 4 percent of the membership of the "hostile" unions in 1940. By 1943, however, women were entering these industries in large numbers. Rather than forfeit them, the unions accepted them as members. By 1944, 76,900 women comprised 13 percent of the membership, and 32 percent of all the locals had some women (see figure 12). In only one industry, construction, were women still systematically excluded. Between 1944 and 1946, the hostile unions lost 43 percent of their women members and 5 percent of their men. By the end of the decade, only 6 percent of the union members in the hostile industries were women. The women had been accepted reluctantly and were quickly dropped.

In contrast, we can identify nine industrial sectors in which the prewar unions were receptive to women (see table 13). Half (54 percent) of the locals had women members who comprised 29 percent of the overall membership. These "friendly" unions also gained members during the war, and the proportion of women rose to 38 percent in 1944. The dramatic difference came after the war when the number of female members rose 12 percent. Thus, while the female membership of the "hostile" unions declined from 76,900 to 39,600 between 1944 and 1949, the corresponding totals in the "friendly" unions showed a gain from 105,200 to 144,610. Nine out of ten women who belonged to unions as the war began were in friendly unions. At the peak of the war only six out of ten were in the friendly camp; by the end of the decade, eight out of ten were in friendlies (see figure 13).

Little evidence of hostility toward women has been discovered in the unions classified as friendly, although job and wage discrimination did exist. But the hostile unions did not hide their true feelings. Studying the hostile unions and the experiences of their women members provides an insight into why the majority of women, then as now, were negative toward organized labor.

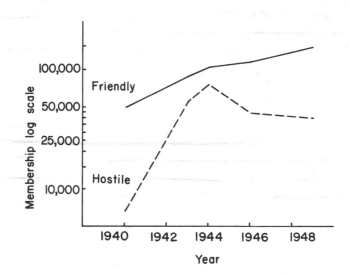

Figure 13. Women in California unions, 1940–1949. Source: Department of Industrial Relations, Division of Labor Statistics and Law Enforcement, Union Labor in California *(San Francisco, 1942–1950), passim.*

Most women who entered factory employment during the war soon learned that they were required to join and pay dues to a union in order to keep their jobs. The unions spent little energy explaining to women the benefits of membership and made even less effort to learn what special problems women had and how they could help. Understandably, the allegiance of most women to the unions was never as strong as that of the older, voluntary male members, many of whom remembered well the bitter strikes of the 1930s. "The women in our plant have never belonged to a union before," one Ohio leader noted. "They have walked into the best wages in the area—the best conditions. They never had to struggle for this."[4]

The hostile unions at first resisted female union membership and then tried to keep women from securing traditionally male positions. These reactions reflected rank-and-file male opinion even more than leadership opinion. In August 1942, for example, the International Brotherhood of Boilermakers and Iron Shipbuilders (AFL) held a referendum on whether women should be admitted to their union. Although the national union approved the innovation, local unions in critical defense areas opposed it by as much as 5 to 1 (Seattle local 104) and 3 to 1 (Seattle local 568). The Seattle Taxicab Drivers Union also blocked resolutions to admit women drivers, with one union official flatly stating that it was "not a woman's job. Taxicab drivers are forced to do things and go many places that would be embarrassing for a woman to do." An enraged applicant countered, "Let us women handle our own morals . . . What's the difference between a drunk man and a sober one? Well, when he's drunk, you have the advantage."[5]

An officer of a Chicago International Association of Machinists (AFL) chapter explained that women did not put out the work that men did and that "women were always having accidents, getting their fingers cut off." (The officer himself had a finger missing.) Other union leaders and shop stewards were equally blunt in their refusal to accept women workers in nontraditional roles. A United Auto Workers (CIO) man in Indiana maintained that "all married women should stay home." A Chicago member of the International Moulders and Foundry Workers Union (AFL) maintained, "Foundry jobs are not suitable for women." A fellow Chicagoan and member of the machinists union argued that, "Women should be out of plants.

[margin note: excuses]

They are interested in money only. They don't catch on, don't buy [their] own tools and are always borrowing." Men in a midwest rubber plant simply announced that they "just did not want women around their work." A Milwaukee AFL affiliate had a more concrete reason to bar women from men's jobs: "It's because women speed up and then the company pushed older men who can't now keep up that pace. Women will speed up and then later have to take 2 or 3 months leaves of absence because they broke down working at such speed." Such uncompromising sexist attitudes were commonplace in most highly industrialized areas.[6]

The relationships of co-workers in a mixed labor force were often very delicate and occasions for friction. Men feared women, resented their lack of experience, worried that they would take and never release men's jobs or that companies would hire cheaper women in place of men. They complained when women obtained special privileges and considerations, such as longer lunches, more rest periods, seats, special lifting devices, clean toilets, and less night work. Employers, like one New York shipyard executive, did not lessen the tension by remarking, "we'll begin with the women, and then maybe later we can have hot lunches for the men too."[7] Indeed, there were no reports during the war of formal or informal meetings between the sexes to come to some understanding. Management, unions, and government were aware of the problem, but, not knowing any quick and easy solutions, they did nothing at all.

As more and more men were drafted, management increasingly hired women for traditionally male positions. The antagonism toward women workers escalated. As taxicab driver Mary Pitts concluded, "The hardest thing about the job was to overcome the hostility of men toward women driving." An aircraft worker recalled the harassment encountered by the first women in war plants. "I never walked a longer road in my life than that to the tool room. The battery of eyes that turned on my jittery physique, the chorus of 'Hi, sisters' and 'tsk-tsk' soon had me thinking: 'Maybe I'm wrong, maybe I'm not just another human. Maybe I'm from Mars.' " The United Auto Workers (CIO), despite the militant equalitarianism of its leaders, at the local level vigorously protested against hiring women in job categories traditionally classified for males.[8]

Hostile unions did provide the usual routine benefits to women, such as negotiating grievances with management, remedying hazards, and ensuring that protective state laws were obeyed. The unions could do little about wages, however, given the nationwide freeze. Women seldom attended union meetings, for their home duties absorbed all their spare time. "We have never advocated women taking a very active part," said the president of a UAW local with 450 women members. When they did attend these heavily masculine affairs, they seldom spoke, for a core of "old-timers" usually monopolized discussions. To raise an issue unique to women was a sure recipe for ridicule. Not surprisingly, they did not feel part of the union. Strikes did occur during the war; the most dramatic were in coal mining, where no women were employed. Of all the strikes, 61 percent were all-male affairs; only 2 percent involved women exclusively.[9]

Occasionally unions would take the side of women but had to decide whether to support single women, who did not want married women as competition, or the married women who wanted to work. The Brotherhood of Railway Clerks (AFL) had a sizeable female membership, and at the behest of single women after World War I had negotiated contracts that forced women to quit when they married. In 1939, however, the Brotherhood adopted an equal rights policy, although it did not immediately eliminate the discrimination between single and married women from all its contracts. The old rule was waived during the war, but when in 1946 one company tried to resurrect it, the Brotherhood fought it before the National Mediation Board and won. Newlyweds could keep their jobs.[10]

The lack of understanding of working mothers' needs was exemplified by UAW vice-president Richard T. Frankensteen when he denounced day-care centers at the 1942 CIO national convention. He argued, "What better way is there for a paternalistic company to control the destinies of their workers than to set up child training centers, to open up nursery schools and allow these women to place their children there, and then training those children on the basis they want them trained upon?" Frankensteen, like many other militant union leaders, saw every issue in terms of class conflict; he was blind to the sex dimension. Nor would he support the establishment of union-run day-care centers; apparently he saw no reason to consult with women directly about their needs. Even the Woman's Bureau of the UAW put class ahead of sex, as when it denounced the use of women counselors in plants because they provided capitalistic advice to employees—such as sending them to a real estate agent when they needed housing. The UAW started training its own counselors, but in very few plants could it even manage to organize a women's committee.[11]

Another factor contributing to the clash between men and women workers was the primary reason women served in wartime factories: their wish to make money. Regardless of patriotic posters and emotional propaganda, most observers agreed with a Rockford, Illinois, labor editor's conclusion that women were attracted primarily by "a fat pay check with a small touch of patriotism."[12] Although this money usually supplemented family income, it was possible that a woman might become so proficient in her job that she made more money than her husband and other family men. This could be disastrous, for as one Indiana union leader put it, "It just don't set very well with the men."[13]

Ironically, women were paid excellent wages during the war in part to slow their entry and maintain high wage levels for men. As the *CIO News* stated, "the Los Angeles CIO asks equal rights for women so there will be no repetition of the blunders of 1918 when women were used to create a fluid labor market and to beat down wage scales." A Chicago UAW official boasted that, "The company asked us about hiring women—yes, at equal pay, we said; they lost interest." An AFL unionist explained, "We tried to maintain the rate of the job for women, otherwise, the companies would hire women and men would not have jobs." Similar statements were made by spokesmen for the Amalgamated Clothing Workers, United Auto Workers, United Electrical Workers, and United Rubber Workers— all CIO unions—during congressional hearings in the late 1940's. Moreover, all of these unions had a very large female membership.[14]

Equal pay for equal work policies became possible in the interwar period when management began analyzing and categorizing jobs. The logic was that optimum pay scales should reflect productivity, regardless of the characteristics of the worker. Unions typically opposed job classification, emphasizing instead the basic equality of all workers. The success of union drives in the 1930s had in large part resulted from worker resentment against the arbitrary power of foremen to hire, fire, and set job rates. Management did not try to preserve the foremen's powers; instead it accelerated the classification of jobs in the wake of unionization, thus shifting decisions from foremen to personnel departments and plant superintendents. The Army and Navy mandated equal pay in their own munitions plants, where large numbers of women were employed. In 1942 the War Labor Board (which had strong union representation) allowed industry to increase the wages of women to bring them to parity with men. The unions welcomed this move, for it meant an aggregate increase in wages. The CIO unions also began promoting equal pay contracts. Although the response of locals might vary, by the end of the war equal pay provisions were standard throughout munitions and in many other heavy industries. Promotion rates, however, were always higher for men, and women rarely qualified for the best-paying skilled positions. Unions were vigorous advocates of equal pay provisions only when women were doing work that men would want to do in the future. "We men have not got used to women in the plant yet," confessed a UAW official in Lansing, Michigan. "We try to give them equal rights but don't understand women's problems too well."[15]

Many women workers had a negative image of unions because unions were an integral part of an unpleasant experience—factory work. Among all American women in the nation aged twenty to thirty-five, those who wanted to switch from factory to office work were much more hostile toward unions than those willing to remain in factory positions. Women who associated unions with blue-collar jobs, and blue-collar jobs with lower status and less attractive working conditions, were thus reluctant to join unions. "They gave me a choice," recalls a woman who had quickly moved from tube bending to forelady status in a Los Angeles aircraft plant. "I could work on the line . . . or I could be the general foreman's clerk—naturally I took that." Why? "I could stay clean. I could stay dressed. I could do the paperwork."[16]

Another reason most women disliked factory jobs, and, by association, unions, was that they were often assigned to the dullest and most menial jobs. "It was a monotonous job, I didn't really like it," a North American Aviation worker recalled.[17] At best, women served as inspectors, whereas male workers were trained to handle the machinery. White-collar workers who filled the bulk of the new female jobs created after the war shared the traditional middle-class hostility toward labor organizations. Until women changed their views about unions, there was little hope for organizing the growing force of clericals and saleswomen.

The war was not yet over when the male policymakers—government authorities, management officials, and labor leaders[18]—attempted to return to normalcy. They assumed that women would consider men's work their part in winning the war, and be willing to release their jobs, especially if married, to men returning from the war or displaced by lack of war work. "Our first interest," a UAW local leader concluded, "is in interesting male members in union activity since women very likely will not be employed in our shop after the war."[19] As early as 1943 a labor leader argued, "we should immediately start planning to get these women back where they belong, amid the environment of home life, where they can raise their children in normal, healthy, happy conditions."[20] A Chicago shop steward of the Electrical Workers union (AFL) reflected prevailing attitudes when he insisted that "there should be a law requiring that women who have taken over men's jobs be laid off after the war." A fellow shopman added that their union had a verbal agreement that if a man were available when a vacancy occurred on a man's job, he had the right to it. Personal as well as professional reasons explained some unionists' desires to see women go back home. One midwestern union man demanded that his wife quit work because "My experience has been that married women generally get too independent when they earn their own money and they won't do what you want them to do. They get too bossy."[21]

It is not surprising that most women workers lost their lucrative positions as the wartime emergency ended. In Detroit's Hoover Company in 1944, 85 percent of the workers fired or rehired for inferior positions were women; at the Metal Stamping Job Shop, 98 percent were women; at American Brake and Block, 90 percent were women; at American Leather Projects, Asbestos Manufacturing, and Baker Rouland Company, 100 percent were women. Across the nation similar patterns emerged. For example, in Wilkes-Barre, Pennsylvania, two-thirds of the workers fired from an ordinance plant were women; in Indiana, over half of the 11,700 workers fired from the

Evansville Ordinance Plant were women. In New York state, 300,000 women lost jobs in the first six months of peace.[22]

While most factory jobs held by women were tedious and boring, some women enjoyed the work as well as the high pay. A west coast welder discovered that "there's a thrill in turning out a good piece of welding." A coremaker agreed with her, "You're proud of your work when it's done—like an artist with a picture." A machine operator commented, "I feel as if I have really accomplished something by staying on the job." And a riveter maintained, "I wouldn't trade my job for any other. I'd like to make a career of it." One aircraft employee even claimed that factory work was "easier than lots of girls' work."[23]

Women who fought back or refused to quit ran into a wall of union opposition. The hostile unions tried to freeze out all women. Four women in the Seattle area refused to accept new assignments at a substantially lower pay level and were consequently denied unemployment benefits. When an unemployment officer called Welders local 541 to check the claims of one of these women, he was informed that while she was in good standing with her union, all job requests called for male workers. Another Seattle union, local 104 of the Boilermakers, made it perfectly clear that women had been accepted in the union only as temporary mechanics and were not "bona fide members of the Union."[24]

The friendly unions after the war did not eject their women members, but instead encouraged the classification of jobs as male or female, with the latter low-paying and dead end. The United Electrical Workers (UE-CIO) did pursue an equal pay policy, which partly reflected a concept of "comparable worth" but primarily was designed to protect its male members. An employee at South Bend's Singer factory explained that the union leaders were not openly hostile toward female workers, but, she argued, they "put themselves first and women could take the leavings (if there were any)."[25]

To stay at work women with wartime factory experience were forced to return to the segregated female labor market and accept low-paying positions. The United States Employment Service estimated that women across the nation had to take pay cuts of up to one-half their former salary to find employment after the war plants closed. Women who had made 85 to 90 cents an hour were offered jobs at 45 to 50 cents.[26] Even when they performed essentially the same duties as male workers, they still received lower wages. Indeed, after the war it was apparently a widespread practice for unions to formalize the dual labor market by signing contracts that stated: "When a job has been established by custom in the Los Angeles plant as a female job and females or males have done the same work, the female rate shall apply for females."[27] With the dual labor market frozen into union contracts as well as by custom, women lost their chance for job equality.

Many unions had urged women to support the seniority system, arguing that it benefited both sexes. However, the majority of women in munitions lacked sufficient seniority at the end of the war to be rehired when plants reconverted. Indeed, even those with seniority, according to a UAW leader's admission, often "were not being given the support they deserved in terms of union readiness to protect their seniority status."[28]

Some contracts reflected the dual market by carefully distinguishing between male and female seniority rights. This had several ramifications for women workers. They might be placed on a separate list and compete only for "female jobs" after the war's end. Alternatively, women with seniority in their prewar women's jobs would have protection, but the majority of women who were employed on "male" jobs would have none. In the Connecticut Valley, the issue of female seniority appeared to be an academic one. With the number of workers in one factory set at 500 in peacetime, and with an estimated 1,200 returning veterans eligible for first consideration for jobs, the possibility of rehiring women was remote.[29] Frieda Miller, director of the Women's Bureau, summarized the charges against both labor and management leaders. She testified in 1948 that management and unions alike had refused to give women an equal opportunity for supplementary training, upgrading, and supervisory work.[30] Distrust, bitterness, and resentment on the part of women who wanted to keep their factory jobs festered rapidly.

Officials of both friendly and hostile unions often justified their postwar favoritism toward male workers by arguing that the law said that veterans must be given top priority when workers were hired. However, union policy gave preferences only to male veterans. As one female veteran explained, "Everywhere I have been here I have always received the same answer—we don't know about WACS—WAVES—SPARS—In other words no one knows anything abut the woman veteran." Many women learned new skills or exercised managerial responsibility in military service. As a result, only 22 percent wanted to go back to their prewar jobs (in contrast to 44 percent of the male veterans). Those who had developed technical skills, such as radio operators, mechanics, and aircraft specialists, could not obtain similar employment in the female sector of the dual civilian market. Moreover, those who wanted to extend their training were often told that there "weren't any jobs open for this type of training for women." Veterans' administration interviewers heard many complaints from women about their "inability to find work which seemed really vital."[31]

Such experiences had a marked effect on women's attitudes toward unions, and throughout the war women were more negative toward unions than were men. In December 1941, only 25 percent of all women favored labor unions. By age categories, 54 percent of those aged twenty to thirty-nine, 53 percent of those aged forty to fifty-nine, and 65 percent of those sixty and over were definitely hostile toward labor unions. Another element of ill-feeling stemmed from the disruptive effect of strikes on women's role as consumer, but whether the direct effect of union sexism or the indirect effect of strikes was more important in shaping women's attitudes we cannot tell. The public focused its hostility on union leaders, rather than unions as institutions. The leaders, especially John L. Lewis, were seen as unpatriotic strikemongers. By contrast, executives and corporation leaders had the strong backing of a majority of the American people (see figure 14).[32]

A 1943 survey provides penetrating data on young women's attitudes toward work roles, careers, and unions.[33] The survey not only illuminates the views of young women aged twenty to thirty-five, but also serves as a microcosm of the attitudes of the entire population toward unions. Americans, regardless of age and sex, were negative toward unions during the war and young women held views a few points more negative. Each person was asked: Which of these kinds of places would you personally rather work in—a place where there is no union and everyone deals directly with her boss/foreman; a place where there is a union of only company employees but no

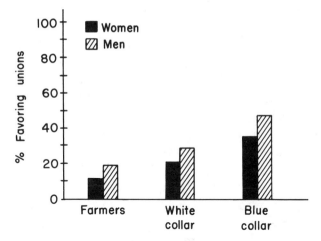

Figure 14. Support for unions by sex and occupation. Source: AIPO (Gallup) poll #254, Dec. 19, 1941, Roper Center.

national union; a place where there is a strong national union, but nonunion people can also work there; a place where everyone must belong to a national union? Nearly half the women surveyed (44 percent) preferred to work in a place where no union was present; 16 percent opted for a company union; 15 percent had no opinion on this question. Only a minority of one in four wanted to be near a strong union, with 12 percent choosing strong national unions and 12 percent a closed union shop.

To discover which groups of women were more or less positive toward belonging to a union, the responses to the question on union membership were converted to a 200-point scale that ranged from −100 to +100.[34] Socioeconomic and occupational status, educational and religious background, and geographical location strongly influenced women's attitudes toward unions.[35]

Lower-middle-class and working-class women scored 8 points higher than those of upper-class and 32 points higher than those of upper-middle-class backgrounds. Black women, displaying a relatively high prounion stance, scored 9 points higher than working-class whites. It was ironic that they had the least chance of gaining membership in a union. Young women who currently held blue-collar jobs scored 13 points higher than nonworking housewives and 24 points higher

than white-collar workers. Women with only grammar school educations were most likely to favor unions; college alumnae were least
likely. High school graduates adopted a position midway between
the grammar school and collegiate groups. Jewish women favored
unions most strongly, followed by Catholics and those marking "other"
as their religious preference. Protestants were much more negative
toward unions than the other denominations. Southern and western
women had stronger objections to joining unions than midwesterners
and northerners. Unions had never made much headway in the South.
They were relatively strong in the West, but the young women there
did not find them attractive. Women from the largest cities and small
mill towns displayed friendlier attitudes toward unions than those
from rural communities, but no simple pattern emerges.

In sum, unions received their greatest support from working-class
women, those who were poorly educated, those of the Jewish or
Catholic faith, and those who lived in northern or midwestern urban
centers. But even these women were on the whole more hostile than
friendly toward labor unions and labor leadership.[36]

At the end of the war and far into the postwar years, women
workers and labor union leaders disagreed on the proper role of
women in the labor force. Unions grudgingly supported women
workers, especially heads of households, in areas where their concerns coincided with those of male workers. Thus, when women were
not being systematically forced out, they were covered in contract
negotiations regarding job security and seniority. But the contracts
were always written to benefit high seniority long-term union members, and thus heavily favored the sort of uninterrupted lifelong work
pattern that most men but very few women followed. Union leaders
feared that, instead of accepting the male career style, women were
merely "until workers." "They are always working until they get
married, until they have a baby, until the house is paid off, or until
they retire."[37]

As a result, women members remained invisible to the all-male
union leadership. Women's auxiliaries, composed of housewives
married to union members, always played a greater role at conven-
tions than actual working women. A typical resolution at the 1942
CIO convention opened with a reference to "the wives, mothers,
and sisters of our union members."[38] However, there were no "hate"

strikes against women the way there had been against blacks—though one episode did occur on the eve of Pearl Harbor. The United Automobile Workers union called a strike at the Kelsey-Hayes machine gun factory in Detroit and successfully demanded that women be removed from traditionally male jobs.[39]

Much debate about the meaning, the justice, the expediency, and the social implications of "equal pay for equal work" took place in the 1940s, and, of course, continues to this day. In the first place, strongly held norms, in part codified into law, held that in the American way of life equal performance should yield equal returns. Or, in terms of work, equal jobs should get equal pay.[40] For white males in a single labor market, this generalization held in practice. However, the norm did not seem to be working for women and blacks.

Employers often explained that women were paid less than men because they were working for "pin money"—that is, for luxuries rather than for the basic necessities supposedly provided by the husband or father. The Women's Bureau frequently found it necessary to issue rebuttals to the "pin money" idea, explaining that many women needed to work to provide necessities for their families. Actually, the whole argument was a red herring. Large companies did not hire workers on the basis of family needs, nor adjust their wages accordingly. The labor economics of modern industry (forgetting unions for the moment) were simple: companies hired as much labor as they needed at the prevailing market wage.

However, there were *two* labor markets, one for men and one for women.[41] Jobs were classified accordingly, and before the war boom little direct competition existed between the sexes. With the huge increase in demand for labor in war industries, and with the transfer of increasingly large numbers of men out of the labor market, industry could no longer supply its needs from the male labor pool; hence it turned to the female labor pool. There were two ways to fill the need: reclassify jobs by sex or hire women for men's jobs. The Army reclassified many of its clerical and maintenance jobs and gave them to Wacs, which released men for combat or other exclusively male roles. Industry also attempted to reclassify certain jobs as women's work, as the grocery stores had done with clerks. However, fierce resistance to juggling blue-collar jobs developed, especially on the part of unions.

Labor unions considered their male members to constitute the bona fide union; any move that undercut the permanent (postwar) job opportunities for men was fought. Furthermore, the American public would not support any move that might reduce the number of jobs available to returning veterans. Most union leaders feared the development of a very poor job market in the postwar period. As poll after poll showed, the prospect that women would hold some of the scarce male jobs at the expense of men greatly troubled Americans. It was considered barely acceptable for a woman to hold a scarce male job if no one else in the family was employed. If a woman's family already had one breadwinner, then her job would come at the expense of a breadwinner in another family. During the labor scarcity of the war, working women did not deprive any breadwinners of a livelihood. The problem would be what to do in peacetime.

Industrialists generally adopted the second approach to tapping the female labor pool: hire women for the same entry-level jobs and wages as men. Hence women's wages rose relative to men's during the war. The newly opened airplane, artillery, and other munitions plants were considered temporary; obviously there would be little need for battleships and bombers after the war. Thus their hiring women for traditionally male jobs did not pose the direct risk of postwar family unemployment. Plants that had converted from civilian to military items, however, could just as easily reconvert. In this case, how to treat women became a delicate matter. Sometimes, jobs were revised and reclassified as female (usually by eliminating heavy lifting). In other cases, women were placed on separate union seniority lists, with the implicit understanding that they would be eliminated when the men returned from war. Most of the time, whatever the promises for postwar, women who performed traditionally male jobs were paid the same as men, at the start. In a sense, then, women were keeping these slots open for men. If one assumed, as most did, that men were superior workers, then it would follow that as soon as the men returned, they would replace the women—provided their jobs were still available.

Women workers were rarely allowed to advance to more skilled jobs or to become foremen. Once a male had some experience, he could be promoted or get a better job at another factory. In contrast, women seemed less credible when they claimed to have experience with machinery. Furthermore, a majority of women, but only a minority of men, were hired at entry-level positions. The men involved were often high school dropouts or older persons returning from retirement. Thus, even though there was some equality at the hiring gate, within a few months there was sex-based inequality on the plant floor.

Two fundamental conflicts separated the women from the unions. First, the rank-and-file men held strong views on the proper role of women, which the female invasion of the factories violated. One view was rooted in their notion of family roles. The husband should be head of the household and the only breadwinner. Wives might work if the husband could not; they ought not work if the husband did. The feared postwar shortage of jobs reinforced this attitude, but even during the postwar era of full employment it remained strong. Men who thought this way were not merely concerned with their own wives—any breadwinner's wife on the job undercut the ideology. The social teachings of the Catholic church, furthermore, provided moral support for this notion of proper family roles. The UAW agreement with Nash-Kelvinator in Kenosha, Wisconsin, exemplified this thinking. "Due to the man-power shortage," the local explained, "we opened up part of our agreement to allow Management to hire married women." But if for any reason the plant could not maintain a forty-eight-hour week, then "married women must be laid off so as to maintain a 48-hour week for all male and single female employees." The contract further stipulated that the restriction applied only to "those married women who have visible means of support."[42]

A complementary viewpoint among many men went beyond family roles to the basic notion of masculinity. Hard physical labor defined manhood. If a woman did the same work, the man was not as masculine as he could be. "They are taking the man out of a man."[43] Masculinity could be manifested through physical prowess, field sports, heavy drinking, and strong swearing. The men did not want any women to try to match them. The engineers in management, more sensitive to the technical needs of production than the nuances of sex roles, evaluated jobs in terms of their physical demands. Meticulous precision work and routine operations that required no strong muscles were denoted "light" work, and women were assigned to them. Heavy work was almost exclusively given to men. Though this technical solution satisfied the masculinity theme, it caused friction when men had customarily done "light" work to which women were now assigned. As the engineers broke down jobs into complex, heavy, and light categories, giving women only the latter, sex segregation on the plant floor crystallized. The division of labor enabled men to be classified higher and paid more, which comported well with their sense of self-worth. The problem was what would happen in the postwar period, when millions of breadwinning men would need jobs. Would the designation of jobs as "female" freeze out men? To a certain extent it did. Women's employment in the automobile industry, for example, was twice as high after the war as before, while male employment was roughly the same.[44] Much of the tension between men and women during reconversion involved crude efforts to reclaim male jobs by upskilling—that is, by adding skilled or heavy components to "female" jobs so that women would be unable or unwilling to handle them.

Situations in which women were doing light jobs that men had traditionally handled posed a more subtle challenge in the quest for male supremacy. The unions came up with a solution early in the war, equal pay for equal work. The theory was that women were inherently less productive than men, and, given equal pay requirements, management would always prefer men. The men, especially union leaders taking a long view, feared that if management could replace highly paid men with poorly paid women, they would do so, and the wages of the remaining male workers would be pulled down. The War Labor Board adopted equal pay requirements, and several industrial states passed equal pay laws, but union efforts to secure federal legislation failed after the war.

Equal pay for equal work appealed to people's sense of fairness, but was fraught with difficulties from the outset. As applied in wartime, it raised the wages of women assigned to "male" jobs. They appreciated the money, but it did not help cure their more pressing problems of juggling two jobs at once. It also signaled that they would be replaced by men later. "Female" jobs may have paid less, but they had far more long-term security. In 1946, so many women quit the labor force that New England textile plants began training men for traditionally female jobs.[45] Leftists in the auto, electrical, and other unions promoted equal pay as part of their equalitarianism, though they too realized it endangered women's place in industry. The CIO women's auxiliaries likewise favored equal pay both because of the immediate benefit for women and the long-term protection of male jobs. On the other hand, elimination of a pay differential would undercut masculine self-conceptions of superiority. The more traditional-minded men, especially those in the AFL, found this threat more alarming than possible replacement with low-wage women. The AFL unions consequently were far less interested in securing equal pay.

2. The second fundamental point at issue between women and unions involved seniority and part-time work. The priority women gave to the family roles meant that their work careers were discontinuous. They would return home for months or years at a time to rear children. Seniority rules that gave a premium to continuous employment were inherently discriminatory. Family responsibilities also meant that women were often interested only in part-time jobs. Many businesses came to recognize this, hiring these women for jobs that had special seasonal demands (such as retail store work before Christmas), or that could be scheduled for ten or twenty hours a week. The unions usually opposed part-time work. They sought contracts that favored full-time workers.

Why were the unions so adamant about seniority and full-time jobs? The explanation seems to lie in the experiences of the depression. Before then, unions rarely emphasized seniority. They emphasized instead provisions like the union hiring hall or the closed shop, which guaranteed that members would be given the first opportunity for hiring. If jobs were scarce, the earlier union policy had favored shorter hours (for example, the eight-hour day and thirty-hour week) or job-sharing. But industry changed in the 1920s. Management realized that high turnover wasted on-the-job experience. As the level of skills of the labor force increased, it was too wasteful to hire and train a revolving work force. Much more efficient were policies designed to keep the best workers. Hence Ford's famous $5-a-day wage in 1914 and the pension plans of the 1920s. By the 1930s it had become standard practice for industry to use years of experience as the criterion for keeping employees in time of cutbacks. The industrial unions, virtually children of the 1930s, seized upon this policy as a device to secure the loyalty of the workers with the longest membership, yet still be in harmony with management policy. Overnight, seniority became an unquestioned dogma for unions, and their indifference to the needs of women guaranteed that it would not be modified during the war. Job-sharing likewise was rejected. Switching from the old AFL emphasis on conditions within a single industry, the unions adopted a macroeconomic outlook. The goal of national policy—pushed by the growing political power of unions—would be full employment at adequate wages (adequate, that is, for a man to support his family).[46]

Union policy implicitly placed gender ahead of class. The needs of the bona fide members, the men, came regardless of the cost of divisiveness among the working class. The mutual hostility between women and unions cost the labor movement heavily in terms of coverage of the entire labor force and aggregate political voting strength. In part, the unions were endorsing the male supremacy component of working-class culture. Vigorous efforts to attract women would have cost the support of many male members. During the war, serious tensions had already created a chasm between union leaders and the rank and file. More trouble was not needed. Yet this is not the whole story. American unions in the 1940s were not a salient part of working-class culture in the first place. The political, social, cooperative, and recreational activities that interlocked unions and working-class culture in other countries was absent in the United States. Unionism, as historians have come to recognize, was simply a narrow band in the total experience of American male workers, and even narrower for the female. The unions worked hard for their men; it was all they could be expected to do.[47]

Women workers also suffered for holding views that clashed with those of labor leaders. Wages for women consistently lagged behind men's; high-wage blue-collar positions remained closed to them until the 1970s and beyond; and very few women ever achieved leadership positions within the labor movement. The primary commitment to marriage and a family was a critical factor that separated women from their male co-workers. The vast majority of working women put the role of housewife and mother first, even if it meant surrendering accumulated seniority to return to the home for child-rearing.[48]

Nearly all single women held paid jobs after leaving school, but they were no more friendly toward unions than married women. Indeed, they were slightly more hostile than married women, regardless of education and socioeconomic status. The sex factor had an effect all its own. Blue-collar women were consistently more hostile to unions than blue-collar men, just as middle-class women were more hostile than middle-class men. Women of all backgrounds and interests had a more negative image of labor unions than men of similar backgrounds and interests.

Forty years later, both labor leaders and women workers have been only partly successful in securing their long-term goals. Women have increasingly entered the labor force, but have not achieved the same wages as men workers. Despite equal opportunity and affirmative action laws, women have gained only the slimmest foothold in such traditionally hostile male bastions as construction, automotive repair, engineering, mining, railroads, police, and fire fighting. Unions have barely managed to maintain their strength in static or declining blue-collar sectors, and have been unable to make substantial gains in the newer fields dominated by women workers. The fastest growth has come in the National Education Association—a militant teachers' union with a predominantly female membership that has carefully avoided calling itself a labor union. Both union leaders and women workers have failed to take advantage of the challenge and opportunities provided by World War II. This legacy, an inability to work in tandem, has continued to haunt both groups, even after federally mandated equal opportunity rules have become commonplace and union leaders have tried to present a more favorable image to women. It may be a long time before union leaders learn how to answer requests such as the one from a UAW local in Battle Creek, Michigan, plaintively asking in 1944 for ideas on "how to prove to them that the Union is as much theirs as it is the men's."[49]

6.
Heroines of the Homefront
The Housewives

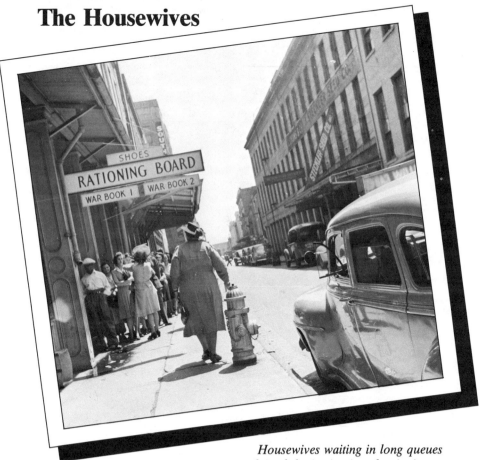

*Housewives waiting in long queues
explained the intricacies of rationing to
each other in New Orleans, March 1943.*

"Oh, I was just a housewife** during the war," is the answer of countless women when asked today to describe their wartime activities. No one has written their history. The housewife herself believes history is something that happened in Europe, in Washington, in town—anywhere but her home. The work of the housewife is seemingly so simple, so regular, so obvious, so trivial that it goes unnoticed, unrecorded, and unappreciated. As we shall see, the activities of this third of the American people were not so simple and obvious, and they certainly were not unimportant. The roles of homemaker, consumer, cook, nurse, shopper, laundress, and child-rearer had never been easy. The wartime shortages, the disruptions of families by migration to war centers or by military service, and the anxieties of global conflict made everything more difficult. The depression years had thrown up the challenges of poverty and unemployment, which the war helped cure. The ways housewives met the challenge of maintaining family life in the war years is an unknown story that is important to explore.

The problems encountered by housewives represented more than just individual difficulties. The entire logic of full wartime mobilization depended heavily on the behavior of housewives. The gross national product expanded enormously during the war, but all of the expansion had to be channeled into military spending. The only way to do this without radically transforming the nation's economy was to first distribute the extra income to households, and then to take back about a third of that income through compulsory taxes, voluntary bond sales, and inflation. Income taxes were imposed that for the first time reached beyond the well-to-do and affected nearly every family. Withholding was first put into effect. Purchase of government bonds, while never compulsory, was made highly attractive, and found favor in even the remotest corners of the land. It was firm national policy to avoid the runaway inflation that had accompanied previous major wars. Hence the Office of Price Administration (OPA) set prices for all items (including rent) at both the retail and wholesale levels, and efforts were made to restrain wage increases.[1]

By and large, the anti-inflation program succeeded in holding prices down. However, the flow of large amounts of new income into the consumer sector threatened to increase the demand for meat, coffee, sugar, housing, fuel oil, gasoline, rubber, automobiles, appliances, and other consumer goods in short supply because of the needs of the military, the conversion of factories, and problems in shipping. It was easy enough to stop the construction of housing and durable goods. The problem for the society was how to allocate shortages of other items without inflation. Although the New Dealers were being squeezed out of power in Washington, they did manage to control the allocation process through rationing handled by the OPA. Equality was the watchword, as all men, women, and children were assigned the same basic set of ration coupons. Regional variations in supply and demand were ignored by the rationing system, which did not take into account hardships caused for automobile drivers in the Plains states or city folk who did not have their own gardens for growing unrationed food.[2] To keep the price controls and rationing system effective, a strong enforcement program was set up to inform customers and retailers and gain pledges of their support, thus undercutting the black market. A small black market in meat and gasoline did emerge, and corners were cut by housewives who bought meat for illegally high prices. But on the whole, compliance was excellent and rationing worked as it was intended.

Taxes, bond sales, rationing, and price and wage controls all depended upon acceptance by consumers. Passive resistance to the war in the form of tax evasion, refusal to buy bonds, or participation in the black market could have seriously weakened the war effort, and concern over this possibility perhaps led to far tighter governmental controls on the lives of the people. The Office of War Information (OWI) constantly monitored the mood of consumers, looking for trouble spots that might provoke anxiety, disgruntlement, or scapegoating against Jews or blacks. (The British and Germans had similar programs to monitor their civilian morale.) The evidence assembled by the OWI is not dramatic. There were no food riots or demonstrations by angry consumers anywhere at any time, nor did the level of discontent over consumer issues ever threaten the overall morale of society. The history of these wartime regulations has been thoroughly documented from the federal point of view. What has never been studied before is the history of the war from the point of view of the consumer, particularly the housewife.

In early 1944, 32,500,000 married women, together with 2,700,000 widowed or divorced women, were running households. Their median age was forty-one; 10 percent were black. Only 8 percent of the wives had husbands in the service, another 4 percent were separated from their husbands or abandoned, so 88 percent had husbands at home throughout the war. Slightly more than half (57 percent) lived in cities; 21 percent lived on farms. At any one time in 1944, one-fourth of the married women and one-third of the widowed and divorced women had full-time paid jobs.

The most common household arrangement was an intact nuclear family of husband, wife, and sometimes children, living in their own household. In September 1945, there were 28,200,000 married couples, of whom 5 percent were living temporarily with relatives.) The average family size was 3.2 members, which obscures the fact that in nearly half (46 percent) of the families there were no children in residence. The situation was changing constantly during the war years, as marriage rates fluctuated (from 1.4 million in 1939, to 1.8 million in 1942, to 1.5 million in 1944, to 2.3 million in 1946); divorces increased (from 251,000 in 1939, to 485,000 in 1945, to 610,000 in 1946); several million husbands entered and then returned from the armed forces; and the number of births increased sharply (from 2.5 million in 1939 to 3.1 million in 1943).[3] Nevertheless, unbroken families were the norm for Americans during World War II.

A rapid drop in unemployment rates and an increase in real dollar family budget expenditures stimulated a surge in family prosperity. Unemployment declined from 17 percent in 1939, to 5 percent in

1942, and stabilized at 2 percent for the duration. Family budgets for urban families in 1935, 1941, 1944, and 1950, show a dramatic wartime gain on the part of the lower third (see tables 14–17). They were no longer as ill-fed, ill-clothed, or ill-housed as they had been in the doldrum depression years. Family income rose 48 percent and spending per person in poor families jumped 52 percent between 1935 and 1944, after inflationary effects were taken into account. Figure 15 shows the narrowing between the richest third and the poorest third that took place between 1935 and 1944 in the areas of income, total spending, and spending for food, housing, clothing, and medical care. A Florida survey showed that "since the war started the Negro men had higher incomes and they could afford to have a higher standard of living. Therefore, their wives and children no longer had to cook for the whites." By contrast, the richest third increased its after-tax income only 32 percent, and its spending only 1 percent. The underlying causes, besides rationing, involved the heavy demand for blue-collar labor in war industry, with fast-rising wages, contrasted with the slack demand and stagnant salaries of office workers and salespeople. During the war, wages rose 30 per-

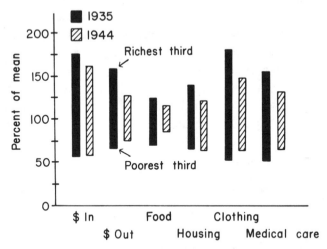

Figure 15. Per capita budgets of urban families, 1935 and 1944. Source: Bureau of the Census, Historical Statistics of the United States *(Washington, D.C., 1975), pp. 210–324. (The rich and poor groups have equal total numbers of persons, not equal numbers of families.)*

cent faster than salaries. The wives of blue-collar workers thus could put a decade of unemployment and uncertainty behind, while the wives of white-collar workers fretted about their relative decline in living standards.[4]

The major responsibilities of the housewife as wife, mother, consumer, and homemaker, were made complicated and difficult to fulfill under wartime conditions. Although American families had more money than ever before, inflation, rationing, shortages, and shoddy goods took so heavy a toll that most families denied they were better off economically. A 1944 survey asking Americans whether they were living better than before the war found 90 percent saying no.[5] The housewives' reports and the national surveys for wives in all classes of society reflected moods of frustration and heroic efforts to meet family needs.

One major depression problem that became worse in wartime was inadequate housing. As 4 million workers and their families migrated to war production centers, they discovered that the housing shortage was acute and getting worse. Within a thirty-five-mile radius of boom town Seneca, Illinois, all the existing housing facilities were filled to overflowing. In other war production centers, between 20 percent and 40 percent of the families lacked adequate housing facilities.[6] According to a nationwide survey, over 90 percent of Americans realized that housing shortages existed in their communities. Over 1,200 communities began housing programs during the war. From 1942 through 1945, only 1 million new housing units were constructed in the country, compared to a postwar pattern of 1 to 2 million each year. Mobile homes and trailers were not produced in sufficient numbers to meet the desperate needs of boom towns. Construction of 700,000 emergency war housing units helped only a little. In Detroit a reporter discovered, "People are living in old abandoned gas stations, and chicken coops and tents. You can't build bombers this way." Another reporter found "people living in stores which had been remodeled, tool sheds, tents, cellars, unfinished houses—almost anything. Nine times out of ten, the toilets and sewage disposal were completely inadequate and the water supply questionable. It is something of a miracle that an epidemic of dystentery and typhoid has not broken out." While men, women, and children all suffered from the housing shortage, the burden of coping fell hardest on the housewife. Making a home out of a chicken coop or a tent bordered on the ridiculous and produced sheer frustration. Being forced to buy a house at inflated prices because nothing else was available also played havoc with family budgets and dispositions. Rent controls made it more advantageous for landlords to sell than to rent. Between April 1940 and October 1944, the number of home owners increased 15 percent. In 122 congested cities, ownership increased 28 to 36 percent. As one Brooklyn housewife concluded, "The buying of homes is no longer for the stable—but rather for the desperate."[7]

Children made the search for rental housing far more difficult. As one newcomer complained, "People have hunted for weeks and weeks and found no places which would take children." Another explained, "They (the owners) got all these rules: no children, no dogs, no cats . . . Why I know one family that lived in a hotel room for two months—couldn't rent a thing—and had to board their kids out." A third maintained, "They won't take children in. No children here! No children there! What's the matter with those people? Don't they have a heart?" Even if one did find a house to rent, it could be sold out from under the family with no advance notice and no provision for another accommodation. The burden of moving the family was often placed on the housewife, since few husbands could afford time off from work to make the necessary preparations. One woman recalls she wore out three pairs of shoes (more than a year's worth of ration coupons) just looking for a new home for her family.[8]

House trailers provided some relief, albeit cramped, from the acute housing shortage near military camps and shipyards. Between 1940 and 1943 the federal government purchased 36,000 trailers (at an average cost of only $945). Trailers camps elicited strong animosity from established families. Trucks hauling units to a town signaled an influx of transient workers, exactly what areas still fearful of unemployment were anxious to avoid. The influx seemed to threaten the local labor and real estate markets and promised to further burden the schools. As vehicles, trailers were not liable to property taxes; to avoid restrictive zoning laws they were typically sited outside the city limits. Few camps had adequate water, sewage, or laundry services, not to mention landscaping or playgrounds. Hygiene was bad. The camps tended to lack neighborhood social controls and were rumored to be hotbeds of juvenile delinquency, sexual license, heavy drinking, and semicommercial vice. The tiny 8-feet by 22-feet homes provided scant privacy and were usually inconveniently far from stores and shops. Housewives trapped there could become lonely very quickly.

Although the tires were usually removed for use on automobiles, the trailers were ultimately mobile. The family could move on when opportunities changed. The very freedom to move on marked trailer camp life as transient, unreliable, and perhaps dangerous, in the view of nervous townsfolk. Yet with the elimination of private home construction, and the temporary surge of population to certain areas, the trailers represented a good emergency solution to the problems of boom towns, and to the shortages of low-cost housing that would not be solved for years to come. Political pressures resulted in a nationwide ban in mid-1943 on the manufacture of trailers. Together with other "temporary" housing, such as Quonset huts, the trailers served far beyond their expected lifetime.[9]

In response to the housing crisis, families often doubled or tripled up. By October 1942, 1,200,000 families had already doubled up. A Colorado housewife described the consequences of three babies in one shared household: "if one cried, they all started. The house was not big enough so they wouldn't hear each other. One bathroom was not enough, etc., it was hectic." A New York mother complained of the lack of privacy in row houses: "They're living on top of each other . . . How can shift workers get their rest—suppose the neighbor wants to play the radio! And what about the children!" Another woman reported, "it is not unusual to find children of all ages, including adolescents, either occupying the bedroom of the parents or sleeping together where no provision can be made for various sexes or age groups." American families eventually found some sort of housing by living with relatives, using trailers or tents, or commuting fifty miles to work, but their choices were severely limited. By November 1945, virtually no vacancies existed: nothing for rent and nothing for sale in most urban areas. As tension mounted, one housewife exploded, "a Christian woman cannot say on paper what people think."[10]

The housing shortage proved an even greater problem in the postwar period. Brides of veterans were especially inconvenienced. Half the soldiers were married at the time of discharge; 47 percent of the black and 36 percent of the white couples did not have a house or apartment to call their own. As late as the spring of 1947, 53 percent of all married black veterans and 39 percent of all whites were living doubled up with relatives, or in trailers or small rented rooms. The GI bill and the postwar housing boom eventually solved the shortages, but only after millions of families had been forced to live in cramped and crowded conditions.[11]

The housing crisis focused attention on the urban centers. Meanwhile, back on the farms, the war generated mixed blessings. In contrast to the urban dweller's problem of housing shortages, wartime repair was the key rural need. Three times as many farm wives as city ones lived in houses needing major repairs. Newfound prosperity in agriculture, coupled with an exodus of the poorest farmers, made it possible to reduce the proportion of homes needing repairs from 34 percent to 22 percent between 1940 and 1945 and to wire nearly half the farmhouses for electricty. Yet, at the war's end four-fifths of the farm wives still had no bathtub, no flush toilet, no central heat; half had no running water (see figure 16). Whether on farms or in cities, black housewives had the most difficult time securing and maintaining a decent shelter for their families.[12]

Scarcities of household supplies and repairmen plagued both city and country homemakers. Imagine a newlywed being told that after

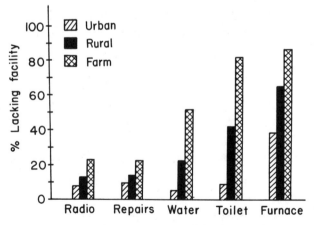

Figure 16. Housing, 1945. Source: Bureau of the Census, Statistical Abstract of the United States *(Washington, D.C., 1946), p. 797.*

September 1942 production was prohibited on electric refrigerators, vacuums and ironers, radios and phonographs, metal household furniture, water heaters, lawn mowers, and a variety of smaller equipment, including waffle irons, toasters, percolators, food mixers, and juice extractors.[13] Even can openers became virtually impossible to find. Linens and towels cost double prewar prices, lasted only half as long because of poor quality, and necessitated several trips to "chase down." One San Francisco housewife reported that "the many brides here wail, 'But what am I going to do,' when they learn there is not an egg beater or a paring knife in town."[14] The scarcity of all basic household equipment meant more drudgery and longer hours for cooking and cleaning.

Even women who owned the basic household machinery might be hard pressed because replacement parts and repairmen were both needed at the battlefront. Very few women seem to have been hired to do the repairs, and wages were much higher in the war factories. The federal government prohibited the use of steel to repair sewing machines or replace bed springs. "We bought light fixtures—tawdry and overpriced—and found on calling an electrician that he may not be able to come as he is short of material and help." A New Mexico housewife discovered that "almost everyone in town is doing their own furnace tending and I certainly am having a lesson in applied mechanics . . . I am learning all about coal stokers, hot water heaters, wells and pumps, together with frozen pipes." Even though American families made more money than ever before, and more had electricity, the percentage owning refrigerators actually dropped during the war from 73 percent in 1941 to 67 percent in 1945; washing machine ownership fell from 65 percent to 59 percent; and those having vacuum cleaners went from 53 percent to 47 percent. The reasons included scarcity of new equipment, wearing out of old, the shortage of spare parts, and the lack of servicemen.[15]

Half the housewives used to having domestic servants lost their help. Before the war, 70 percent of the rich, 42 percent of the upper middle class, 14 percent of the lower middle class, and 6 percent of the poor (in times of sickness) reported hiring help. Southern women became alarmed over the supposed formation of "Eleanor Clubs" by black maids to demand higher wages. No such clubs actually existed, but the bargaining position of domestic servants greatly improved. The domestics who were available charged twice as much as before the war, and they were less willing to live in, provide free overtime, or do the windows. Those who left domestic work for high-paying factory jobs observed that Lincoln freed the Negroes from cotton picking and "Hitler was the one that got us out of the white folks' kitchen." Thus a major wartime contribution for hundreds of thousands of housewives was to serve as their own maid at a time when housework was becoming far more time-consuming.[16]

The weekly wash created headaches and backaches. Soap of all types was scarce throughout the war. Lacking help or working machines, housewives often resorted to commercial laundries; seven of ten Americans used outside laundry services. However, laundries soon became overcrowded, short of supplies and helpers, and generally unreliable. The draft and poor wages accounted for the exodus of laundry workers. Believable rumors circulated across the country that tons of dirty clothes and linens were stacked in laundry facilities. Some shops required a month to complete their orders, others promised two weeks. One Baltimore housewife complained that laundries were "very choosy about whose work they will do, careless with the goods received and slow to make reasonable adjustment for goods lost." A woman from Norfolk, Virginia, wailed, "What is not ruined (torn, scorched, or streaked) is lost." Small families found it took extra time to amass the twenty-pound minimum for damp wash, requiring otherwise unnecessary purchases to eke out the two-week period between clean clothes. The old washboard, washbasin, and homemade concoction of soap particles were all recalled to duty for the duration.[17]

Outside of cities and war-boom centers, particularly in rural areas, the allocation of time to various household tasks changed only slightly during the war. Indeed, except for a gradual decline in food preparation time and an increase in shopping and managerial tasks, the pattern of housework remained quite constant in the United States from the 1920s to the 1960s. In Vermont farm homes, 25 percent of the work went to food preparation (85 percent done by the wife), 22 percent to cleaning and upkeep (75 percent by the wife), 15 percent to dishwashing (only 60 percent by the wife—the children helped a lot), with 10 percent each to family activities, care of family members, and laundry or sewing work. The most enjoyable task was cooking; while cleaning, mopping, and ironing were the most tiring, boring, and disliked duties. Women with electric washing machines were delighted with the convenience. Many said they made doing the laundry a pleasure. Presence of a small child, of course, sharply increased the work load. Vermont households without children under eight required seventy-two hours of work a week; those with little ones necessitated ninety-five hours a week. As mothers across the country discovered, to their relief, a second, third, or fourth child increased their work only slightly, as the older children could entertain each other and help with dressing and supervision. Clearly the main attraction in housework was the pride in working hard and effectively for the direct benefit of loved ones.[18]

How much time housework consumed varied according to the number of people and rooms that had to be cared for and the equipment available. In rural Vermont, 95 percent of the housewives had washing machines; in rural Mississippi, almost none did. Three-fourths of Mississippi whites had kitchen sinks and running water, compared to one black housewife in forty. The laundry still had to be done, so half the whites sent theirs to black washerwomen, while the black women lugged water from the well, boiled it in tubs, and scrubbed clothes by hand. Household help patterns in Mississippi and Vermont (see figure 17) show that housewives did 70 to 80 percent of the work themselves, with some help from children and, among whites, from hired maids. Husbands had responsibility for yard work, most repairs and maintenance, and especially driving and caring for the family automobile. They helped with gardens, canning, and other food production, but rarely did any "women's work."

Shortages, shoddy quality, and soaring prices were triple threats to housewives shopping for family clothing. Women found it "almost impossible to outfit babies and children," and mothers were "frantic over the problem of children's underwear and cotton clothing," advising other mothers to "write their Congressman about the lack of underwear for children." Housewives stood in long queues to buy rubber pants without elastic and shoes that fell apart in a month instead of lasting a school year, only to discover that their orders had been lost or written incorrectly. A survey of shoe stores showed that deliveries averaged ten-week delays. As one shopper explained, "Adults are urged not to buy for themselves, but children outgrow

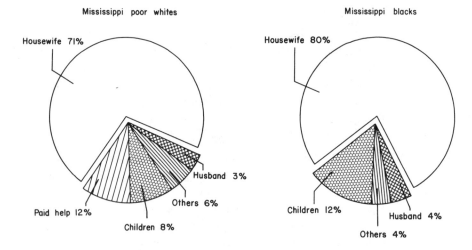

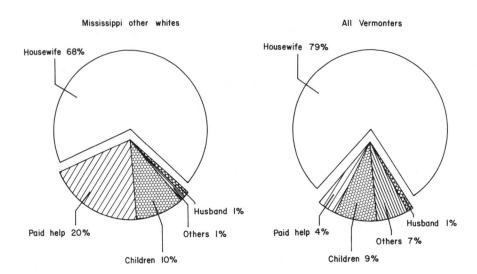

Figure 17. Household help patterns in Mississippi and Vermont, 1943. Source: Dorothy Dickens, Time Activities in Homemaking, *Mississippi State College Agricultural Experiment Station Bulletin 424 (1945), pp. 5–17; Marianne Muse,* Time Expenditures on Homemaking Activities in 183 Vermont Farm Homes, *University of Vermont Agricultural Experiment Station Bulletin 530 (1946), pp. 18–24.*

their clothes and it is imperative that they have new clothes." One could get extra ration coupons for children, but it was difficult for many mothers to travel downtown for them, and then they had to waste so much time standing in line that they got nothing else done that trip. Housewives asked: "Why have pajamas for large men been discontinued?" "Why can't there be clothes for tall people?" "Why can't I find anything in a ladies size 50?" "Why is there *no* underwear for my oversized man? There isn't even any good material to be used in making some." Shortages hit hardest on the housewife who purchased just enough clothes each year to make do. One result of the general shortage was a sharp increase in sales of specialty items such as maternity clothes. These proved popular because they permitted certain frills forbidden on regular garments; a woman who was not expecting could alter the waistband and enjoy the extra fullness in the skirt. One social commentator suggested that the OPA might "start requiring certificates of necessity or letters from attending physicians before such garments could be purchased." Sales of yard goods and sewing patterns soared during the war until these materials became scarce. Woolen clothes, rugs, and blankets disappeared from department stores as production of wool for civilian use virtually ceased.[19]

In an attempt to keep up with demand, hastily made, poor quality goods flooded the stores. Fifty-five percent of the respondents to an American Home Economics Association survey complained about the deterioration of clothing and shoes. New dresses pulled out at the seams, shoes would not stand up under heavy wear, and stockings came with shorter leg lengths and tore out at the top. One shopper purchased a white rayon blouse that on the first wearing pulled out at the seams, and on the first washing shrunk and had to be given away to a friend. Housewives spent extra time sewing simply because the material wore out so quickly. One woman complained, "We are supposed to buy less and we certainly would if we could get anything that would wear a while." A District of Columbia woman reported, "The quality deterioration is even worse, if possible, in negro neighborhoods." A Pittsburgh housewife recounted that during her "last trip in search for a coat for my daughter I saw a rack of winter coats—marked down to $29.95—with all their velvet collars as skinned as great-grandfather's green-black great coat which he had worn for forty years."[20]

Though clothes were of poorer quality, prices went up; "more trash than ever is in the department stores at constantly increasing prices." Criteria changed: "Good shoes are something you judge by price alone—and take to the repair shop with rapidity." Such high-priced clothes "present a problem for working mothers and workers on a stable salary such as school teachers." Families with children discovered to their regret that "children's clothing is both hard to get and expensive . . . People with several children are really finding that the cost is pretty high." What hurt even more was the "scarcity of necessities . . . when luxury items are abundant on the counters of department stores." The cost of living index showed a 36 percent increase in overall cost of clothing between 1939 and 1944. To add to their frustration, women shoppers experienced a decline in the quality of department store service as well as the disappearance of bargain sales.[21]

Housewives grew "very weary of the eternal standing in line." Recreation and leisure activity had to be sacrificed—an occasional movie, perhaps, but no more drives in the countryside and far fewer summer vacations. Working wives and mothers who were tied down with young children were at a distinct disadvantage. Even getting to the store became a real undertaking. Gasoline rations of three gallons a week for the average family drastically limited the use of cars for shopping (70 percent of American families had access to a car in early 1942, only 61 percent in 1944). Bus service became erratic and overcrowded, as the number of riders doubled between 1941 and 1944. The manpower shortage forced grocers and merchants to curtail delivery service. Even the paper bags the shopper had to lug were thinner. Uncounted millions of miles of extra walking, carrying heavy bags, proved the only recourse. However, some families did find imaginative solutions. One young boy's father took his tire swing for the automobile, mother commandeered his wagon for groceries, brother took his skates to help with his paper route, and older sister borrowed his bike to ride to her new job at the shipyard. For this youngster, such sacrifices meant total war![22]

Unfortunately for the American mother, measles, mumps, and other childhood diseases did not go to war; they stayed home. While 1941 was a peak year for measles, children continued to stay home from school with measles in record numbers throughout the war.

Mumps hit hardest in 1942, reaching 50 percent more children than in either 1941 or 1943, while scarlet fever peaked in 1944. Presaging a grave postwar epidemic, acute polio cases doubled and trebled, afflicting 14,000 children and adults in 1944. Meningitis, commonly referred to as a disease of children and soldiers, was double the World War I rates and twelve times the rates immediately before or after the war. Fortunately, new sulpha drugs and penicillin brought the danger under control by 1947. Shortages everywhere of doctors and medicine often meant that diseases lingered on and that the housewife became nurse or even family doctor. Many physicians were drafted, but each state tried, though not with great success, to keep a ratio of one doctor per 1,500 citizens. Twenty-nine states reported serious shortages of doctors. Farm families were especially hurt by the doctor shortage.[23]

The doctor shortage and gasoline rationing forced a permanent change in health care practices. Individual house calls in maternity cases virtually disappeared, so the overwhelming majority of babies were born in hospitals. Although not solely a product of the war, the trend toward hospital birth suddenly became the established practice. Nationwide, the percentage of babies born in hospitals rose from 45 percent in 1937 to 56 percent in 1940 and 82 percent in 1946. The increase in rural hospital births was most striking. Nationwide, the percentage born in hospitals skyrocketed from 17 percent to 61 percent in farming areas and increased from 85 to 91 percent in urban areas.[24] Midwifery and home delivery remained the norm in rural southern black communities. For example, in boom town Pascagoula, Mississippi, 119 black babies were delivered by midwives and 37 by physicians in 1942. Of the 37 physician cases, 26 were delivered at home and 11 in the hospitals. In Alabama, 62 percent of black children were delivered by midwives, in South Carolina 80 percent, in the 1941–1942 period. As late as 1949, midwives delivered over half the black babies in Alabama.[25]

The impact of sickness, as well as clothing and housing shortages, was felt by most Americans, but food shortages brought the war closest to home. The federal food rationing system, begun in 1942, forced shoppers to change their buying habits, memorize ceiling prices, calculate points, and guard colored coupon booklets. By January 1943, only half the women had mastered the bureaucratic maze, but three months later, 88 percent were on top of the system. Understanding the system did not make it attractive; in most parts of the country, food shortages and rationing led the list of civilian grievances.[26]

More housewives had coupons than storekeepers had meat. A fourth of all consumers in May 1943 had been unable to obtain beef; one-tenth could not find steaks or lamb; and 7 percent could not buy pork or bacon. A woman worker complained that she could not "get enough meat to put up lunches and have some for dinner, too." Another noted, "My old man won't eat liver and stuff like that. You can't get pork. Don't know how I'll get enough meat for him." Adult eaters created a shortage of baby food, which was not rationed. Winter weather brought shortages of fresh fruit, vegetables, and even milk. Women trying to do their canning often walked all over town in search of sugar. As one complained, "they urge us to save and preserve everything and then let this occur." By October 1943, 50 percent of all housewives could not buy as much food as they desired for their families, and only 45 percent said that the food system was working well.[27]

Americans were well fed in comparison with citizens of other countries at war, but homemakers worried about the deterioration in the quality of their food. As one Pittsburgh housewife argued, "I've seen meat in otherwise clean large markets covered with fly eggs . . . under such conditions low point liver, etc., is not an economy but a sad mistake." A Norfolk housewife commented that "chickens that make their appearance are so yellow, so tiny, and so peculiar looking that even people who have eaten frozen chickens for quite a while refuse them." A third reported, "The meat markets soon run out of 'good' pieces, and while there are cold cuts some of them are pretty weird— they must have drafted the man with the recipes." When they got the stuff home, millions of women had to cope with the refrigerator shortage. The rationing system most affected families with growing adolescents and small families with only two or three coupon booklets. Those with special dietary needs or restrictions had major problems. As one Baltimore housewife explained about her mother, "She *needs* gelatin every day and we are having a very difficult time getting it." When asked if they were actually buying as much food as needed to maintain a healthy family, only three-fifths of American housewives answered yes. Thus, for a majority of families, food rationing and shortages were constant if not critical reminders that Americans were engaged in war.[28]

"Make Do" became the American housewife's slogan. As one Hoosier explained, "No one is suffering from undernourishment but the experience is new for many to have to do without those things formerly taken for granted." In response to the food shortage, some families began looking for new sources of nourishment. By May 1943, two-fifths of the housewives were buying meat substitutes, and one-fifth were using "stretchers," preparing meat differently, and making greater use of leftovers. Many admitted that they were eating foods that they used to discard. Large portions of Americans swallowed their prejudices and used oleomargarine. One housewife reported that women were "unanimous in their praise of oleo . . . All had been against it at the start. Our butcher can't keep up with the demand." Victory gardens could be found in two-thirds of all back-yards, especially those in rural areas or small towns. Two-thirds of the new foods tried by white and black homemakers in Mississippi were vegetables, mostly from their own gardens. By 1943, three-fourths of America's housewives were canning vegetables, fruits, jams, jellies, and meat products. "I was canning until midnight, night after night," a North Carolina woman later recalled, "and I frequently said, 'I wish I had Hitler in that pressure cooker!' " The restaurant business, which remained unrationed, flourished during the war. One survey reported that a fourth of the public, typically the more affluent, ate out once a week or more and another quarter once a month or every other month. Over half the general public and 70 percent of the frequent diners did not want restaurants to be required to collect ration points for the food they served.[29]

The ultimate solution to shortages, for those who had the money, was a visit to a black market or, more likely, a store that obtained some of its supplies illegally. Over half the public stated that black markets existed, a third admitted that they would pay a little extra for a scarce item, a fifth agreed that some black market "was justified" and that they had paid over the ceiling price for groceries or meats. While few consumers actually purchased items on the black market, many a customer, pleased to find a special food, often forgot to check the ceiling price. The Home Front Pledge, the government's attempt to swear women to its policies, was honored when convenient but broken, in minor ways, when homemakers felt it necessary. In order that "some soldier will have that much more to eat," Americans tightened their belts. In 1945, surveys in Philadelphia and Iowa showed that 80 percent of the citizens were willing to ration at home and to send food abroad. Seven out of every ten Americans were prepared to go further and eat 20 percent less food in order to send more food to European allies.[30]

What housewives feared and resented most was being duped. As a Taos, New Mexico, woman explained, "The thing that I have heard the most comment on is the fact that the country went along, heroically doing without coffee and then last week there was a news item saying that coffee had been dumped because there was no room for storage for it." Her friends "don't mind doing anything, however hard, if they know what it is all about, but they do not like being made to feel that they have to be rationed unnecessarily to make them realize we are in war."[31]

Given the frustrations, difficulties, and adjustments required by wartime economy, one might wonder how successful the housewife was in providing a balanced diet for her family. In fact, Americans were better nourished during the war than ever before. Thanks to the general level of prosperity—the substantial increase in wages of blue-collar workers, the increased number of workers, and the low percentage of unemployment—the dietary habits of the poorest Americans began to resemble those of the most prosperous Americans. Consumption patterns of meat and poultry showed a trend toward homogeneity (see table 18). The rich were still eating juicier cuts of meat, especially good steak, and the poor were relying heavily on utility beef, but it is important to note that for the first time, high nutritional standards for Americans became an achievable goal.[32] Urban diets in 1936, 1942, and 1948 show a narrowing of class differentials (see table 19). Many who a few years before would have found it inconceivable to think of eating steak could now complain about the shortage of it. The differential in the calories, calcium, and protein consumed by the poorest and richest third of Americans was cut in half between 1936 and 1942. The gap in iron intake shrank 75 percent. The statistics on other vitamins consumed reflect similar trends.[33]

To find the human meaning of the gross statistical trends, we must look at the individual level. In rural Mississippi, for example, black and white housewives began substituting corn syrup, molasses, or condensed milk for white sugar in recipes. Fruit and fruit juices were used in desserts. Planting new vegetables and preparing them in different ways was popular. Store-bought breads and cereals (now fortified with vitamins A and D) also became part of the family meal. More families than ever ate salads and included vegetables in them. Black and white homemakers of all incomes broke with their up-bringing by learning to prepare food differently. New vegetable dishes such as baked eggplant and scalloped squash became part of the family diet. Women learned that shorter cooking times for vegetables retained both flavor and nutritional values. They were most likely to experiment with new recipes after their friends recommended them. Besides relying on friends, upper-income whites also tested recipes that appeared in magazines, newspapers, or a recently ac-quired cookbook. Black housewives, in contrast, were likely to turn to relatives or white employers after their friends to find out about new techniques and new food items. The results were the same for all socioeconomic classes: new recipes, new food items, more nutri-tional meals.[34]

By no means were all dietary deficiencies overcome during the war. A U.S. Public Health survey carried out through the public schools in 1945 revealed that one-fourth of the white children showed signs of vitamin A deficiency, 16 percent showed signs of rickets (a vitamin D deficiency), and 9 percent showed signs of goiter (a de-ficiency of iodine). Improvements were striking, however, for a 1948 survey discovered that three-fourths of the urban families surveyed had diets meeting the recommended calcium levels compared with one-half in the spring of 1942 and one-third in 1936. The quality of diets in the rural South, especially among blacks, remained prob-lematic. In the rural North, however, good nutritional practices were widespread, especially where women had some exposure to home economics through high school or rural extension programs.[35]

The federal government aided housewives by teaching them the basics of nutrition and by requiring the fortification or enrichment of basic foods such as bread and milk. By 1943, iron, thiamine, riboflavin, and niacin had been added to white flour, enriching it 65 percent. Nearly all margarine was fortified by 1943, up from 65 percent in 1938.[36] Agitation for national nutritional standards, which had begun in the 1930s, reached fruition during World War II. The National Research Council's Food and Nutrition Board began to issue its "recommended dietary allowances" in 1941. Throughout the war it joined other government-sponsored nutrition programs and locally formed health organizations, such as the Kips Bay–Yorkville Area (New York) Health Committee, to distribute posters, hold classes, generate "nutrition bars," and sponsor radio programs and newspaper stories talking about the "basic seven" and the different vitamins.[37] A survey taken at the beginning of the war showed that only 12 percent of Canadians, 16 percent of Americans, and 19 percent of the British could explain the difference between a vitamin and a calorie. A later survey showed that almost half the Americans were now reading or hearing about vitamins B, B1, and B2. American housewives practiced what they learned, though they remained overly satisfied with the quality of diets that too often had nutritional deficiencies.[38]

The change in American dietary patterns that reached a high point during the war continued into the postwar period. These trends were reflected in both the nutritional value of food consumed and in the dollar amount spent. For example, the ratio between what the richest third and poorest third spent for food in 1941 was 2.18:1. By 1944, the ratio had dropped 30 percent to 1.36:1. In 1950 the ratio had only increased to 1.58:1. While the period 1949–1952 saw a leveling off and decline from the peak year, it still represented a substantial overall improvement over the prewar years. War had a lasting and equalizing effect on American dietary habits, and American housewives could claim their share of the credit for this nutritional revolution.[39]

The roles and responsibilities of American housewives demonstrate that most did not give up family life for the duration nor send their husbands off to war. They found family living doubly difficult and time-consuming. Children and shopping lines both multiplied during the war and grouchy husbands abounded. Even with the highest family budget ever, most housewives found it difficult to care for their families or to use the extra cash to lighten their work load. Whether describing housing, appliances, medical care, laundry, clothing, or food, the story was much the same: inflation of work loads, hidden price increases as shoddy goods replaced durable items, shortages of amenities and necessities, and deterioration in the overall quality of life.

The housewives were not alone. They coaxed assistance from children and, occasionally, from husbands. They helped each other supervise children, shop, tend the sick, and repair appliances, and explained to each other how ration coupons worked. It was illegal to sell or swap coupons, but if one family had surplus sugar points and another did not drink coffee, a simple trade made life easier for both, and the economy more efficient. While the amount of visiting among neighbors and relatives was another casualty of the war, needed assistance and advice was as forthcoming as ever. Most women belonged to small informal cliques that formed the basis of community life. Younger women were often called upon for fashion advice, older ones for advice on cooking, shopping, and child management. Opinion leadership on governmental matters, however, was provided chiefly by men. The block clubs set up as civil defense operations in many large cities and the school district meetings sponsored by farm groups facilitated scrap metal collections, car pooling, victory gardening, and the eradication of neighborhood nuisances.[40]

In leisure moments—or more likely, during their sewing, washing, and ironing chores—housewives enjoyed listening to soap operas on the radio. The plots typically involved intricate family problems that had to be solved by a mature woman. Every show began with a new challenge, to be solved within fifteen minutes, followed by a new crisis whose solution would come tomorrow. It was easy to identify with radio heroines whose lives were so much like their own.[41]

What is striking about these women was their flexibility, creativity, and general competence. They tried to make a warm home life in flimsy trailers, crowded apartments, and overpriced houses. They repaired, mended, and conserved. They stood in long lines, lugged home their purchases and children, and devised ways to keep their families clothed, healthy, and well fed. They organized their households more efficiently and coaxed extra chores from family members. They relied upon friends, kin, and neighbors for advice and material help, and in turn gave freely of their own resources. When they were frustrated, they complained to neighbors, friends, butchers, and storekeepers, but they met adversity head on. In some areas they coped; in others, such as feeding their families nutritional meals, they triumphed.

What of the service wives whose husbands were away in the military? Their incomes were lower and their housing much worse. Housework was more difficult, and—far more important—loneliness and insecurity were constant. How well they coped, and how they helped move American society in new directions, must be examined in depth.

7.
War and Victory Inside the Home
The Service Families

*Trailer homes were a way of life
for many servicemen's families as well as
other families who had to move frequently.
Jim Hogg County, Texas, June 1946.*

In the 1940s, millions of husbands, wives, children, and kinfolk attempted to reorder their lives in a disordered world. The challenge to the historian is to discover the ways people successfully coped or failed in that attempt, and to gauge the long-term impact of the wartime experience.[1] Our best evidence comes from meticulous interviews conducted at the time by sociologists. We have seen how housewives from intact families coped with the war. By now concentrating on servicemen's families, in which the psychological stresses were greatest, we can more readily see the mechanisms of coping that all families used. Although there were many wartime disruptions caused by a husband leaving his family at home while he worked in a defense plant in another town, our concern here is with those caused by the draft.

These families disrupted by military service were a special group. The wives, some 4 or 5 million in all, were young, ranging from their late teens to early thirties. As children of the depression, they had dim memories of prosperity and had become accustomed to hardships. Many had postponed marriage or childbearing. Their husbands could remember the difficulty of finding a first job, or of advancing on a career ladder. Military service caught most of the husbands just as the war boom was generating high-paying employment; the draftees were paid far less than the men who remained home. The government's modest family allotment of $50 per month (plus $20 per child) represented a depression era standard of living for the wives who did not find jobs. Most of the childless wives did take jobs, as did some of the mothers. Even so, income among service families was low. They did have one advantage: they were better educated than their elders, and as a result they had more intellectual resources to help them chart their lives.

The contemporary interviews of service wives used here come mostly from the state of Iowa, the Hyde Park neighborhood of Chicago, and the small town of Morris, in northern Illinois. Although the geographical spread is not great, and all the families are from areas that prospered during the war, the data nevertheless encompass the full range of problems and adjustments encountered by separated families.

The Iowa study involved sophisticated interviews with a cross-section of families with children. Most of the 135 families lived in towns or small cities; few were on farms.[2] (Iowa agriculture played a critical role in food production; few farmers were drafted.) The Chicago study examined 100 families in the vicinity of the University of Chicago. Half the families had children, most were middle or upper middle class, almost all were highly educated.[3] The Morris project sampled families of all socioeconomic levels from one small town. Focusing on the postwar adjustment of 500 servicemen, it included interviews with 60 wives.[4]

Most of these couples were married during the depression and had postponed marriage and even children for economic reasons. Of the 135 Iowa families, 16 percent were psychologically unprepared for the husband's induction and panicked, 12 percent of the husbands voluntarily enlisted with the wife's consent (2 percent without it), 11 percent actually looked forward to the separation. At induction, couples separated with a variety of problems unresolved. The major trouble points were jealousy, budget shortages, disputes over who would make spending decisions, tensions with in-laws, drinking, housing, child discipline, number of children, sex satisfactions, and clashing temperaments. But all families have troubles, and the Iowa couples scored higher on measures of marital adjustment than the national average.[5]

"My two biggest problems right now are loneliness and money," explained a serviceman's wife interviewed in Chicago, echoing the sentiments of many of her peers.[6] Most wives had been dependent on their husbands emotionally as well as financially and had to make major adjustments during the separation. What forms did the dependence take, and how did the women cope?

Two-thirds of the Chicago wives experienced from moderate to extreme signs of loneliness. Meeting the new responsibilities intensified the loneliness. Anxiety over having to make all decisions concerning money, work, children, and the household could be acute. "I try not to worry and if I can't sleep at night I just take a sleeping pill. Life seems more like existing to me than living." Time also played tricks on her, the same woman observed, "it passes quickly but accumulates endlessly."[7] Loneliness struck servicemen's wives whether or not they worked or had children. However, most workers experienced only moderate or little loneliness, while most full-time mothers experienced considerable loneliness. The children simply could not fill the need for adult companionship.

A wife in Amarillo, Texas, took an evening job explaining, "I want to work till I'm so tired I'll just drop." Part-time work helped a barber's wife with two small children while her husband was overseas. "With the children, it is so confining and my vocabulary has to be limited with them." Therefore, she volunteered as a nurse's aide. She enjoyed her work, meeting new people and escaping a bit. In contrast, a lonely mother resented being tied down with the children. "When my husband was home he would stay in some nights and relieve me, but now I must carry all the responsibility, worries, and work without any help." She especially missed the conversation and the sharing of the day's troubles and discoveries. "Lack of companionship is the biggest problem I have." The Chicago study found no correlation between the degree of a wife's loneliness and length of marriage or length of separation. In other words, newlyweds and older wives of all backgrounds experienced similar feelings of loneliness.[8]

Loneliness was not the only symptom of strain. In Chicago, 29 percent of the wives reported symptoms of nervousness, irritability, restlessness, insomnia, loss of interest, feeling subdued, or feeling older. Several of the Iowa wives suffered from insomnia, two had serious breakdowns, and another found her migraine headaches intensified. A pharmacist's wife married two and a half years could not get to sleep when she was alone in the house. "I just lay awake all night listening to the water faucet drip, and the window panes creak, and finally when it starts to get a little light outside, I fall asleep for a few hours."[9] A wife of a sailor stationed in the South Pacific complained that her personality and temperament had drastically changed since her husband left. "I smoke like a fiend and chew my nails like mad. I knit all the time and never finish anything. I have severe headaches. I was nervous before but not that bad."[10] In the San Francisco area alone, 2,500 wives underwent treatment for psychoneurosis in 1944. With simple psychotherapeutic treatment, most recovered from their depressions very quickly.[11]

Increased participation in social activities proved the best cure. Servicemen's wives opted for social activities based on their class background. One middle-class woman, a Navy wife, recounted her days: "I don't have too many periods of loneliness because I keep myself busy and do a lot of arranging of recreational activities over here and so spend my spare time helping out with the plans for parties and dances."[12] Servicemen's wives in Morris, Illinois, showed the narrow range of activities of the less-educated working-class women in small towns: "My girl friends and I visit back and forth and go to shows. Well, there's roller-skating, but I don't skate. And there's bowling, but I don't bowl. And there's dancing, but I don't dance. There's a couple of movies in town, and I go to them once in a while."[13]

Some found that they had more in common with other war wives than with members of their own social class, and they formed informal clubs. At Lookout Mountain near Chattanooga, Tennessee, the clubwomen left the children with grandmother or a maid, caught the cable car into town, and took in a movie. While on these outings, they first talked about their husbands. "Then we talk of the wash, the children, some more about our husbands and then about the wash again."[14]

Half the Chicago wives kept busy socially. They had a wide range of friends and participated in a number of activities. The other half, however, had few social outlets and limited their visits and activities to immediate family or a few friends. Not one was totally isolated. (A totally isolated women would not have been visible to the sociology graduate students who selected and interviewed the wives.)

The most active were the happiest. Although the forms of activities were different, there was no difference in the range of activities between working wives and full-time housewives.[15]

Visits with friends and relatives were welcomed by all wives. "His family took good care of me, they always took me out and were very considerate." While most servicemen's wives were close to their own parents and siblings, relationships with in-laws ran the gamut. At one extreme, a Chicagoan complained that her in-laws "weren't very nice." In fact, "I felt that I was solely their son's wife, that they took no personal interest in me, had no deep feelings toward me as a daughter."[16] Another Chicagoan was more specific about her complaints: "Recreation—I don't have any. My husband's family lives downstairs and they watch me constantly. If I do go to a show once in a while (I have only gone three times since my husband left), they tell me that I should stay home and not leave the child crying all night.[17]

The importance of neighbors in helping ease the separation depended on the location. Rural and small town wives reported visiting neighbors frequently, but only 2 percent of the wives in inner-city Chicago mentioned neighborhood contacts. Those from urban areas tried to find other servicemen's wives to socialize with or spent time with their childhood girlfriends. One gregarious wife had been rushed in college by a sorority but had not pledged. Now members of that sorority were her neighbors. With all of their husbands overseas they formed a support group. Yet going out with the girls was no substitute for going out as a couple. When these husbandless wives tagged along with couples, they felt like a fifth wheel. Since their husband was the only escort "allowed" them, they stayed home at night.[18] One wife learned a bitter lesson: "I became very depressed, nervous, and a little smarter. I found out that once you are down, friends leave you out. I discovered who my friends really were, and that they did not mean very much."[19] Another wife went back to nursing school and lived in a dorm surrounded by unmarried women. Her unusual status made her an outsider. "Your topic of conversation is narrow here because other girls talk about dates, but no one wants to hear about my husband eight hours a day."[20]

Fiancées experienced less loneliness than wives. They had not built up the psychological interdependence that grows with marriage, were not tied down with children, and did not suffer quite so much over-sight of their private lives. But they too had to wait for their men to return, and they usually waited longer because single men were drafted first and released last.

The men in service got lonely too, despite everyone's best efforts to keep them busy and entertained. Some women had to contend with husbands whose loneliness was even greater than their own. As one women described her predicament: "Twice he came to Chicago AWOL to see me. Of course I was glad to see him, but I sure did fuss and fuss at him for doing it . . . He cried and said I just wanted him to be in the Army . . . I write him letters five or six pages long every day just to keep him cheerful. Goodness knows I try to build up his morale."[21]

Most wives were able to make adequate emotional and financial adjustments to their husband's absence. However, the Morris study suggested that wives with higher socioeconomic status had an easier time adjusting. They coped better because of their superior educa-tion, not because of their money. Indeed, affluence alone did little to ease the process of adjustment.[22]

Prewar financial dependence on the husband meant that many servicemen's wives were forced to learn the fundamentals of budg-eting. When a financial crisis hit, wives borrowed from their parents, used up their family savings, or got a job. About one-third of the wives took each option. One-fifth of the Chicago wives expressed real dissatisfaction with their financial situation; 12 percent found the allotment from the government insufficient. The most difficult financial reports came from families who maintained their own homes. However, two-thirds of those living in their own household reported no major difficulties. Wives who had been married two to five years had less trouble balancing budgets than those married less than two years. Mothers had more extreme cases of financial difficulties than wives without children. To ease the financial burden, many wives moved in with their relatives. In Morris, one-half of the couples had never set up a home and the wife simply stayed with parents or parents-in-law for the duration. As one wife explained, "We have never set up a home of our own, of course, and we have no children. So I just continued to live with my mother." Another quarter of the wives in Morris gave up their own homes to move in with relatives for the duration. Iowa families also doubled up. One-fifth of the families moved in with parents or had their parents move in with them.[23]

In Chicago, over half of the service wives moved in with parents or relatives (a few moved out again), and 43 percent stayed in their own apartment but lived close to relatives and called on them for help frequently. Less than half (45 percent) of the mothers, but 62 percent of the childless wives, lived with parents. This contrasts with American society in general, with only 5 percent of all families doubled up. Many found the doubling up arrangements satisfactory even though at times trying. One in ten wives claimed that this doubling up caused a real hardship. However, in at least one case, a wife enjoyed living with her mother more than she had with her husband.[24]

The most recently married women seemed to adjust better to doubling up than those who had been married the longest. Younger wives, however, had to face the problem of getting their parents to treat them like independent adults. In Hyde Park, about one-fourth of the childless wives and one-half of the mothers found doubling up a hardship, especially if they had to stay home all day. As one wife recounted, "I get along well with my mother, but I had my own home long enough to develop my own methods of keeping house, so Mother and I have altogether different ideas on how a house should be run." However, only 11 percent of the working wives were extremely dissatisfied, in contrast to 46 percent of the wives who did not work outside the home. Having outside employment and interests thus provided a safety valve for tensions building up around the house.[25]

Arguments with kinfolk and uncertain division of authority were the most commonly registered complaints. One Atlantan who lived with her husband's family and worked part time worried that her daughter would be so spoiled by the time her husband returned that he would notice the difference. "I have to fill my letters with fake stories about her for when I come home I find that if she wants to play outside without her sweater on, or if she wants candy, Herb's parents let her."[26]

The community neglected the needs of the service wives. Over half the servicemen's families were helped by their relatives, friends, and neighbors, but almost no one mentioned getting support from any community or welfare agencies or even religious groups. America poured out its heart to servicemen. Women's organizations were especially supportive of USO service centers and sent vast quantities of cookies, kits, and knitting to the soldiers in camp and overseas. Astonishingly, most organizations neglected the service wives in their midst. Established private welfare agencies, especially the Red Cross, Salvation Army, and Traveler's Aid, did provide some help in hardship cases, such as arranging for emergency furloughs and discharges, assisting indigent wives, and helping stranded camp followers return home. However, most women who could have used these services either did not know about them or avoided them. The loneliness of the typical service wife could have been assuaged by club facilities operated by churches, local governments, or community groups, but few if any were established. "I've often thought they could form some sort of USO right here in town," noted a wife in Morris, "but the people around here don't seem to go in for that sort of thing.[27]

One major new federal program did provide significant help—the Emergency Maternity and Infant Care Program. EMIC paid prenatal care, doctors' fees, hospital costs, and infant care for mothers of servicemen's babies. The couple did not have to be married. Wacs, nurses, and other servicewomen were not covered, nor were officers' wives. From 1943 through 1947, EMIC spent $127,000,000 for 1,223,000 maternity cases and 230,000 infant cases. About 70 percent of all service wives took advantage of EMIC, which covered the costs of every seventh baby in the country. The Children's Bureau, which ran EMIC, had long pushed for a comprehensive national maternity program. Before EMIC began in the spring of 1943, the maternal and child health services program in the states (funded under social security) had already assisted hundreds of thousands of mothers and children, mostly relief cases. Congress, nervous about socialized medicine, approached EMIC as a wartime emergency measure, considering it to be primarily a benefit to the fathers in the military. Proposals to provide case benefits directly to the mothers were blocked because "there would be no way to assure the enlisted man that care . . . will be available for either his wife or infant."[28]

The best support for the serviceman's family came from the grandparents—the grandmothers who shopped and babysat and the grandfathers who did repairs and served as role models to the little boys.

They took back into their homes their wedded daughter and provided for her and her children, or sent her money to help her maintain her own dwelling. Help from families and relatives in the form of sharing houses or giving money made it possible for most servicemen's wives to make do. Such family help was not measurable in dollars and cents. Family members watched children so that mothers could go to school or go out with friends. The ways families helped out were countless.[29]

A service wife's first impulse was to follow her husband from base to base until he was discharged or shipped overseas. Among the wives in Morris, two-fifths became camp followers and lived as near as possible to their husbands for as long as possible. Another third saved up money for visits. Only a quarter did neither.[30] By 1945, enlisted Army husbands reported that half of their wives lived near or on the post. Unfortunately, housing on most bases was never plentiful. Even for the semipermanent soldiers and sailors, housing officials ranked family needs near the bottom of the list. In Wilmington, North Carolina, two hundred pregnant Army wives at one stage planned a sitdown strike to protest their treatment. They had been allowed to rent the summer cottages of Wilmington citizens for the fall and winter and refused to move once summer returned. "The war worker's wife gets a house and a big salary," they fumed, "What do we get?"[31]

In many congested areas, wives with children faced severe problems, since landlords could be choosy and did not want to have crying babies in their apartments. Navy wives in Portland, Maine, were bluntly told that those with children were not welcome. After spending a month looking for a house in Great Falls, Montana, an Army camp follower "arrived at the conclusion via slammed telephones and shaken heads that army couples generally were unwelcome and army couples with children were absolutely unclean." Rental restrictions often included no kitchen privileges, which meant that the women had to spend precious money to eat out. Food in town was neither cheap nor appetizing; even worse, eating in public restaurants indicated that women were not performing the normal cooking duties of a wife. In one apartment building, "The men weren't allowed to come up to our rooms and you had to hide in a telephone booth to kiss your husband good night."[32] Desperate wives rented almost anything that resembled an apartment. Indeed, the overwhelming majority of enlisted soldiers complained that the living facilities for their wives near them ranged from pretty poor to very poor.

Roving journalist Agnes Meyer reported that a building in Leesville, Louisiana, condemned before the war, now had fourteen families in rooms "no larger than the pig runs. There were twelve babies under a year—'all boys' as the mothers told me proudly."[33] Each cramped room was equipped with only one light bulb and no water save on the ground floor. In another servicemen's ghetto, each family lived in a shed big enough for one double bed. Thirty-five families shared one toilet and shower. Even then the toilet was kept locked and "every inhabitant had to run to the landlady for permission to use it." Meyer concluded that "Old barns deserted by construction gangs, chicken coops, improvised structures thrown together with a few boards, a piece of corrugated iron and whatnot, were all brought into use for this purpose." The exorbitant rents charged servicemen's wives were similar to those paid in Negro slums. For these apartments, many not larger than 10 feet by 12 feet in size, the wives paid $30 to $35 a month from their monthly allowance of $50. Near Truax Field, Wisconsin, one flyer's wife was succinct, "I'm sick of living in a hole in the wall and seeing him only once a week. I want to have some fun!"[34]

Finding a job, especially for wives not tied down with small children, became as important as finding a place to live. Here again, servicemen's wives often encountered discrimination. Many served as waitresses and even as taxi dancers in the night cafés. Better jobs were hard to find, since any prospective employer knew that a serviceman's wife would quit whenever her husband was transferred, which could be at any time. Some pretended that their husbands were part of the permanent cadre at the post. But perceptive employees would usually reply, "There can't be that many cademen at Crowder. No you girls aren't very good risks from the hiring end."[35] For most, camp following soon became intolerable, so they drifted back to their hometowns.

In Iowa, 43 percent of the wives worked, 29 percent full time, 14 percent part time. The 35 percent who considered work a hardship worked solely for financial reasons. The remaining 65 percent said that they enjoyed their jobs. Some had even started work in order to meet new people and begin new activities. In Chicago, only one wife was absolutely "miserable" because she had to work. Much more typical was the comment from a department store clerk: "I like my job and all of the people I work with. Everyone is so pleasant, and that helps me so much."[36] Women without children were much more likely to work than mothers. In the Chicago sample, drawn from a university neighborhood, 57 percent of the childless wives worked full time, 30 percent were full-time students, and 13 percent did not work or go to school (one-fourth of these were pregnant). Of the Chicago mothers, 11 percent worked part time, and 72 percent stayed home.[37]

Even though their wives needed money and adult companionship, many husbands opposed their working on principle. One Iowan explained that he would rather starve than have his wife work. Another made his wife promise at their marriage that she would never work. In this case, the husband finally gave his consent because they were so financially strapped, but the wife promised to quit work when he returned.[38]

Since many wives enjoyed work, and gained confidence as well as learning new skills, their husbands now had another worry. What if their wives would not quit when they came home? The wives themselves were eager to return to homemaking and motherhood, however. As one interviewer reported, "Mina explains she will gladly quit when Virgil returns, but Virgil's letters indicate he is afraid she won't."[39] A Chicagoan explained, "I'm now working steady. I enjoy working. I'd rather work than stay home. When my husband comes home I'll quit."[40]

To reach a joint decision on whether a wife should work as well as on other important issues, couples had to develop ways to communicate long distance their feelings, attitudes, hopes, and fears. Letters, furloughs, and visits to the base by the wife, were the most common sources of communication used by the separated couples. The quantity of the letters was not as important as the quality, and no letters could alone patch up years of difficulties. Yet correspondence was vital. Among the well-educated Chicago wives, 63 percent wrote their husbands at least once a day, 9 percent wrote every other day, 5 percent twice a week, 3 percent once a week. Only 2 percent did not write; they were waiting for postwar divorces. For many wives, correspondence was just like keeping a diary. The main topics were daily activities, children, friends, families, past and future together, assurances of love, and general discussions of topics of mutual interest. Fourteen percent simply said that they "wrote everything"; 14 percent also added that they sent clippings, pictures, or packages. One of the wives who wrote her husband about everything she did said that her letters were "about two typewritten sheets of letter paper and just tell him everything I've done to that point."[41]

Only a handful of wives attempted to improve and advance their relationship further through their letters. Most tried to hold on to what they once had. Those who did brave forth adventurously were pleased with the results. As one explained, "We have both written and joked about the adjustments he will have to make because he will probably be changed, but we're both mature and don't think we'll have very many problems of adjustment."[42] Another provided a detailed account: "I wrote every day and he wrote every day. I wrote about everything I read about, my feelings for him, and described my activities. Those letters really helped us to continue our relationship. He is repressed in some ways and had a hard time talking about the things he could write about."[43]

How effective were couples in communicating by letter? On a three-point scale, 9 percent of the Iowa couples scored very good, 73 percent adequate, and 18 percent fair to poor. Chicago couples reflected similar rankings on a five-point scale, 9 percent scored very good, 24 percent above average, 41 percent adequate, 17 percent fairly adequate, 7 percent weak communication or none at all. One-fourth of the wives were dissatisfied with their letter-writing abilities. A long separation took a toll even on the best communicators. Correspondence became more difficult as the months and years went by. A handful of wives got to the point that they felt that they no longer knew their husbands, and therefore stopped writing to them. A few felt inhibited from writing their intimate thoughts because they knew that censors would read all letters. Those who became dissatisfied said it was harder to communicate as time passed, difficult to remember things to tell about, and not easy to "find the time." Moreover, for some it became increasingly difficult to remember just how their husbands used to look. A Bostonian knitted her 6 foot 3½ inch officer husband a sweater. His next letter contained a snapshot showing that the sweater came halfway to his knees.[44]

Furloughs or visits by wives to a military base smoothed the way to a good postwar reunion. A New Yorker thoroughly cleaned her apartment and planned the perfect dinner, the mood to be set with dry martinis, only to discover, "Darling, don't you remember? I never drink martinis." While furloughs could be temporarily disruptive and hard on couples and children who were not sure how to behave, they often helped reassure family members that any changes detected would not prove insurmountable barriers to a successful reunion.[45]

On top of the emotional and financial hardships, most wives worried about the safety of their husbands. They feared that their husbands would be captured, killed, or missing in action. One wife's dreams foretold that her husband would be kept in the Army during the postwar occupation of Europe. While women were reluctant to talk about their anxieties, they often gnawed just below the surface.[46]

The popular culture of the era, reflected in songs, soap operas, and movies, quickly picked up the themes of separation, loneliness, and the need for inner strength to carry on. A new religious tone was evident in Hollywood, as indicated by the enormous popularity of Catholic pictures like *The Song of Bernadette* (1943) and *Going My Way* (1944). While there were no major films that adopted a particularly Protestant approach, Hollywood did produce a series of movies in which spiritualism was a theme. In *A Guy Named Joe* (1943) pilot Spencer Tracy dies, but his spirit guides a new generation of air men and air women (Irene Dunne plays a WASP pilot). Tracy is fatalistic about warfare: "Men must die and women must weep." In *The Human Comedy* (1943), a faithful rendition of William Saroyan's 1943 novel, the women on the home front must maintain their morale in the face of telegrams of death delivered by Mickey Rooney. Knowledge that their departed loved ones have eternal life sustains them. As the fighting in France reached a crescendo in the summer of 1944, the Lux Radio Theater presented Jeanette MacDonald and Nelson Eddy in a version of "Maytime," originally a 1937 movie, updated to emphasize the power of love over death in wartime.[47]

During the war, parent-child relations and child-rearing meant different things to middle- and working-class families. Middle-class mothers were more likely than working-class mothers to bottle feed than to nurse infants, to set strict schedules, and to expect their children to assume greater responsibilities at a younger age. After the war, however, middle-class mothers became rather more permissive in rearing infants. The popularity of Dr. Spock's new "Baby Book" typified this trend.

Throughout the war, middle-class mothers were more permissive in fulfilling their older children's requests and more equalitarian in dealing with the child than were working-class mothers.[48] The middle-class parents spanked children much less often than the working class did, preferring instead to encourage internalized guilt feelings in those who misbehaved. They felt standing in the corner was a more effective technique, and better for the child's moral growth, than a whack on the rear. Middle-class parents were more concerned with the child's motivations, working-class parents with the child's overt actions. Thus the middle class stressed internalized standards of conduct, such as honesty and self-control, as well as postponement of gratification. Upward social mobility, especially through educational achievement, continued to be a strong ideal among the middle class.[49] Working-class children, by contrast, were trained to obedience, neatness, and respectability. The class differences must not be exaggerated; compared to other cultures, the differences were small and the overlap was large. But when children reached high school, teachers and laymen alike felt they could fairly easily tell the class background of each youth.[50]

In some families fathers actively participated in child care. Before induction, one-third of the Iowa fathers had been helpful, especially in feeding and dressing the youngest children. Two-fifths of the men believed that fatherhood had made them "more responsible." For at least a third of the servicemen's families, then, the husband's part in child care during wartime was sorely missed.[51] Civilian fathers in defense jobs also found it difficult to participate in child-care responsibilities. Hundreds of thousands moved to large war production centers in search of work and left their families back home. Others commuted several hours each way to and from work, usually with overtime added, and were too tired to help with child care. Still other fathers worked the graveyard shift and were sleeping when their children were awake. Yet the problems remained most acute in servicemen's families.

What seemed to worry America more than absent fathers was

absent mothers. Newspapers were filled with horror stories about children locked in cars while mothers worked, or youngsters wandering the streets with latch-keys around their necks. Older children, it was feared, would become juvenile delinquents because their mothers were no longer home to properly supervise them. Editorialists discovered a new problem, one of "parental delinquency, currently aggravated by war conditions." They recommended an awakening on the part of the parents to their responsibilities and, in some cases, a vigorous application of the old-fashioned woodshed treatment. A sampling by the Office for War Information of newspapers in December 1943 and January 1944 revealed that 11 percent of all editorials dealt with juvenile delinquency. The press divided about equally between blaming parents and blaming the community.[52]

Was juvenile delinquency on the rise? Yes, for both boys and girls. A sample of eighty-three courts showed an increase in cases from 65,000 to 75,500 between 1940 and 1942. This 16 percent increase was not shared equally by boys and girls. Although four-fifths of all crimes were committed by boys, the percentage increase was much greater for girls (38 percent) than for boys (11 percent). Moreover, growing cities showed higher increases. The increase for boys in cities with a growing population was 13.5 percent, with decreasing population, 4.5 percent. For girls the figures were 40.5 percent and 30.1 percent. Delinquency increased twice as fast among white girls as black girls, and three times as fast among white boys as black boys.[53] The crimes boys and girls committed were also different. Boys were most likely to steal or be caught in an act of vandalism or mischief. Girls, on the other hand, were most likely to be picked up for running away from home or "ungovernable behavior," which usually meant intimate association with disreputable boys. Delinquency reached a peak in 1943, but in 1944 and 1945, the peak years for employment of mothers, juvenile delinquency actually decreased one year and rose only slightly the other.

Temporary disruption of family life could lead to problems that adversely affected children, but the real roots of juvenile delinquency were much deeper. A study early in the war of five hundred hard-core juvenile delinquents and a control group of five hundred non-delinquents from the same deteriorating low-rent neighborhood in Boston concluded that the nondelinquents were not just undetected delinquents, but rather came from a very different home environment. Delinquent children moved from tenement to tenement twice as often as the nondelinquents and were twice as likely to come from broken homes. Nondelinquents' homes were characterized twice as often by internal cleanliness, well-planned household routine, and self-respect for family members. Nondelinquents were four times as likely as delinquents to have deep emotional ties with both mother and father and ten times as likely to have experienced firm but kindly discipline in contrast with lax or no discipline (6 percent of the fathers of delinquents were characterized as firm, 56 percent of the fathers of nondelinquents were firm). The parents and grandparents of hard-core juvenile delinquents had a much higher history of mental retardation, emotional disturbances, criminality, drunkenness, and serious physical ailments. Though many differences existed between delinquent and nondelinquent families, one thing was constant, the same percentage of mothers worked in both groups.[54] In sum, disrupted families and working mothers were blamed far more than was appropriate for their part in the rise of juvenile delinquency.

Most servicemen's families did not include teenagers or even many children because older men and fathers of large families were usually immune from the draft. In the Chicago study, 88 percent of the children were under age seven; only half the families even had children. Three-fourths of the Chicago service families with children had only one child, a fifth had two children, only one family had more than two. In Iowa, the sizes were slightly higher, one-fourth had one child, one-half had two children, the remaining one-fourth had three or more.[55]

Mothers emphasized repeatedly how much company their children provided. One Morris woman explained: "I don't know what I'd do without him. He keeps me busy all day, and even though he does go to bed early at night, it's about eight o'clock before I'm really through for the day. That helps to make it less lonesome." Another mother's daughter was "just about at the creep stage now, and gets into everything. She's so happy all the time and gets around so much that I just enjoy having her here. I'm just so happy with the baby. She keeps me so interested and occupied all the time."[56]

But the feeling of satisfaction was not universal. The wife of a former policeman who was in the Navy explained, "since I am tied down with the kids I get very little opportunity to go out . . . I am very nervous and irritable, worry more than I ever did and feel very unhappy." Another recalled that after being with the kids day and night, "I was very nervous and high strung and let it out on them."[57]

The area in which a father's absence caused the greatest trouble was in the disciplining of children. "The kids don't seem to mind as much as they did when he was home," was a typical lament. In Iowa an interviewer reported that Mrs. J. "was so accustomed to having her husband rule the children that she did not know how to manage them alone, and always missed him when a disciplinary situation arose."[58] The Chicago study could not determine if it was the age of the children or the number of the children that caused the greatest problems. Mothers reported special trouble disciplining their children after the age of three. In Chicago, 19 percent of the mothers with one child and 70 percent of those with two or more children reported considerable difficulty in discipline. Furthermore, the longer the separation, the more serious the problems.[59]

Of the 51 percent of the Iowa families reporting disciplinary problems, almost one-third reflected prolonged maladjustment. The war hit little Sally H. in Iowa hard. Her daddy had gone away, maybe to be killed. Mommy worked every day, leaving grandmother to care for her. She was frightened—maybe nobody loved her, maybe everyone hated her and wanted to get rid of her. Not until daddy returned and the old three-way companionship had been restored did Sally regain her zest for life.[60] Although five out of six of the mothers did not report such serious problems, they did tell how the children got on their nerves, how it was hard to manage and discipline the children without a father around, how tied down they were, how the grandparents spoiled the children, how the mother's full-time occupation made caring for the child difficult, and how much the children missed the father. The mothers who had limited social contacts reported even more problems with their children.[61]

How much of the problem with children was related to father's absence, how much to mother's adjustment to his absence, and how much would have happened even if the father had stayed home is hard to determine. Mothers did, however, worry that children would complicate a smooth reunion, and they were often right. Some children might hold back and not immediately recognize or accept their fathers. Others might simply be confused about family roles and responsibilities. For some, fears became realities; for most, the problems would work themselves out over time.

When the day finally came for the homecoming and reunion, the great majority of the wives expected postservice readjustment would work out satisfactorily. Half the women expected no significant change in either spouse. "No sirree, it won't be hard to get used to him when he comes home . . . I know I'm certain I wouldn't want to spend my life with any other man." One in five foresaw a happier family. "He is more broad-minded . . . He wants to spend more time with his family. I have become much more capable and I think it is a very good thing."[62]

Military service helped many black families break out of the cycle of poverty, recrimination, and psychological depression. Before the war, the Browns were an atomistic and unhappy family in Des Moines. Howard Brown, an unemployed porter, spent his time as a volunteer in Boy Scout and YMCA work, yearning for a law degree and a political career that seemed beyond reach. Sarah's work supported Howard and the three children, and it also made her psychologically independent of him. For the sake of the children she did not seek a divorce. Howard spent his Army years in New York, where he was drawn into the excitement of the Harlem scene. He wrote lengthy letters, full of longing for Sarah and dreams for the future. The new mood continued upon his return, as Howard began helping Sarah at home and playing with the children. Howard attended college on the GI bill, and drew Sarah into his community projects. She could not quite grasp his dreams of becoming a lawyer, but she went along and succeeded in becoming a much more sociable person herself.[63]

A minority of wives, about one in four, predicted trouble ahead. Long years of separation made the marriage seem like a dream. "I can't remember what he looks like." A few feared that a stranger would come home. Others detected an unfavorable personality change in their absent spouses, perhaps caused by the miseries of military life, perhaps something permanent. "I just don't feel that common rapport anymore . . . I don't see how we can bridge over basic differences." One Chicago woman recognized they both had changed: "Our ideas and interests . . . will now be changed because he has seen too much and I too little." The new sense of independence might also be threatened. "He will feel superior and will insist on being the boss in the strictest sense of the word . . . Now I speak my piece regardless of the consequences."[64]

A small number of wives, 3 or 4 percent, planned on divorce: "And now everything is in the lawyer's hands. I'm getting the divorce on grounds of desertion, because he hasn't written for over a year now. I couldn't get a divorce on the grounds of cruelty or adultery or any of the other grounds allowed in the State of Illinois because he isn't guilty of any of those things."[65] Another discovered that her husband was going with a nurse in England; he wanted a divorce. The Iowa families who divorced all had had major preservice problems. Not one of these divorces was due to wartime causes.[66]

Even successful reunions could be rocky at first. The men anticipated with some trepidation the challenge of reestablishing their roles as breadwinner, husband, and father. Many wives reported that their husbands took to drinking, gambling, and going out with their veteran pals when they came home. In Iowa, 8 percent of the men found it hard to settle down, 6 percent more were upset because of the lack of adequate housing, 5 percent could find no jobs they liked, and 4 percent were chronically ill. Many wives worried because of this inability to settle down. "He'd go up to town and come back again—just fidget around—it seemed like that was all he'd ever do. It got on his nerves, and it got on my nerves."[67]

In these studies the same indicators that predicted successful adjustment to separation also predicted adjustment to reunion. The only difference was that for reunion, the couple's adjustment to separation, the length of the separation, and the number of hardships encountered by each person had to be taken into account. The Iowa study also looked to see if the childhood happiness of the wife had any effect on her adjustment to separation (no) and if it was related to poor adjustment to the reunion (yes). The Freudians are still working on this finding. Age at marriage did not help predict adjustment to reunion, but the larger the family, the poorer the adjustment. The men did not expect the trouble they would have becoming a father to children who never knew them. The war-separated children were more aggressive, anxiety ridden, and distant from their fathers than children in families that had not been disrupted. As sociologist Reuben Hill concluded, "Children are burdensome."[68]

Self-sufficiency on the part of the wife during the separation sometimes helped and sometimes hindered the adjustment during the reunion. The ideal balance was to achieve a moderate amount of maturity, confidence, and self-sufficiency. If a wife had become highly self-sufficient or independent, the couple had trouble adjusting to the original family roles, as did couples where the wife was too dependent.[69]

The contacts husband and wife made with members of the opposite sex during the separation generated discussion and debate within servicemen's families. Sexual mores were generally looser during the war. Many a teenage girl was told that having intercourse with a soldier before he was shipped out, perhaps never to return, was a way to contribute to the war effort. Apparently these "Victory girls" would not think of having sexual relations with a civilian, but felt they were "doing something for their country" when they had sex with soldiers. They refused money for their services and some picked up the spirit of the Army-Navy rivalry by "specializing in the Army" and refusing to have anything to do with a sailor or vice versa.[70]

The Army and Navy alarmed at the skyrocketing rates of VD reported in 1941, and determined not to repeat the World War I losses, started sex education classes and issued prophylactics. The military also did a thorough job of clearing out the red light districts, at least those in close proximity to their bases and stations. However, pick-up girls and Victory girls soon replaced prostitutes, especially in urban areas. Eliot Ness, in charge of Venereal Disease Control, maintained that the promiscuous girl was typically "a casual, fun-seeking girl, wanting male companionship; a young experimenter, somewhat lonely, easing her conscience by quixotic references to 'patriotism.' "[71]

How many servicemen could resist the temptation to take advantage of the V-girls? The Army's experts concluded that "15 percent to 30 percent won't, 15 percent will, 70 percent shift back and forth under the influence of this or that circumstance including upbringing, availability of companionship, mass or group morale, work interest and fatigue, normal recreation and distraction, feeding and above all alcohol."[72] About one-third of the married soldiers engaged in extramarital affairs while they were in uniform. In civilian life, only one of every six of these same men carried on extramarital affairs. One wife in six had an extramarital affair during the war, about the same proportion as in the 1930s.[73]

Although few husbands told their wives about their extramarital affairs while in the service, many couples did reach an understanding concerning what contacts were allowable for each partner during the separation. According to a survey of the Twelfth Corps, part of Patton's Third Army, the officers were more likely than enlisted men not to object to their wives having contact with members of the opposite sex as long as it remained platonic. A favorite soldier's song was "Don't Sit under the Apple Tree" ("with anyone else but me"). In the Iowa study the overwhelming majority of couples opted for fidelity for both husband and wife, 12 percent for a double standard, 6 percent for "friendly but not intimate." Those opting for fidelity or a double standard adjusted best to separation and reunions. Women who dated other men during the husband's absence had the hardest time readjusting to the reunion.[74]

If soldiers discovered that their wives had been cheating, nearly half said that they would forgive and forget: "you're damn right I would, for I've been no saint." Yet the majority of soldiers accepted a double standard. A soldier's indiscretions need not affect a marriage permanently; a wife's indiscretions would be intolerable. Communities usually sanctioned the double standard; while tolerating a soldier's extramarital affairs they were quick to notice and condemn any suspicious activity by a serviceman's wife. Indeed, many wives complained of overzealous community watchdog policies: "A friend called me over to his table and asked me who the sailor was. I told him it was just my cousin, and he said, 'Oh, heck! That takes all the fun out of it.' If I ever had any intention of going out with anyone when my husband was away, I certainly wouldn't bring my family along!" Another summed up the exasperation of many, "It doesn't matter what time it is, the people upstairs jump to peek whenever I go out or come in."[75]

Gossip abounded in small towns: "I'm worried about my daughter-in-law. Two different women have been to see me and tell me that they've seen her out with a man in town who's married and has three children . . . Of course, I wouldn't dream of telling Dan. But I'm so afraid that someone in town might just be malicious enough to write him about it. If Dan ever hears there was anything the least bit wrong about his wife while he was gone, he'll never forgive her and he'll never go back and live with her."[76] More soldier husbands had suspicions than wives had affairs. More accurate was the observer who noted, "I know of eighteen wives and sweethearts of servicemen and I don't know of anyone stepping out."[77]

The general loosening of personal morals continued into the post-war period. It affected not just the relationship between husbands and wives, but also that between parents and children. In the postwar period, adolescents were generally more independent and practiced more flexible moral codes than did their parents.

A 1943 survey of women aged twenty to thirty-five asked a series of questions about attitudes concerning personal morality: "Do you feel women's morals should be the same as men? Should men/women require virginity in a girl/boy for marriage? Do men require virginity?" The survey found that a woman's education and location (size of city) were the best predictors of her response pattern; region ranked third. The highly educated servicemen's wives who lived in Chicago were therefore more open to change and more likely to approve equal standards for men and women than those wives in Morris, Illinois, or in Iowa.[78]

The college-educated, big-city dwellers, and westerners held views on morals that were more equalitarian. Those with little education and southern or rural background remained tied to the traditional double standard. Small-city, high-school-educated, northern Americans held intermediate views in the area of morals. To the extent that they differed from their sisters, the college-educated, big-city dwellers, and westerners pioneered the future.

These servicemen's families whose wives and children were forced to become more independent, more skilled in finances and handi-work, and more mature reflected what was happening to American families in general but much more slowly. Servicemen's families were more disrupted and more traumatized during the war, and they were, therefore, the first group to reflect the future trend toward equali-tarian marriages.

A 1946 poll captured this trend. Interviewers asked a series of questions about how decisions were made regarding when to have children, how the family money would be spent, where the family would locate, how to discipline the children, and where to spend a vacation.[79] How to discipline the children split the American public between people who felt it ought to be a wife's prerogative and those who preferred a joint decision. Women were more insistent than men on the joint nature of the decision. Americans answered that spending the family income and taking a vacation should be joint decisions. In contrast, few thought women should decide where the family would live.

To discover which sociocultural factors most influenced a person's answers, all five questions were pooled together. Those who answered by maintaining that these be joint decisions were scored highest. The average score was 62 percent, which means Americans tended to give equalitarian answers. Three sociocultural factors tied for best predictor of a person's equalitarian responses. Educational background split respondents into those without and those with a high school education. The better-educated gave more joint decision answers. The impact of high school education was becoming noticeable in the values of the people. A person's occupational background also influenced his or her answers. Farmers ranked higher than white-collar and blue-collar workers. Tying with education and occupation was a person's religious affiliation. The more traditionalistic Catholics scored lower than those of the other faiths. The nondenominational were most likely to favor an equalitarian husband-wife domestic relationship.[80]

The millions of couples whose lives were disrupted by military service did not consciously attempt to restructure the American family. They tried their best to cope with uncertainty, to gain fuller control of their own destiny. For a few, their marriages crumbled with the return to peacetime. Problems already apparent before the war, or, less often, hasty unions made during the war, accounted for the majority of divorces. In the sample of servicemen's families in Iowa, Hyde Park, and Morris, less than 1 percent of the marriages ended in divorce upon the husband's return.

In the vast majority of cases, both partners discovered untapped reserves of strength, courage, and wisdom. Better educated than older generations, they were better equipped to analyze their problems, weigh the options, and find solutions. The loneliness suffered by both wife and husband taught both how central companionship was to their marriage. The assistance rendered by parents and parents-in-law was wisely designed to strengthen the nuclear family, rather than pull the wife's loyalties back toward an extended kin group. The many problems caused by children reinforced the wife's realization that the husband was needed as a father, not just a bread-winner. Separation forced both husbands and wives to become more mature, independent, and self-reliant. The way they balanced their new strengths with their heightened realization of the importance of companionate marriage was to seek and accept more sharing of power and responsibility within the family. Many husbands accepted the growing strength of their wives and were ready to share more. The intrusion of public needs into the private sanctuary of the home accelerated the acceptance of equalitarian norms inside the family.

8.
The War and Beyond
Women's Place in American Life

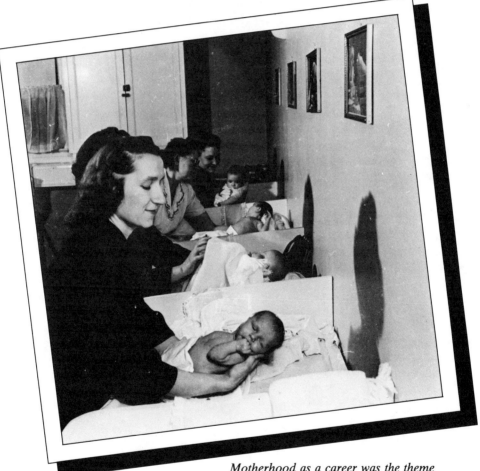

Motherhood as a career was the theme of the baby boom. Bayway Community Center, Elizabeth, New Jersey, April 1944.

From **1941 to 1945,** American women were at war with America in a double sense. In households, the labor market, and the services, women cooperated with—sacrificed for—national goals; in the same arenas, women also waged their own wars against those goals, which they frequently viewed as subversive of their own most deeply held values. Throughout the period, private goals remained overwhelmingly important for many women. Yet women's experience of and attitudes toward the war cannot be explained simply as a struggle between the claims of patriotism and those of private interest. Both patriotism and private interest informed women's cooperation as well as their conflict with national priorities. The two sets of categories do not mesh neatly, but rather cut across each other like a grid. In their evaluation of national goals, women responded from their own deeply rooted moral evaluations of good and evil, which they associated intimately with what they considered proper or improper behavior for women in society. American women responded to the demands of the war as women.

Women, like other Americans, answered the call of patriotism, and felt themselves to be patriotic. Yet women, also like other Americans, reinterpreted the public definitions of patriotism in relation to their own values, experiences, and goals. At best, patriotism is an elusive concept, and especially hard to identify during the war years. Women's patriotism, understood as their support for the war against the Axis, resulted both from a willingness to offer unquestioning support to national policies and, perhaps more important, from a sense of moral outrage at the perfidy of the attack on Pearl Harbor, the atrocities of the Japanese, and the immoral conduct of the Nazi government. These contemporaneous justifications for the war were captured in the media's depiction of Tojo and Hitler as personalized enemies. The emphasis fell on the personal and the concrete. In recent years, it has become common to judge the barbarity of the war by more general criteria, such as genocide—the Holocaust or total war on civilian populations—but it was not at the time. And women expressed their patriotism in concrete personal ways also. Women felt patriotic when they volunteered for USO work, took a war job, saved fats, bought war bonds, or sent a loved one to the Army. Other women felt patriotic when they resisted the intense propaganda for women to take war jobs. "I have plenty of defense work myself taking care of the nine-month-old baby and the five-year-old boy," explained the wife of a welder in Pittsburgh. In May 1943, 58 percent of all women thought they could best help the war effort by staying home.[1] The government was concerned by the proliferation of individual interpretations of patriotism that assumed the virtues of loyalty while resisting specific directives. Business shrugged; to coax more women into the labor force it raised pay scales and improved working conditions.

In effect, for most women, universal moral values probably carried more weight than patriotism, which they most readily assumed out of moral concern and the dictates of which they persisted in defining for themselves. Women's concern with conforming to their own understanding of moral imperatives helps to explain the confusion between the categories of patriotism and private interest and cooperation and conflict. The private decisions of women and their families normally reflected a balance between particular self-interest—both economic and psychic—and universal moral beliefs. But women's understanding of morality itself requires careful investigation.

By 1940 (and probably earlier) the special link between morality and gender roles had largely dissolved. Americans of the late nineteenth century had, by and large, accepted the notion that women inherently possessed a superior sense of morality to that of men. This ideology associated moral purity with the home, in which female values should dominate; less spiritual male values held corresponding sway in the public realm of work and politics. Women leaders of the Progressive era had relied upon this view to argue that women should have the right to vote in order to protect the home and to purify politics.[2] By the third decade of the twentieth century, however, the special association of women with morality had largely dissipated, a casualty perhaps of the fiasco of prohibition, perhaps of woman suffrage, perhaps of the steady increase in women's labor force participation, perhaps only of the more relaxed social mores of the 1920s, perhaps of the blow of the depression. Whatever the causes, by the 1940s, with the exception of the literature of the Women's Christian Temperance Union, few references to the notion of inherently superior female morality could be found. Claire Boothe Luce's smash Broadway hit *The Women* (1937) openly proclaimed that the fair sex could be inherently nasty, if not actually evil. The polls of the war years still showed that women displayed greater pacifism than men, but the national commitment to fighting, hating, and unconditional surrender submerged the possible impact of this tendency. No women peace leaders of the stature of Jane Addams or Emily Balch emerged, nor did anything resembling the large peace movement of the 1920s. When, after the war, Eleanor Roosevelt earned a place as an influential peace leader, she did so on new grounds.

The central moral issues of the war were not specifically linked to gender. Equality, in particular, assumed the proportions of a central moral value, but equality of sacrifice appealed to both liberals and conservatives, and to both men and women. Both the Roosevelt administration and labor unions strongly promoted economic equality. Rationing, taxes, and selective service appeared far more tolerable to those who believed that the rules were being applied uniformly to everyone regardless of status. Indeed, in practice the rules were seen as equitably administered. Americans' main moral complaint concerned labor strikes, which appeared as illegitimate efforts to profiteer from the emergency. Union spokesmen emphasized their "no-strike" pledge, pointing out how small a proportion of work time was lost through strikes. But not even the most militant unionists tried to explain away the massive coal strikes that threatened the fuel supply of homes and factories. The public mood of hostility toward unions, especially on the part of housewives, grew.

The claims of racial equality for blacks aroused little support outside the black community, the CIO leadership, and leftist groups. The reason seems to have been a remarkable misperception on the part of white America that blacks actually did enjoy equality in terms of jobs, housing, schooling, police protection, and welfare services. The white, segregated South was more aware of the reality of inequality, but vigorously defended it, arguing that blacks, being morally and intellectually inferior and lacking ambition, were getting all they deserved. The contradictions of southern racism were already beginning to unravel, although black women had little reason to discern signs of change, except perhaps for the improvement in salary scales for black teachers.[3]

For the American population as a whole, inequality of actual living conditions lessened during the war. The share of family income going to the top 5 percent declined from 30 percent in 1929 to 21 percent in 1944.[4] During the war boom, working-class families with two or three wage earners frequently reached the $100-a-week level that placed them in the top fifth of income distribution. The diminishing inequality of standards of living proved even more dramatic: rationing, price and rent controls, the relative rise of blue-collar versus white-collar incomes, selective service, EMIC, and the rapid spread of hospitalization insurance all combined to narrow the gap in consumption between the richest and the poorest thirds of the population. The evidence on narrowing gaps in food consumption and nutritional standards underscored the implications of the changes for housewives. Other forces also tended to lessen inequality. The exodus out of rural American transferred millions of families from areas with poor prospects for men and few jobs for women into a more promising urban or small town environment.

Minority families made especially dramatic gains during the war. The labor force participation rates for the major ethnic and racial groups of women living in cities and small towns had begun to converge by 1950, though black women stood out as especially committed to paid employment. The rate at which the groups held white-collar jobs reflects the strong impact made by differential access to education and by the lingering effects of discrimination (see table 20).

The income of black families more than doubled between 1939 and 1945, though their incomes and opportunities still fell far below whites. The wretched poverty on Indian reservations had worsened during the 1930s; of the New Deal welfare programs only the Civilian Conservation Corps had reached the reservations. During the war, military service rates were high among Native Americans, and several hundred women enlisted. Their family allowance and dependency checks poured welcome cash into the community, as did the earnings of men and women who found jobs at nearby military installations or who trekked to industrial centers. Extensive military activities in Alaska also provided job opportunities for Eskimo, Indian, and Aleut families, although many of the latter were forced to resettle in camps when the Japanese threatened the Aleutian Islands. On the whole, blacks were able to hold their wartime income gains, though fierce discrimination blocked them from further advances. The reservation Indians, however, relapsed into poverty after the war boom ended. The only permanent gain they made was the acquisition of skills that would permit them to survive in the cities when they eventually decided to abandon the reservations. Incomes doubled in over-crowded Puerto Rico, thanks to higher sugar prices and new military installations. Continued rural poverty, combined with rapid popu-lation growth rates, set the stage for large-scale postwar migration to New York.[5]

In the southern Appalachians, 700,000 moved north to industrial centers such as Dayton, Detroit, and Muncie. In the face of consid-erable hostility toward "hillbillies," they clung to strong extended kin networks, often driving back and forth to the mountains after a week's work in the city. The remittances from war workers and soldiers helped ease the poverty in the mountains. The Appalachians responded to their new contact with cities by a dramatic change in fertility. In 1940, mountain women had a birth rate 50 percent higher than the national average; by 1950 they were only 20 percent higher, and by 1960 were slightly below the national rate. The women also sharply increased their labor force participation rates, and, to some degree, helped nudge their families away from patriarchy.[6]

To the extent that an economic leveling took place during the war, the sense of injustice regarding structural inequality seems to have dimmed. Certainly the moral fervor of liberalism faded, and the postwar political mood became distinctly more conservative, a trend reinforced by the grudging acceptance of the income tax that was now routinely withheld from the paychecks of all classes. During the war, little attention was paid to economic inequality. In any case, far more attention centered on the equality of personal sacrifice. With every neighborhood in the land displaying blue stars and gold stars, the immediacy of the sacrifice was clear even to those who did not have a loved one in uniform. Women shared a bondage of grief, a point constantly reiterated by media images of servicemen saying farewell to their mothers, wives, and sweethearts, which further strengthened the sense of sisterhood in their sphere of suffering. But a deep spirit of equality and community in general resulted from the hardships imposed upon everyone and the complex adjustments needed to meet the challenge, especially on the part of housewives. Long after the war, the generations who had lived through it would wax nostalgic about their equality of sacrifice and of suffering, and about the resurgence of a sense of civic duty and community participation.

The big loser in the wake of equality of sacrifice was the Red Cross. Its elitist social pretensions offended average Americans, while its disdain for its own volunteers relegated society women to make-work tasks. Blacks were outraged at its segregated blood policy. The Red Cross lost its important role in controlling nursing to the military nurse corps on the one hand, and the newly invigorated civilian American Nurses' Association on the other. Most damaging of all, the Red Cross had alienated its most important clients, the soldiers. They returned home with a highly negative view of the bureaucratic aloofness (and alleged promiscuity) of the agency's staff, producing a sharp decline in public support. Although the Red Cross desperately reorganized itself after the war, allowing more of a voice to local chapters and concentrating on blood supply and disaster services, it never regained its status as the nation's premier social service agency. Its place was taken by more representative local organizations, especially the Community Chest, which built on the more open, more democratic wartime experience of volunteers.[7]

But what of equality between the sexes? While the labor force participation of women increased sharply, and remained permanently well above previous levels, the breakdown of historic sex roles in the workplace was marginal at best. Only in obviously temporary sectors, such as munitions, airplanes and shipbuilding, were large numbers of women holding jobs traditionally held by men. Even there, gender segregation was high, as the men held the skilled and supervisory positions. In the blue-collar realm the men, and their unions, reluctantly accepted women as temporary co-workers, but they effectively blocked them from permanent entry into their shops and assembly lines. In the white-collar realm, however, women did make permanent gains, especially in retail sales jobs and middle management. The status of so many women as part-time or part-year workers give them a weak bargaining position for factory jobs, but made them ideal workers in the retail, office, and service sectors of the economy.

The labor unions, cresting in size and political power, yet fearful that postwar reaction would sweep away their astounding new gains, distrusted and even feared women. No one who switched into and out of the labor force, and who proclaimed primary loyalty to the family, could fit the intensely masculine image of the brotherhood banded together. The willingness of wives and single women to work for less pay than men demanded was even more disturbing. The equal-pay clause CIO leaders sought was only partially a reflection of equalitarianism; the men who ran the unions were so certain that women were inferior workers that they figured companies would not displace men if they had to pay women the same wage. Blinded by a historic shop-floor sense of male supremacy, and fearful for their sudden gains, most unions refused to take advantage of the opportunity to embrace a major element of the labor force. Conversely, the weakness of unions in the increasingly feminine white-collar sector raised a barrier to union expansion for decades to come.

Management, long accustomed to the luxury of picking from a surfeit of qualified male job applicants, discovered by 1942 that women would have to be hired in large numbers, trained, and supervised if war contracts were to be filled on time. The federal government offered some generalized advice and lavish publicity, and provided some vocational training, but had little direct influence on how women should be handled. The chief state contribution was suspension of "protective" legislation for the duration. The unions, abjuring any direct involvement, divided in their response to these ninety-day wonders. The unions failed even to educate their men on such elemental matters as sexual harassment and the common courtesies of the workplace.

The engineers who ran industry soon appreciated the need for suitable sanitary, rest, and eating facilities and for the installation of devices to increase safety and reduce heavy muscle work. They also tailored job tasks so that unskilled women could learn them quickly. The importance of human relationships had become more apparent to management in the 1930s. During the war the newer, more technologically sophisticated industries making aircraft, ships, and electrical equipment hired matrons to patrol the shop floor, used interviewers to assist in personnel offices, and occasionally—as in the Kaiser shipyards in Oregon—provided day-care centers and grocery shops. While women were added in staff roles, they were rarely given line responsibilities. The women workers themselves preferred male supervisors, provided they avoided the crudities that had historically marked the way foremen dealt with workers.

The wages in war industry were high. Women marveled at their take-home pay, even if men in comparable jobs were paid more. Women knew about the wage disparity (which lessened during the war), but blocked from having a voice in union affairs, did little more than grumble. A feminist consciousness was scarcely visible in the factories.[8] Women participated in official strikes, and occasionally led walkouts against the hiring of black women co-workers, but few agitated for equal pay or equal rights. Numerous factors were involved. The turnover of women was so high that a leadership cadre seldom formed; men who totally controlled the unions rarely listened to women; and the lack of specialized skills meant women had weak bargaining advantages. Women, furthermore, were typically more dissatisfied with unequal burdens caused by home duties. They responded to bad conditions not by voice but by exit—switching jobs or returning to the home. Black women, who had vastly fewer job options and who needed to work, were more likely than whites to protest, even to the point of organizing strikes in Atlanta laundries.[9]

Paid employment was not a new experience for women. Their opportunities shifted during the war, however, with more jobs available at much higher pay, and women responded accordingly. When asked if they planned to continue work after the war, the unmarried women said "yes"—and they did continue. The married women were more ambivalent. About half needed to work to help support their families; the permanent lowering of barriers against employment of wives was a significant gain for them. But other wives worked because their husbands were away, and they eagerly looked forward to the day when they could become housewives again. After the war, most of them did quit readily, although a large fraction were responding to their husbands' demands that they stay home. In a relatively small number of cases, notably in the automobile industry, women were forced out of good jobs by a combination of hostile unions, indifferent management, and the favoritism shown to male veterans. Some became housewives; others scrambled for poorly paid, traditionally female jobs. The unemployment compensation system, biased against women workers who had taken up housekeeping, or who had nontraditional skills, provided little protection to women.[10]

The feminist dream of equal opportunity seemed for a brief while to hold most promise in the military. The systematic planners in the high command, especially the more daring aerial services, readily overcame the traditional prejudices against women in uniform when their calculations showed how significant the manpower advantages would be. However, the WAAC/WAC, WAVES, Spars, and women Marines were so hurriedly organized that an experienced leadership cadre never matured. The dispersal of women into small groups inhibited the emergence of support networks, mentors, and role models upon which leadership skills must be based. Perhaps that would have come in time, but no time was allowed because the men resisted the challenge to their masculinity (or, more often, their status and their very lives) by a vicious slander campaign. As successful as it was false, the slander campaign kept women from enlisting. Those who did serve were largely assigned low-level stereotypical female jobs, despite their superior education, skills, and versatility. While the pay was good, the oppressive atmosphere and absence of training programs, together with the favoritism shown civilian women, undercut and finally destroyed the women's morale. The generals and admirals after the war, on looking over the same manpower calculations, decided they wanted women permanently in uniform. However, the women veterans and the feminists had become uncertain about the wisdom of the experiment, and the rank-and-file men remained so obdurate that full utilization of women by the military remained a distant goal even after the feminist revolution of the 1970s.

The nurses, by contrast, made striking feminist gains. Slanders there were aplenty, especially by corpsmen relegated to a traditionally female role under the control of women. Yet the structure of the situation was favorable. The nurses were virtually drafted, so they could not avoid the challenge. Military service was congruent with their technical skills, their careers as nurses, and their humanitarian motivations. Most soldiers and sailors were not corpsmen threatened by loss of status but potential casualties who welcomed the availability of expert treatment. Most important, the Army and Navy Nurse Corps were distinctive, semiautonomous, all-female units, with a female chain of command, clear-cut career stages, unique traditions, and a structure that facilitated the development of support networks, administrative skills, de facto command over men, and pride in accomplishing a highly valued, difficult job. After the war, the civilian nurses, encouraged and eventually led by their veterans, seized control of their own profession and emerged as the only major institution in American society controlled by women.

To understand American women in the 1940s, it is essential to concentrate, not on the formerly male roles that some women occupied, but on the family roles that the vast majority of women at the time defined as central to their lives. The housewife, not the Wac or the riveter, was the modal woman. As purchaser and consumer, women had never been as important. With the purchase of automobiles at a low ebb, husbands had a drastically reduced role in deciding family expenditures. With strict rationing, severe shortages, overcrowded stores, jammed transportation facilities, and hidden cost increases, the task of shopping became far more complex, though the abundance of money meant that the privations of depression could at last be left behind. The government's policy of diverting all of the increase in GNP to the military necessitated an elaborate structure of taxes, bond sales, price fixing, and allocations of scarce goods. Housewives accepted the system realistically, and soon were able to decipher the mysteries of coupons and controls. Despite shortages, the nation's nutritional practices and standards of health care improved sharply during the war, as a result of government and media information campaigns, Red Cross programs, the spread of health insurance (Blue Cross especially), EMIC, and above all, the awareness by housewives that their patriotic and family interests were identical. Had the war lasted another five years, the impact on morale generally might have been adverse, but the housewives would have maintained a highly supportive consumer sector.

Housekeeping and purchasing duties, while important, do not reach the core of what married life was like in the 1940s. To interpret the meaning of marriage for women we must inquire what it implied in terms of a woman's self-image and her relationship to husband, children, and community.

Why did women marry? The question may seem superficial—sociologists in the 1940s did not even bother asking. But we must ask, because women clearly changed their behavior in the decade: more of them married, they married at younger ages, and they had more children. Three types of explanatory factors can be considered: changes in external factors, notably the economy and the draft; new social pressures, as expressed through the media and informal interpersonal contacts; and the emergence of different values among young couples. Statistical techniques that could weigh the importance of each factor require detailed data that does not now exist (though possibly it could be created by very ingenious oral histories),[11] so our conclusions must be tentative.

The improved economy certainly provided the jobs and income that made marriage feasible for millions of couples, including many who had been forced to delay their plans by the depression. The psychology of war seems to have encouraged quick marriages, until the sheer physical segregation of young men by 1943 or 1944, together with the severe problems faced by camp followers, had their impact. The good jobs available for civilian husbands, furthermore, encouraged working women to leave the labor force and become housewives. The sense that newlywed women, and especially new mothers, should quit their jobs, at least temporarily, remained strong. In making their ideal life choices, young women in 1943 preferred the housewife role (75 percent) over being single with successful career (6.5 percent) or combining marriage and career (19 percent). If forced to choose, only one woman in five in the last group spoke of career over marriage.[12] Evidence from cohorts of college alumnae, as well as from the census reports, shows that marriage and motherhood were more favored by the younger women than the older; the increases in both marriage and fertility in the 1940s were greatest among the best-educated, urban women—the ones with the most privileges and the most opportunities in life. The chief critique younger alumnae made about Barnard College was that it had not given enough preparatory training for family life.[13] The greater opportunity to combine marriage with a career doubtless played a role in their planning, but something more profound was also involved.

Young women were discovering marriage to be not just a social obligation or a mechanism to provide children and financial security. It was increasingly seen as a vehicle for independence and self-fulfillment. The daughters of these women, who today seek similar goals through careers or companionate relationships rather than marriage, might find the 1940s quaint, or even systematically oppressive. For young women emerging from the high school and college campuses in the 1940s, marriage represented a declaration of independence from the traditional family economy in which parental control was strong over the behavior and the wages of unmarried daughters.[14] Marriage provided release from these constraints and marked full entry into the adult world. Of course, marriage had long provided a measure of independence, but we can hypothesize that the growing gap between the generations quickened the desire for freedom.

The war hastened a major transformation in a significant aspect of American family life, the relationship of parents and adolescents. A growing proportion, probably a majority, of the nation's teenagers were part of an emerging "youth culture."[15] Older observers at the time noted the new phenomenon with alarm; much of the concern over "ungovernable" youth and "juvenile delinquency" reflected, not young hoodlums, but large numbers of young people struggling to break free of family and social controls. The military had siphoned off a majority of men aged eighteen to thirty, so teenagers now constituted a larger percentage of the home front population and their activities were more conspicuous to law enforcement. "It's odd," complained one bobby-soxer, "how grown-ups stress the wrong things. They're blind to the dangers of race discrimination, but they get terribly excited about the effects of boogie woogie."

Even more important was the rapid increase in length of stay in school, including the colleges, of course, but especially the high schools. Unlike their parents, the great majority of the World War II adolescents started, and many finished, high school. While there, they were subjected to peer group pressure that molded their behavior in a far different fashion than would have been the case had they entered the work force. Instead, in high school, adolescents were among their peers for at least one-third of each day. Cliques and small informal support groups provided both support and pressure to conform. As one student observed, "This school is full of cliques. You go into the hall or the common room and you will find the same kids together day after day."[16] High school cliques controlled the personal grooming, dating patterns, and general behavior of their members. The students acknowledged that peer group pressure determined what they wore at parties and how they acted when out with the gang or on a date. "You buy loafer moccasins because your friends do . . . You go to Joe's grill . . . or Doc's for cokes not because those places are charming, or the food good—but because the crowd goes. Most of your surface habits are picked up from people your own age."[17]

Farm boys and girls reacted differently to high school than did city students. The girls reported being "too nervous" and worrying excessively about their possible social inferiority. They reported more difficulty in expressing themselves well. As a result, farm teenagers did not enjoy classes as much as city students, nor were they as likely to make plans to continue their education by attending college. Farm girls also complained about too few social activities and more trouble than other girls with their parents about outside activities. Farm boys, however, seemed to have less trouble than other boys in getting the family car or resisting parental interference with their private lives.[18] Rural black teenagers had a different set of priorities than whites; they sought to escape the oppressive environment of the rural South. The young women wanted to marry any man except a farmer. They had begun working in earnest in the cotton patches and tobacco fields as five- and six-year-old children. Few finished grammar school; even fewer considered high school. Rural and black youth, therefore, were less likely than their urban white counterparts to have participated fully in the emerging youth culture, but their yearnings for independence were also quite strong.[19]

Besides more education, young adults had more money. During the depression, any income they generated went into the family till. Now money was plentiful and youth who had jobs could spend far more than ever before. At seventeen or eighteen, they could earn as much as many adults. Since high school students were at school much of the day and worked in the evenings, they were not supervised very closely by their parents, nor did they obey automatically any longer. Teenage girls continued to date older boys, but now these boys were in uniform and from out of town. The girl's usual form of community protection no longer worked. If she got pregnant, the soldier did not "have" to marry her. He might be transferred at any time and never be heard from again.

The development of a youth culture speeded the transformation of the family structure from authoritarian to equalitarian. More and more parents consulted with children, advised and suggested rather than commanded. Parents still tried to guide their children, especially in the choice of friends. The older youth, aware that the draft was imminent, turned increasingly to their peers for standards of behavior, fashion, entertainment, and morality. The youth culture did not peak until later decades, but by the end of the 1940s it had already made its mark on the American family. Young adults found more freedom, more responsibility, and more autonomy than their parents had known.[20]

The popular image of marriage and the family involves a timeless, unchanging institution. Historians of the family, however, have discovered dramatic changes, particularly in the psychological interactions among husbands, wives, children, and other kinfolk. Did the 1940s mark a watershed, ushering in a new American family? Changes do not come so quickly. The working out of roles and responsibilities takes years for every family, and it seems likely that little change took place in the majority of established marriages in the 1940s. Younger couples were much more likely to adopt new relationships. The combination of the emergent youth culture and the unprecedented stresses faced by service families doubtless hastened the transformations that shaped the main family forms of the 1950s and 1960s.[21]

A permanent equalitarian shift in the war generation could still be detected three decades later. Asked in 1977 whether male and female employees should be treated the same during cutbacks, or whether wives whose husbands have jobs should be laid off first, the men and women who came of age before 1940 were much less equalitarian than the war generation. Of the older women, 36 percent were equalitarian, compared to a much higher 56 percent among those who became twenty-one during the war. The men showed the same difference (47 percent and 69 percent). The youthful experiences of each generation thus tend to fix their values permanently.[22]

The most valuable aspect of marriage for half of all American wives at mid-century was "companionship in doing things together with my husband." The chance to have children was most important for a fourth of the wives, with considerations like love, understanding, and standard of living trailing in importance. The severe loneliness of the separated service wives, and the difficulties children caused during reunions, suggests the women correctly understood their needs. But the historian must raise another issue—one seldom openly discussed at the time—the distribution of power within the family. Interviews during the 1940s and 1950s consistently indicated that women were acknowledged to have the major responsibility for raising children and maintaining the family budget. In practice, however, the power within the family could be hoarded by the husband (or, less often, the wife), or parceled out with little communication, or used in democratic fashion after full mutual consultation. The experiences of service wives suggested an increased equalitarianism owing to their experiences. What of labor force participation? Did it enhance the power of wives? Did it help liberate women?[23]

In blue-collar households in the 1950s, employed wives exercised a bit more power over decisions than full-time housewives. In some cases the pattern was a statistical artifact: very dominant husbands disproportionately prevented their wives from working in the first place and, conversely, more dominant wives could successfully insist on taking a job. But in other cases, outside employment itself increased the power of the wife inside the family. In 25 percent of Detroit families in the early 1950s, the husband dominated decisionmaking: the rate was 37 percent when the wife had never been employed, 24 percent when she once worked but was now a housewife, and 13 percent when she was employed. Equalitarian decisionmaking characterized 31 percent of the families (28 percent when the wife never worked, 29 percent when she previously worked, 39 percent when she currently was employed). A few families (3 percent) were largely dominated by the wife, while in 42 percent the husband and wife were each dominant in their separate spheres. In terms of money decisions, the wife was dominant in 40 percent of the families, had equal say in 34 percent, and was subordinate in 26 percent. The war generation (wife aged thirty to thirty-nine in 1954) was more equalitarian overall (40 percent) than either older (27 percent) or younger (24 percent) couples. The wives in equalitarian marriages were more likely to report high marital satisfaction (61 percent) than others (45 percent).[24]

The paycheck itself increased the value of the woman's contribution to family finances but did not necessarily give her a stronger voice. In the first place, the great majority of wives rejected the notion that if a man brings in all the income he has more right to be boss. Her paid hours involved costs—to her leisure or that of the husband and children, or to the level of services she performed inside the house. Furthermore, the fact of employment frequently gave rise to new quarrels and new tensions between husband and wife; most husbands wanted their wives to quit war jobs when the war was over. Working daughters had long been accustomed to turning over their paychecks to their fathers and remaining under paternal control. More likely, the enhanced power of working women derived from their broader contacts with the larger world, which increased their intellectual input during conversations regarding spending decisions. Power was not a fixed quantity, to be divided one way or another. It could be expanded so that everyone had more of it, and the increased exposure of women to a wider world beyond the home did increase the total power. However, the learning experience that was most valuable came *before* marriage, in school, jobs, and voluntary activity. Less-educated women could gain useful new experiences through paid employment, but the better-educated, with a limited range of jobs open, typically preferred to learn through voluntary work and informal social contacts. It seems unlikely, therefore, that higher labor force participation during the war—or lower rates after the war—significantly affected the distribution of power inside the family.[25]

Jobs had other implications for women besides power. Most important was the money itself, most of it saved, which enhanced the family's financial security and fueled dreams of postwar comfort. Before she took a job a housewife might entertain thoughts of gaining independence, escaping troublesome children, exercising rusty talents, and relieving boredom by meeting new people and seeing more of the world. The quest for independence was especially keen on the part of women in unhappy marriages, particularly if divorce loomed as a possibility. For most, however, the reality of war jobs was tedium, compounded by transportation and shopping difficulties. The dream of escaping housework was simply unrealistic. Working women held two jobs and were forced to curtail their recreation, visiting, and passive leisure. As for the high pay, the women who decided not to take jobs had predicted correctly that it would prove only temporary.

Some feminists at the time believed that deep down housewives wanted to escape their confines and that paid employment would be a panacea for liberation. "If we free women now from the care of children, it is like letting the stopper out of a bottle of carbonated water. Women will come pouring out of the home—permanently—and will never be satisfied to go back home once they get accustomed to a paycheck, to the satisfaction that comes from productive work, and above all if they know their children can be better cared for by professionals than by amateurs."[26]

The misperception about children was striking. The vast majority of mothers enjoyed their children immensely and were highly dubious about "professional" day-care center employees, especially in comparison with their own "amateur" skills. Their standards of right behavior made them feel guilty if they could not be confident of the supervision their children received, or if their own activities made them inaccessible in time of emergency.[27] Those women who had trouble with their small children often did enroll them in day-care centers, which in turn made the centers less attractive to other mothers. The government propaganda encouraging use of the centers was as systematically ignored as the massive media campaigns to coax women into war jobs or the Army. Feeling that motherhood was not only patriotic but typified the right to a private life for which the war was being fought, mothers could in good conscience devote themselves to the needs of their families.

Asked whether running a home or a full-time job was more interesting for women, 50 percent of the entire population said the home, 30 percent picked the job, the rest were unsure or thought them equally interesting. A half dozen reasons typified the responses of the first group: more activity, rearing children, extra leisure time, more independence, sheer enjoyment, and the basic duty of women. Those who thought a full-time job might be more interesting usually cited the opportunity to meet more people and do more things, only occasionally mentioning independence or becoming better informed.[28]

The broad consensus after the war was that women with children should not work unless circumstances were severe. What if there were no children under sixteen? Of a cross-section of the entire adult population, 39 percent said she should work, 44 percent said no, and it depended on circumstances for the rest. Why should she work? One in eight pointed to a more interesting life (13 percent), one in six cited equal rights (9 percent) or freedom of choice (6 percent), while the extra income was only occasionally noted (5 percent). Why she should not work prompted one American in five to warn that it would cost someone else a job (22 percent) or that it was just not the way things ought to be (15 percent). To make a hypothetical situation more realistic, interviewers asked about Mrs. Jones: "The Jones family lives in a small modern home. Mr. Jones earns a good but not a high salary. There are two children, both in school. Mrs. Jones would enjoy doing something besides running her home if she could arrange it. [What] do you think Mrs. Jones should do?" Only a handful thought Mrs. Jones should take a full-time job (4 percent); most recommended a part-time job (32 percent) or suggested volunteer work (30 percent). But one in three (35 percent) would tell her to stay home.

The hypothetical nature of questions about wives working was underscored by the strong consensus that homemaking was (or ought to be) a full-time job. Seven out of eight adults thought so in 1946. With regard to their own situation, two out of three wives said that housekeeping was indeed a full-time task. One-third of all wives (33 percent) said they had enough spare time to do other things, and one in seven did have paid employment. In truth, housewifery, in contrast to gainful employment, offered a peculiar opportunity for autonomy. The housewife could set her own standards of performance and her own schedule, subject not to time clocks and deadlines but to her perception of the needs and demands of family (and, perhaps, the neighbors). If women themselves insisted that women's work was never done, women themselves also defined that work. Just as farmers valued their autonomy, despite the hard work, so too did housewives. With marriages more companionate, and family life so psychologically rewarding to the vast majority of women, it required no mysterious packet of social or economic forces to keep women at home.[29]

The historian of the 1940s who accepts the primacy of family and agrees that paid employment produced little liberation might still ask about freedom of choice. What about the minority of women who did have a taste for male jobs, or aspired to a rewarding career? Did not society systematically discriminate against them? Yes, it certainly did. The dominance of men in all sectors of employment gave them a decisive advantage, for they were protecting historic patterns and could laugh off women's efforts or, if necessary, assault them with sexual innuendoes. Not many men had read Freud, but they did feel that anatomy was destiny. Women were too small, too weak to handle the inner core of a "man's job." They could and did point out that few women had the technical training requisite for a crafts or managerial position, and they immediately concluded that women had no aptitude for such matters. The constant movement in and out of the labor market could be cited as evidence that women lacked the drive and ambition to stick to careers. Counselors, employment bureaus, and personnel officers who steered men one way and women another did not create the culture, they merely reflected it, and they often had elaborate evidence to show women that they would be unhappy in certain lines of work. As the labor market changed, so did the advisers. Early in the war, they had to convince women that domestic skills could be put to good use in industry, that anyone who could run a sewing machine could operate a drill press. As clerical jobs became feminized, the advisers began to steer men away from them, even veterans who had been trained as clerks in the Army.[30]

"Social forces" are sometimes assumed to have generated the socializing mechanisms that steered girls away from aspiring to male jobs. But what are "social forces"? The media could be examined, but it would not explain very much, for images of women were often ambiguous and could be interpreted in many ways. As the failure of the propaganda drives proves, even intensive media campaigns had little effect in changing deeply held values. The ways in which girls were raised by their families to become feminine clearly counted more. Here the socialization intended to replicate in the child the values of the parents. Girls who deviated could be gently rebuffed. One Chicago mother explained in 1944 that Santa gave her five-year-old daughter a doll house so she could learn "feminine interests." The mother recalled that she had grown up a tomboy, and did not want her daughter to do so. The little girl had asked Santa for a Wac uniform. Churches, schools, and clubs further facilitated the transmission of parental values, especially middle-class values. The peer pressure of other girls, especially during adolescence, could operate as a countervailing influence. However, in this instance peer pressure strongly reinforced notions of femininity and effectively prevented the vast majority of girls from developing "masculine" tastes. With all, the prevailing mood was neatly captured in a hit 1946 movie, *It's a Wonderful Life.* When the despondent hero (James Stewart) contemplates suicide, a heavenly angel reveals to him what would have happened had he never lived. The idyllic small town would be in the grasp of an evil moneylender; it would be ruined by poverty, violence, hatred, and alcoholism. To climax the horrible image, the fate of Donna Reed, Stewart's faithful wife and marvelous mother of his children, is shown: she would have become a spinster career woman, the town librarian. Stewart decides not to jump off the bridge, the movie ends happily.[31]

Freedom of choice was highly regarded as a democratic value worth fighting for. But in the 1940s it meant freedom to choose within strictly defined guidelines that emerged from the people, particularly from the women who were charged with responsibility for guiding children to do the right and proper thing.

Suppose the wartime government had been more successful in inducing women to join the Army, or to take jobs, or to keep them when they married, or to place their children in day-care centers. What might have been the results? Possibly the GNP would have been a bit higher and more desk-bound servicemen could have been shipped to Europe or the Pacific. It appears highly unlikely that the war would have ended any sooner, or that the necessary massive intrusion into private lives would have had no deleterious impact on American morale. What of the postwar era, assuming that the government relaxed its direct controls over people's lives but instituted effective equal-pay rules? The closing of the munitions plants still would have thrown millions of women out of work, though many would have clung successfully to factory jobs in automobile, machinery, and electrical plants. Unless unions somehow had reversed their male chauvinism, however, it is difficult to guess how many women would have persisted in hostile work places. The impact on white-collar employment patterns of these hypothetical reforms would have been nil, unless the early motivations and training of women changed drastically or the people of the 1940s had somehow managed to envisage and implement an "equal-worth" standard of pay for women in predominantly female occupations. Structural reforms such as those imagined here would have had, at best, a small impact on the lives of women, if, indeed, women were motivated primarily by internalized, private goals and ambitions.

But what if women's attitudes toward childbearing and family life had changed, and men's too? Then we would not be dealing with history, but with a utopia set in the past, or perhaps the 1980s magically transposed four decades back, and the history books would tell us more about ourselves than about the people of the 1940s. Women of the decade did not seek to break barriers or change their own values; rather, women sought and fought for companionship, and security within the home. A remarkable number achieved their goal. Eleanor Roosevelt said it best: "The circumstances that surround women as a rule force most of them into certain channels . . . The best she can do is to use the opportunities that come to her in life to the best advantage, according to her abilities. This is a little less true today than it was in the past, but nevertheless it still holds true, since women, or the greatest number of women, must subordinate themselves to the life of the family."[32]

The circumstances to which Roosevelt alluded were not unique to America, but were shared broadly in other lands, most notably Britain and Canada. Those nations recognized the urgency of mobilizing womanpower early in the war, and in the case of military service both Canada and the United States studied and replicated the British model. Similar debates about women in factories, equal pay, and day care were played out in each nation. Yet there were differences. In Britain, for example, women members of Parliament caucused to present feminist views. They pressed for equality in the rates of compensation to which civilians would be entitled if injured by enemy action. Surely the human worth of the female equaled the man's, even if she was paid less! No, the government said, for it would lead to equal pay, which both the unions and the traditionalists opposed. But the feminists finally won over the War Cabinet in 1943. They pushed on and in 1944 defeated the government by a vote of 117 to 116 in Parliament to require equal pay for teachers. It was the first and only defeat the coalition suffered during the war. Winston Churchill, the Conservative Prime Minister, and Labourite Ernest Bevin, the Minister of Labour and National Service, immediately threatened to resign unless the vote was reversed. It was, and the principle of equal pay would languish in Britain for another generation. Nothing so dramatic happened in the United States, for the government adopted a policy of equal pay with so many loopholes that opposition was muted. It was a commentary on the state of feminism that no women's caucus emerged in Congress or the state legislatures.[33]

It is difficult to argue that World War II, in itself, constituted a watershed in the experience of American women. During the short term of the war years, women responded to new challenges on the basis of their identities as women, as members of families and communities, that had been forged before the war and would persist after it. An insignificant proportion of American women seized upon the opportunities for new occupations that the war proffered as a permanent break with their past commitments, sense of themselves, and expectations. For the majority of American women, the war years may have altered some specific activities, but they did not change their interpretations of their primary roles. Gender roles—and, even more, gender identities—change in the long, rather than the short, term. For the majority of American women, the war years constituted one more installment in a series of events that shaped their lives. To be sure, the impact of those years on a woman's life depended in some measure upon her age, the moment in her life cycle, the cohort or generation to which she belonged. A married woman in her fifties, a married woman in her thirties, a late adolescent, a child—all experienced the war differently, not merely because of their age per se, but also because of the other events that had already influenced their identities and values. The vast majority of women who lived through those years were doubtless more profoundly marked by the secular changes that were slowly modifying women's experience than by the war itself.

Perhaps the principal impact of the war on women derived from the changes in American society as a whole that the war crystallized or accelerated. The recovery from the depression, the shifting balance between rural and urban populations, the greater equality in distribution of income among the population, among other tendencies, had important consequences for women as well as for men. The social patterns and values of the fifties as well as of the sixties can legitimately be traced to changes that had their seeds in the forties. The growing importance of peer groups in the decisive years of adolescence that was evident during the war years would have important repercussions in each succeeding generation. An array of social, economic, and political changes in American society that can be traced at least from the 1920s were slowly altering the conditions of women's lives in all classes and ethnic groups, albeit at different rates. The ideology of separate spheres and women's special moral mission proved an early casualty of the transformation of American society. But other ideas about gender roles and gender differences did not disappear so fast. In most walks of life and in most organizations, men vigorously warred against equality for women. In this respect, women's occasional access to men's jobs and men's pay rates proved a temporary expedient of wartime exigencies. But men were not alone in their commitment to returning women to women's proper place. Women themselves indisputably placed their highest priority on a family life that could only be sustained by their own special efforts. It would take more than the war for them even to begin to think of their own independence and full equality as a goal that might justify the sacrifice of the "traditional" values of home, husband, and children.

This assessment should not be taken to imply that women did not have personal ambitions and dreams, that they lacked self-respect, that they would not have preferred equal opportunities for jobs and careers, or equal pay for their work. We cannot easily judge what women may have wanted in the abstract. We can better judge the choices they made. If they wanted personal fulfillment in many areas, they clearly judged that personal fulfillment—not to mention economic security—was more likely to result from a solid family life than from independence, and that a solid family life was more likely to result from acceptance of, than from war against, the norms of inherited values. The challenge for the historian remains to recognize that even as the appearance of the conventional relations between men and women persisted, changes in society as a whole were eroding its foundations. When, in 1945, American women of various generations, classes, and races withdrew from choice positions in the labor market, picked up life as usual, and benefited from growing prosperity to devote time to their homes and families, they were not, in fact, returning to the world of their foremothers, but—consciously or not—reinterpreting it as a legacy for their daughters and granddaughters.

Tables

Table 1. Women as proportion of all workers, by occupational status, 1940–1947

Occupation	1940 (%)	1945 (%)	1947 (%)
Professional	45.5	46.5	39.9
Managerial	11.7	17.4	13.5
Clerical	52.6	70.3	58.6
Sales	27.9	54.1	39.9
All white collar	35.8	49.6	38.9
Craftsman, foreman, skilled	2.1	4.4	2.1
Factory operative	25.7	38.3	28.1
Domestic service	93.8	93.8	92.3
Other service	40.1	47.8	43.6
All blue collar	26.2	31.7	24.6
Agriculture	8.0	22.4	11.8
All occupations	25.9	36.0	27.9

Source: Women's Bureau, *Women as Workers, A Statistical Guide* (Washington, D.C. 1953), pp. 15–17.

LIBRARY ST. MARY'S COLLEGE

Table 2. Black women's employment patterns, 1940–1947

Occupation	1940 (percent of 1,656,000[a])	1944 (percent of 2,345,000[a])	1947 (percent of 2,086,000[a])
Professional	4.1	4.2	4.8
Other white collar	1.7	4.6	5.7
Industry	5.8	17.6	17.3
Domestic service	57.0	43.7	44.5
Other service	10.4	18.9	20.5
Agriculture	20.9	10.9	7.2

Source: Seymour L. Wolfbein, "Postwar Trends in Negro Employment," *Monthly Labor Review,* 65 (Dec. 1947), 664.

a. Total number of black women workers.

Table 3. Occupational status changes of women, December 1941–March 1944 (all women 14 and over in 1944, in thousands, read down)[a]

Destination in 1944	Outside the labor force in 1941						Inside the labor force in 1941					All women in 1944
	House-work	School	Under 14	Unable to work[b]	Unknown	Total	White collar	Blue collar	Farm	Unem-ployed	Total	
White collar	1,311	1,331	85	3	117	2,847	4,516	273	13	75	4,877	7,724
Blue collar	2,160	821	134	55	227	3,397	208	4,346	97	155	4,806	8,203
Farm	128	42	4	1	6	181	7	42	340	0	389	570
Unemployed	110	90	10	1	10	221	43	87	0	40	170	391
Inside labor force	3,709	2,284	233	60	360	6,646	4,774	4,748	450	270	10,242	16,888
Housework	25,550	520	120	30	478	26,698	962	1,053	95	50	2,160	28,858
School	20	1,580	2,290	0	30	3,920	8	2	0	0	10	3,930
Other	500	100	30	1,790	40	2,460	60	65	5	10	140	2,600
Outside labor force	26,070	2,200	2,440	1,820	548	33,078	1,030	1,120	100	60	2,310	35,388
Total	29,779	4,484	2,673	1,880	908	39,724	5,804	5,868	550	330	12,552	52,276

Source: Mary Elizabeth Pidgeon, *Changes in Women's Employment During the War*, Women's Bureau Special Bulletin 20 (Washington, D.C., 1944), pp. 5–26.

a. Excludes approximately 1.5 million women who died between Dec. 1941 and March 1944.

b. Chiefly women over 60.

Table 4. 1944 destination of 1941 women (all women 14 and over in 1944)

1944 destination	1941 origin				
	All (percent of 52,276,000[a])	Housewife (percent of 29,779,000[a])	Student (percent of 4,484,000[a])	White collar (percent of 5,804,000[a])	Blue collar (percent of 5,868,000[a])
In labor force	32.2	12.5	50.9	82.3	80.8
White collar	14.8	4.4	29.7	77.8	4.6
Blue collar	15.7	7.3	18.3	3.6	74.3
Not in labor force	67.8	87.5	49.1	17.8	19.2
Housewife	55.1	85.8	11.6	16.6	18.0
Total	100.0	100.0	100.0	100.0	100.0

Source: Table 3.
a. Total number of women in category.

Table 5. 1941 origin of 1944 women workers

1941 origin	1944 destination		
	All (percent of 16,888,000[a])	White collar (percent of 7,724,000[a])	Blue collar (percent of 8,203,000[a])
In labor force	60.6	63.1	58.6
White collar	28.3	58.5	2.5
Blue collar	28.1	3.5	53.0
Not in labor force	39.4	36.9	41.4
Housework	22.0	17.0	26.3
School	13.5	17.2	10.0
Total	100.0	100.0	100.0

Source: Table 3.
a. Total number of women in category.

Table 6. Labor force movement of wives, by status of husband, 1941–1944

Movement 1941–1944	All wives (percent of 32,450,000[a])	Husband present (percent of 28,510,000[a])	Husband in service (percent of 2,580,000[a])	Husband in service[b] (percent of 2,580,000[a])	Difference (percent)
Enter labor force	9.8	8.3	24.0	21.5	+13.2
Quit	5.2	4.7	10.9	9.4	+ 4.7
Stayed in	13.1	10.8	27.1	27.3	+16.5
Stayed out	71.8	76.1	38.0	42.8	−33.3
Proportion in labor force, 1944	22.9	19.1	51.1	48.8	+29.7
Net increase in labor force	1,493,000	1,026,000	340,000		

Source: Mary Elizabeth Pidgeon, *Changes in Women's Employment During the War*, Women's Bureau Special Bulletin 20 (Washington, D.C., 1944), p. 29.

a. Total number of women in category.

b. Expected values standardized by using ages of all wives as a base.

Table 7. Proportion married and with husband absent, by age and race, 1940–1944

Age	Year	Married (%)	Husband absent (%)	War effect (1940–1944)
Native white women				
18–19	1940	20.5	6.8	
	1944	25.6	55.5	+48.7
20–24	1940	50.5	5.3	
	1944	57.0	33.9	+28.6
25–29	1940	74.4	3.9	
	1944	79.4	16.8	+12.9
30–34	1940	80.6	3.9	
	1944	85.1	15.4	+11.5
Black women				
18–19	1940	32.8	16.2	
	1944	37.2	33.6	+17.4
20–24	1940	59.6	14.4	
	1944	64.0	30.3	+15.9
25–29	1940	74.3	15.1	
	1944	73.8	21.8	+ 6.7
30–34	1940	77.0	16.0	
	1944	78.3	23.5	+ 7.5

Source: John Durand, *The Labor Force in the United States, 1890–1960* (New York, 1948), pp. 224–226.

Table 8. Kin at war (number per 100 Chicago women factory workers, 1944)

Cousin	52	In-law	3
Brother	37	Sister	2
Nephew	11	Niece	2
None	10	Daughter	.8
Fiancé	10	Father	.7
Son	8	Uncle	—[a]
Husband	8	Aunt	—[a]

Source: Herbert Fleming, "Women War Workers Look Ahead," *Survey Graphic* (Oct. 1944), pp. 415–419.

a. Not asked.

Table 9. Median money income by size of place, 1947

	1,000,000 +	250,000–1,000,000	50,000–250,000	2,500–50,000	All urban	Rural nonfarm	Rural farm[a]
Families	100[b]	126	113	106	103	106	93	65
Individual outside families	100[c]	156	142	138	80	122	70	66
Families controlling for size	100[d]	—	—	—	—	112	91	63

Source: Bureau of the Census, *Statistical Abstract of the United States, 1949* (Washington, D.C., 1949), pp. 292–293, 296.
a. Not including nonmoney farm income.
b. 100 = $3,031 in 1947 dollars.
c. 100 = $980 in 1947 dollars.
d. Hypothetical incomes if urban and rural families had been same size.

Table 10. Fertility increases, by age and education, 1940–1950 (in percentages)[a]

Age	College graduate	Some college	High school graduate	Some high school	No high school
20–24	+194	+149	+105	+52	+37
25–29	+145	+72	+63	+35	+22
30–34	+83	+45	+40	+17	+4

Source: Wilson Grabill, Clyde Kiser, and Pascal Welpton, *The Fertility of American Women* (New York, 1958), tables 75, 76.
a. Number of children ever born per 1,000 white women. The patterns for black women were similar.

Table 11. Labor force participation rates, by marital status, 1940–1947

Year	Single		Married		Widowed and divorced		Total	
	Size[a]	Rate[b]	Size[a]	Rate[b]	Size[a]	Rate[b]	Size[a]	Rate[b]
1940	27.5	48.1	59.6	16.7	12.9	32.0	100	27.4
1944	24.4	58.6	62.5	25.6	13.1	35.7	100	35.0
1947	22.0	51.2	64.3	21.4	13.7	34.6	100	29.8

Source: Bureau of the Census, *Statistical Abstract of the United States, 1957* (Washington, D.C., 1957), p. 208.

a. Percent of all women 14 and over.

b. Percent in the labor force.

Table 12. Minimum hourly pay rates for hiring unskilled workers, 1943

	Men	Women hired for men's jobs	Women hired for women's jobs
Mean	66.7¢	61.7¢	57.8¢
Standard deviation	10.7¢	11.8¢	11.5¢
Number of plants	155	148	132

Source: National survey of war plants, March 1943, in "Wartime Pay of Women in Industry," *The Conference Board, Management Record*, 5 (Oct. 1943), p. 404.

Table 13. Acceptance of women in California unions

Union group	Locals with any women members (%)		Change in membership, 1944–1946 (%)	
	1940	1944	Men	Women
Hostile Groups				
Misc. nonmfg.	6	25	+23	(too few)
Construction	2	8	+29	(too few)
Air, ship, auto mfg.	9	66	−58	−84
Transport	11	26	+20	0
Misc. mfg.	19	59	+41	− 4
Furniture, lumber	19	56	+36	−31
Machinery	19	66	+21	−45
Utility, transit	20	56	−21	+45
Govt., postal	21	26	+40	+28
Average	10	32	− 5	−43
Friendly Groups				
Misc. services	40	54	+30	+40
Movies	41	53	+27	+72
Oil, chemical	41	76	+44	−42
Printing	43	49	+16	+45
Food mfg.	55	83	+35	+19
Retail, wholesale trade	59	80	+60	+44
Hotel, restaurant	62	71	+37	+18
Clothing mfg.	95	100	+37	+18
Average	54	71	+46	+12
Totals				
All mfg.	32	65	−24	−48
All nonmfg.	21	34	+37	+49
All unions	25	44	+ 7	−12

Source: Department of Industrial Relations, Division of Labor Statistics and Law Enforcement, *Union Labor in California* (San Francisco, 1942–1947), passim.

Table 14. Per capita budgets of urban families, 1935–1936 (1940 dollars)

	Poorest $\frac{1}{3}$[a]	Overall average	Richest $\frac{1}{3}$[a]	Ratio rich to poor
Mean family size	3.5	3.7	3.9	1.11
Income (per capita)	$295.00	$518.00	$896.00	3.03
Spending	307.00	482.00	749.00	2.44
Food	105.00	147.00	176.00	1.67
Housing	106.00	163.00	222.00	2.10
Clothing	27.00	51.00	90.00	3.36
Medical	13.00	24.00	37.00	2.86

Source: Bureau of the Census, *Historical Statistics of the United States, Colonial Times to 1970* (Washington, D.C., 1975), pp. 210, 323–324.

a. Equal total numbers of persons, not equal numbers of families.

Table 15. Per capita budgets of urban families, 1941 (1940 dollars)

	Poorest $\frac{1}{3}$[a]	Overall average	Richest $\frac{1}{3}$[a]	Ratio rich to poor
Mean family size	3.13	3.44	3.89	1.24
Income (per capita)	$339.93	$739.75	$1,260.73	3.71
Spending	341.87	634.00	973.13	2.85
Food	119.17	188.13	259.92	2.18
Housing	106.60	188.63	285.00	2.67
Clothing	34.90	77.20	132.55	3.80
Medical	15.81	30.93	48.33	3.06

Source: Historical Statistics of the United States, Colonial Times to 1970, pp. 210, 323–324.

a. Equal total numbers of persons, not equal numbers of families.

Table 16. Per capita budgets of urban families, 1944 (1940 dollars)

	Poorest $\frac{1}{3}$[a]	Overall average	Richest $\frac{1}{3}$[a]	Ratio rich to poor
Mean family size	2.91	3.42	4.04	1.32
Income (per capita, after taxes)	$437.50	$749.90	$1,181.00	2.49
Spending	467.60	613.60	757.40	1.62
Food	163.30	196.00	222.30	1.36
Housing	105.90	178.60	212.80	2.01
Clothing	54.60	92.04	132.00	2.42
Medical	24.86	38.73	50.27	2.02
Taxes (per family)	86.87	458.30	1,184.00	13.63
Savings (per family)	44.63	494.80	1,448.00	32.44
War bonds (per family)	81.29	288.30	649.20	8.00

Source: Historical Statistics of the United States, Colonial Times to 1970, pp. 210, 323–324.

a. Equal total numbers of persons, not equal numbers of families.

Table 17. Per capita budgets of urban families, 1950 (1940 dollars)

	Poorest $\frac{1}{3}$[a]	Overall average	Richest $\frac{1}{3}$[a]	Ratio rich to poor
Income (per capita, after taxes)	$442.30	$745.60	$1,106.00	2.50
Spending	500.80	727.00	1,005.00	2.00
Food	142.80	184.40	225.90	1.58
Housing	178.00	241.70	316.80	1.78
Clothing	45.67	78.12	187.80	4.11
Medical	34.01	44.23	55.23	1.62

Source: Historical Statistics of the United States, Colonial Times to 1970, pp. 210, 323–324.

a. Equal total numbers of persons, not equal numbers of families.

Table 18. Per capita weekly consumption of meat and poultry, urban population by income class, 1942 and 1944 (in pounds)

Income group	Spring 1942	Fall 1944	Change (%)
Poorest third	2.40	2.80	+ 16.7
Middle third	2.80	2.69	− 4.0
Richest third	3.14	3.04	− 3.3

Source: Wartime Food Purchases, Department of Labor Bulletin 838 (Washington, D.C., 1945), p. 5.

Table 19. Nutritive value of city diets, 1936, 1942, 1948

Income group	Calories	Protein (grams)	Calcium (grams)	Iron (milligrams)
1936				
Poorest third	2,580	66	.64	10.2
Middle third	2,790	78	.83	11.8
Richest third	3,130	90	.95	14.0
1942				
Poorest third	2,670	76	.86	12.8
Middle third	2,870	85	.98	13.5
Richest third	2,920	89	1.01	13.8
1948				
Poorest third	2,930	86	1.02	15.6
Middle third	3,040	91	1.11	15.8
Richest third	3,040	95	1.15	16.2

Source: Bureau of the Census, *Historical Statistics of the United States, Colonial Times to 1970* (Washington, D.C., 1975), p. 328.

Table 20. Employment of urban women aged 24–44, by race and ethnicity, 1950

Census group	In labor force (%)	White collar (%)
Native white, native parents	36	65
Japanese	51	50
Chinese	33	45
Indian	32	31
Black	53	14
Filipina	29	10
Native white, immigrant parents:	36	58
Irish	41	78
Scandinavian	37	73
British	36	70
German	36	65
From Russia	29	62
Czech	37	50
Italian	36	43
Polish	38	42
Puerto Rican (mainland)	37	41
French Canadian	43	35
Mexican	28	31
Foreign-born white	35	46
All urban women	36	55

Source: Donald J. Bogue, *The Population of the United States* (New York, 1959), pp. 367–369, 437, 506; U.S. Bureau of the Census, *U.S. Census of Population: 1950,* vol. IV, *Special Reports,* part 3, chap. A, *Nativity and Parentage* (Washington, D.C., 1954), pp. 58–59, 136–161.

Notes

Introduction

1. The response "being a wife" dropped from 22 percent to 6 percent. 1970 data from Virginia Slims poll conducted by Louis Harris and Associates, Louis Harris Center, Chapel Hill, N.C. 1983 data from *New York Times* poll taken in mid-November; *New York Times,* Dec. 4, 1983.

2. William Henry Chafe, *The American Woman: Her Changing Social, Economic, and Political Roles, 1920–1970* (New York, 1972).

3. Paddy Quick, "Rosie the Riveter: Myths and Realities," *Radical America,* 9 (July–Aug. 1975), 115–132; Joan Ellen Trey, "Women in the War Economy," *Reviews of Radical Political Economics,* 4 (July 1972), 40–57; Sheila Tobias and Lisa Anderson, "What Really Happened to Rosie the Riveter?" MSS Modular Publications, Module 9 (1974); Eleanor Straub, "United States Government Policy Toward Civilian Women During World War II," *Prologue,* 5 (Winter 1973), 240–254.

4. Karen Sue Anderson, *Wartime Women* (Westport, Conn., 1981); Susan Hartmann, *The Home Front and Beyond: American Women in the 1940's* (Boston, 1982).

5. George Martin, *Madam Secretary Frances Perkins* (Boston, 1976); Eleanor Straub, "United States Government Policy Toward Civilian Women During World War II," Ph.D. diss., Emory University, 1973.

6. Bernard R. Berelson, Paul F. Lazarsfeld, and William N. McPhee, *Voting: A Study of Opinion Formation in a Presidential Campaign* (Chicago, 1954), pp. 102–103; Elihu Katz and Paul Lazarsfeld, *Personal Influence* (Glencoe, Ill., 1955); Paul Lazarsfeld, Bernard R. Berelson, Hazel Gaudet, *The People's Choice* (New York, 1948).

7. Office of War Information, Bureau of Intelligence, "Women and the War," Report of Aug. 19, 1942, pp. 9–15; "Personal Identification with the War," Report 27, Oct. 13, 1942, table 26; "Women and the War," Report 31, Aug. 6, 1942, tables 5, 6a, 6c, 10a, 10b, all in Record Group 44, box 1798, National Archives, Washington, D.C. Katz and Lazarsfeld, *Personal Influence;* Richard W. Steele, "American Popular Opinion and the War Against Germany: The Issue of Negotiated Peace, 1942," *Journal of American History,* 65 (1978), 704–723.

8. *Adam's Rib,* 1949, screenplay by Ruth Gordon and Garson Kanin.

9. The largest oral history project on women in the 1940s is Sherna Berger Gluck, ed., *Rosie the Riveter Revisited: Women and the World War II Work Experience* (Long Beach: California State University Long Beach Foundation, 1983). These forty-five volumes of transcripts of interviews with women who worked in Los Angeles war factories have been deposited in various women's history archives on the east and west coasts and in the Midwest. I used the set at the Walter P. Reuther Archives of Labor and Urban Affairs, Wayne State University, Detroit, Mich.

10. Straub, "United States Government Policy Toward Civilian Women"; Chafe, *The American Woman;* Howard Dratch, "The Politics of Child Care in the 1940's," *Science and Society,* 38 (1974–75), 167–204; Anderson, *Wartime Women;* Virginia Kerr, "One Step Forward—Two Steps Back: Child Care's Long American History," in Pamela Roley, ed., *Child Care—Who Cares* (New York, 1973); Joan L. Rothstein, "The Government of the United States and the Young Child: A Study of Federal Child Care Legislation Between 1935–1971," Ph.D. diss., University of Maryland, 1979; Karen Beck Skold, "Women Workers and Child Care During World War II: A Case Study of the Portland, Oregon Shipyards," Ph.D. diss., University of Oregon, 1981; Margaret O'Brien Steinfel, *Who's Minding the Children? The History and Politics of Daycare in America* (New York, 1973); Hartmann, *The Home Front and Beyond;* Sheila Trupp Lichtman, "Women at War, 1941–1945: Wartime Employment in the San Francisco Bay Area," Ph.D. diss., University of California, Davis, 1981.

11. For international comparisons see, in general, International Labour Organization, *The War and Women's Employment* (Montreal, 1946). For Britain see Angus Calder, *The People's War: Britain, 1939–1945* (New York, 1969), and Margaret Allen, "The Domestic Ideal and the Mobilization of Womanpower in World War II," *Women's Studies International Forum,* 6 (1983), 401–412. For Germany see Leila Rupp, *Mobilizing Women for War: German and American Propaganda, 1939–1945* (Princeton, 1978), and Jill Stephenson, *The Nazi Organization of Women* (London, 1982). For Japan see Thomas R. H. Havens, "Women and War in Japan, 1937–45," *American Historical Review,* 80 (1975), 913–934. For Canada see Ruth Roach Pierson, "Canadian Women and Canadian Mobilization During the Second World War," *International Review of Military History,* no. 51 (1982), 181–207.

1. A Crushing Defeat in This Man's Army

1. See Nancy Loring Goldman, ed., *Female Soldiers—Combatants or Noncombatants: Historical and Contemporary Perspectives* (Westport, Conn., 1982), esp. chaps. 1 and 2.

2. Bureau of the Census, *Statistical Abstract of the United States, 1946* (Washington, D.C., 1946), pp. 206–207; Samuel Stouffer and others, *The American Soldier: Adjustment During Army Life,* vol. 1 (Princeton, 1949), pp. 312–313, calculates that of every four men in the U.S. Army, one had a combatant job, one a clerical, one a skilled, and one a semiskilled or unskilled job.

3. By far the best study of women's roles in one branch is Mattie E. Treadwell, *The United States Army in World War II, Special Studies, The Women's Army Corps* (Washington, D.C., 1954); for a longer view see Jeanne Holm, *Women in the Military* (Novato, Calif., 1982). On the creation of the women's units see Susan M. Hartmann, "Women in the Military Service," in Mabel E. Deutrich and Virginia C. Purdy, eds., *Clio Was a Woman: Studies in the History of American Women* (Washington, D.C., 1980), and Hartmann, *The Home Front and Beyond* (New York, 1982), chap. 3. For Canadian material see Ruth Roach Pierson, " 'Jill Canuck': CWAC of All Trades, But No 'Pistol Packing Momma,' " *Historical Papers/Communications Historiques* (1978), pp. 106–133, and Pierson, "Canadian Women and Canadian Mobilization During the Second World War," *Revue Internationale d'Histoire Militaire,* 51 (1982), 181–207.

4. Susan H. Godson, "The Waves in World War II," Naval Institute *Proceedings,* 107 (Dec. 1981), 46.

5. Mildred McAfee Horton, "Recollections of Captain Mildred McAfee [Horton], USNR (Ret.)," 1971, pp. 2, 13, Oral History Collection, United States Naval Institute, Annapolis, Md.; Joy Bright Hancock, *Lady in the Navy: A Personal Reminiscence* (Annapolis, Md., 1972), p. 59; Lt. Col. Betty Bandal, "The WAC Program in the Army Air Force," Nov. 1945, p. 1, WAC Branch Military Personnel Division, Army Air Force Headquarters, Maxwell Air Force Base Library, Montgomery, Ala. Since this chapter focuses on the military, it will not include a discussion of the Women's Airforce Service Pilots (WASP), a civilian group of 1,074 who flew planes for two years for the Army Air Corps during the war. After a long struggle, they received veteran's status in 1977. For an introduction to the WASP experience see Sally Van Wegener Keil, *Those Wonderful Women in Their Flying Machines: The Unknown Heroines of World War II* (New York, 1979); Jacqueline Cochran, *The Stars at Noon* (Boston, 1954); Victor K. Chun, "The Origins of the WASPS," *American Aviation Historical Society Journal,* 14 (Winter 1969), pp. 259–262; Joseph J. Corn, "Making Flying 'Thinkable': Women Pilots and the Selling of Aviation, 1927–1940," *American Quarterly,* 31 (Fall 1979), 556–571, and Len Famiglietti, "How Women Flew in Wartime," *Air Force Times,* April 26, 1976.

6. Treadwell, *Women's Army Corps,* p. 22.

7. Hancock, *Lady in the Navy,* pp. 46, 51, 59.

8. The peak wartime enrollments were 100,000 Wacs, 86,000 Waves, 17,600 Marines, 10,000 Spars, 47,000 Army Nurse Corps, and 11,000 Navy Nurse Corps. The total who served at one time or another during the war was 140,000 in the WAAC/WAC, 100,000 Waves, 23,000 Marines, 13,000 Spars, 60,000 Army Nurse Corps, and 14,000 Navy Nurse Corps. Estimates calculated from data provided by Treadwell, *Women's Army Corps,* pp. 765–769, and Ruth Chenery Streeter, "History of the Marine Corps Women's Reserve: A Critical Analysis of Its Development and Operation, 1943–1945," Dec. 5, 1945, pp. 99, 100, 126, Schlesinger Library, Radcliffe College, Cambridge, Mass.

9. Lt. Col. Pat Meid, "Marine Corps Women's Reserve in World War II," 1964, p. 64, Historical Branch, G-3 Division Headquarters, U.S. Marine Corps, Washington, D.C.

10. General H. H. Arnold, Army Air Force Headquarters, Washington, D.C., letter of Feb. 25, 1944, WAC Branch Military Personnel Division Collection, Maxwell Air Force Base Library, Montgomery, Ala.

11. Meid, "Marine Corps Women's Reserve," p. 64.

12. Treadwell, *Women's Army Corps,* p. 746; Lt. Col. Anna W. Wilson, press release, War Department, Bureau of Public Relations, Feb. 6, 1945, National Archives, Washington, D.C.

13. *America,* April 4, 1942, p. 714, Aug. 14, 1942, p. 507, and Feb. 26, 1944; Louise Edna Goeden, "Women in Uniform: Work of the Wacs," *America,* July 31, 1943, p. 457.

14. Meid, "Marine Corps Women's Reserve," pp. 9, 10, 61; Marie Bennett Alsmeyer, *The Way of the WAVES* (Conway, Ark., 1981), p. 11; Treadwell, *Women's Army Corps,* p. 607; Mary C. Lyne and Kay Arthur, *Three Years Behind the Mast: The Story of the United States Coast Guard, SPARS* (Washington, D.C., 1946), p. 103.

15. Lyne and Arthur, *Three Years Behind the Mast,* p. 103; Bureau of Naval Personnel, Historical Section, "Women's Reserve," Washington, D.C.,1946, in Navy Department Library, Washington, D.C.; Samuel Stouffer, "The American Soldier in World War II," Survey S-194, "Attitudes of Wacs," Feb. 1945, question 14, Roper Center, Williams College, Williamstown, Mass., and University of Connecticut, Storrs, Conn.; Streeter, "History of the Marine Corps Women's Reserve," p. 104.

16. Stouffer, "The American Soldier in World War II," Survey S-194, question 5.

17. "Women in the Air Force: A Study of Recent Enlistees," Department of Defense, Attitude Research Branch, Report 121-344-W, Armed Forces Information and Education Division, Jan. 1952, p. 16; "Women in the WAC: A Study of Recent Enlistees," Department of Defense, Attitude Research Branch, Report 126-345-W, Armed Forces Information and Education Division, May 1952, p. 6, both at Maxwell Air Force Base Library.

18. Meid, "Marine Corps Women's Reserve," p. 60. For a discussion on the heritage of military service for southern men see Morris Janowitz, *The Professional Soldier: A Social and Political Portrait* (New York, 1960), pp. 87–89.

19. Stouffer, Survey S-194, questions 14, 15; Lyne and Arthur, *Three Years Behind the Mast,* p. 67.

20. Treadwell, *Women's Army Corps,* pp. 596, 591–592, 599–600, 777; "Recollections of Captain Mildred McAfee," pp. 44–48; Bureau of Naval Personnel, "Women's Reserve," pp. 31, 156; Florence Murray, ed., *The Negro Handbook: 1949* (New York, 1949), pp. 275–276; Jesse J. Johnson, *Black Women in the Armed Forces: 1942–1974* (Hampton, Va., 1974).

21. Treadwell, *Women's Army Corps,* p. 28.

22. Meid, "Marine Corps Women's Reserve," pp. 95–96.

23. "Recollections of Captain Mildred McAfee," p. 45; Virginia Crocheron Gildersleeve, *Many a Good Crusade* (New York, 1954), pp. 267–284.

24. Treadwell, *Women's Army Corps,* pp. 402, 403, 511, 512, 514; Bureau of Naval Personnel, "Women's Reserve," p. 74; Streeter, "History of Marine Corps Women's Reserve," p. 370. Margaret D. Craighill, "The Women's Army Corps," in Robert S. Anderson, ed., *Neuropsychiatry in World War II* (Washington, D.C., 1966), vol. 1, pp. 417–474.

25. Streeter, "History of Marine Corps Women's Reserve," pp. 381–383; Meid, "Marine Corps Women's Reserve," pp. 40, 41.

26. Bureau of Naval Personnel, "Women's Reserve," pp. 155, 156; Streeter, "History of Marine Corps Women's Reserve," p. 239; Treadwell, *Women's Army Corps*, p. 775.

27. Bureau of Naval Personnel, "Women's Reserve," p. 155.

28. Bureau of Naval Personnel, "Women's Reserve," pp. 75, 77; Treadwell, *Women's Army Corps,* p. 625; Streeter, "History of Marine Corps Women's Reserve," pp. 230, 236, 237; Donald Webster Cory, *The Homosexual in America* (New York, 1951), pp. 43–44, 76–78.

29. Hancock, *Lady in the Navy,* p. 226. On venereal disease see Ruth Roach Pierson, "The Double Bind of the Double Standard: VD Control and the CWAC in World War II," *Canadian Historical Review,* 62 (1981), 31–58.

30. Bureau of Naval Personnel, "Women's Reserve," p. 118; Streeter, "History of Marine Corps Women's Reserve," pp. 226, 227, 245.

31. Bureau of Naval Personnel, "Women's Reserve," p. 121.

32. Treadwell, *Women's Army Corps*, p. 209; oral histories provide many examples of avoiding and enduring discipline.

33. Streeter, "History of Marine Corps Women's Reserve," pp. 167–168.

34. U.S. Navy, "U.S. Naval Administrative Histories of World War II, Commandant's Report, Twelfth Naval District," San Francisco, 1946, manuscript, Navy Department Library, Washington, D.C.

35. Lyne and Arthur, *Three Years Behind the Mast,* p. 116.

36. Meid, "Marine Corps Women's Reserve," p. 34; Hancock, *Lady in the Navy,* 130.

37. Stouffer, Survey S-194, questions 15, 18.

38. Streeter, "History of Marine Corps Women's Reserve," p. 136; Stouffer, Survey S-194, question 17.

39. Treadwell, *Women's Army Corps,* p. 328.

40. Ibid., p. 346.

41. Ibid., pp. 345, 349.

42. *Time,* April 2, 1945, p. 20, and April 16, 1945, p. 24; Treadwell, *Women's Army Corps,* pp. 598–599.

43. Treadwell, *Women's Army Corps,* p. 337; Hancock, *Lady in the Navy,* p. 178.

44. Streeter, "History of Marine Corps Women's Reserve," pp. 276, 253, 270–273, 341, 342; Treadwell, *Women's Army Corps,* chap. 33.

45. Treadwell, *Women's Army Corps,* p. 70.

46. Ibid., p. 71.

47. WAC director's speech, FAF Command Conference, Jan. 26–27, 1944, quoted in Fourth Air Force Historical Study V-4, p. 247, Maxwell Air Force Base Library.

48. Streeter, "History of Marine Corps Women's Reserve," pp. 375–376; "Recollections of Captain Mildred McAfee," p. 71; Hancock, *Lady in the Navy,* p. 189; Stouffer, Survey S-194.

49. Streeter, "History of Marine Corps Women's Reserve," pp. 375–376.

50. Historical Report for 1943, WAC Section Headquarters, Western Flying Training Command, vol. 5 (Jan.–Dec. 1943), pp. 1257–1258, Maxwell Air Force Base Library.

51. Lyne and Arthur, *Three Years Behind the Mast,* p. 84.

52. Ibid., pp. 17, 84. Meid, "Marine Corps Women's Reserve," p. 62. Research Branch, Special Service Division, Services of Supply, War Department, "Preliminary Report on Motivations in Joining WAAC," Jan. 26, 1943, copy in George C. Marshall Research Library, Lexington, Va.

53. Treadwell, *Women's Army Corps,* pp. 186–189.

54. Ibid., pp. 191–218. Ruth Roach Pierson, "Ladies or Loose Women: The Canadian Women's Army Corps in World War II," *Atlantis,* 4 (1979), 245–266.

55. Gildersleeve, *Many a Good Crusade,* p. 267.

56. Streeter, "History of Marine Corps Women's Reserve," p. 105; Lyne and Arthur, *Three Years Behind the Mast,* p. 67; Bureau of Naval Personnel, "Women's Reserves," pp. 82, 84; Hancock, *Lady of the Navy,* p. 210.

57. Goldman, ed., *Female Soldiers,* pp. 55, 243. Madison Pearson to Commanding General, Services of Supply, Nov. 18, 1942, with enclosures; Ray E. Porter, "Memorandum for the Chief of Staff," July 7, 1943, with enclosures; "Report of Civilian Antiaircraft Artillery Personnel Board," Oct. 10, 1942; General Staff, G-3, "Employment of WAAC Personnel," June 16, 1943, all in Record Group 165, boxes 199, 836, National Archives, copies in George C. Marshall Research Library. See also Treadwell, *Women's Army Corps,* pp. 191, 301–302.

58. Marie Bennett Alsmeyer, ed., *Old Waves. Tales* (Conway, Ark., 1982), p. 17; Lyne and Arthur, *Three Years Behind the Mast,* p. 70; Treadwell, *Women's Army Corps,* pp. 211–213; Alsmeyer, *The Way of the WAVES,* pp. 20, 25.

59. Treadwell, *Women's Army Corps,* pp. 184, 232–233; Lyne and Arthur, *Three Years Behind the Mast,* p. 78; Streeter, "History of the Marine Corps Women's Reserve," p. 332. Personal letter to Commanding General, Army Air Force, March 31, 1944, quoted in Fourth Air Force Historical Study No. V-4, p. 248, Maxwell Air Force Base Library.

60. Stouffer, Survey S-215, Methodological Study, June 1945.

61. Treadwell, *Women's Army Corps,* p. 448.

62. Judith Hicks Stiehm, *Bring Me Men and Women* (Berkeley, 1981), pp. 140, 144.

63. Lyne and Arthur, *Three Years Behind the Mast,* pp. 19, 74; Treadwell, *Women's Army Corps,* p. 171.

64. "How YOU Can Enlist More WACS," p. 6, Headquarters Army Air Force Training Command, Fort Worth, Texas, n.d., Maxwell Air Force Base Library.

65. Ibid., p. 7.

66. Ibid.

67. Quoted in E. G. Dennis, "Each Hospital Corps Wave Frees a Fighting Sailor 'And Helps 100 Men,' " *Hospitals,* 18 (March 1944), 38.

68. Treadwell, *Women's Army Corps,* pp. 400, 401.

69. Ibid., p. 402.

70. *New York Times,* Jan. 19, Oct. 2, 1945.

71. Treadwell, *Women's Army Corps,* p. 738.

72. Ibid.; Stouffer, Survey S-194, questions 45, 46.

73. Treadwell, *Women's Army Corps,* p. 739. June A. Willenz, *Women Veterans: America's Forgotten Heroines* (New York,1983).

74. Treadwell, *Women's Army Corps*, pp. 748, 749.

75. George C. Marshall to Orlando Ward, July 28, 1950, copy in George C. Marshall Research Library.

76. Rear Admiral Randall Jacobs, USM, Chief of Bureau, to Senator David Walsh, May 11, 1942, in *Congressional Record,* 77th Cong., 2nd sess., May 14, 1942.

2. Victory for the Angels of Mercy

1. Bureau of the Census, *Historical Statistics of the United States, Colonial Times to 1970* (Washington, D.C., 1975), pp. 69, 76; Nursing Information Bureau, *Facts About Nursing, 1944* (New York, 1944), p. 40. On the status of nurses during World War I and between the wars see Elizabeth A. Shields, "A History of the United States Army Nurse Corps (Female): 1901–1937," Ed.D. diss., Columbia University Teacher's College, 1980; Barbara Melosh, *"The Physician's Hand": Nurses and Nursing in the Twentieth Century* (Philadelphia, 1982); Susan Reverby, "The Nursing Disorder: A Critical History of the Hospital–Nursing Relationship, 1860–1945," Ph.D. diss., Boston University, 1982;

Philip A. Kalisch and Beatrice Kalisch, *The Advance of American Nursing* (Boston, 1978); and Philip A. Kalisch and Margaret Scobey, "Female Nurses in American Wars: Helplessness Suspended for the Duration," *Armed Forces and Society,* 9 (Winter 1982).

2. Esther Lucile Brown, *Nursing for the Future: A Report Prepared for the National Nursing Council* (New York, 1948); Mary M. Roberts, *American Nursing History and Interpretation* (New York, 1954), pp. 489–495; Hans O. Manksch, "Nursing: Churning for Change," in Howard E. Freeman and others, eds., *Handbook of Medical Sociology* (Englewood Cliffs, N.J., 1972), pp. 106–130.

3. Everett Chorrington Hughes, *Twenty Thousand Nurses Tell Their Story* (Philadelphia, 1958), pp. 53–54: Ida Harper Simpson, *From Student to Nurse: A Longitudinal Study of Socialization* (New York, 1979).

4. By 1975 only 23 percent of students were in hospital schools. Howard S. Rowland, *The Nurse's Almanac* (Germantown, Md., 1978), p. 164; Kalisch and Kalisch, *Advance of Nursing,* pp. 594–595, 623–626; Roberts, *American Nursing,* pp. 512–547.

5. Edward L. Bernays, "The Medical Profession and Nursing," *American Journal of Nursing,* 45 (Nov. 1945), 909; Bernays, "What Patients Say about Nurses," *American Journal of Nursing,* 47 (1947), 93–96; Bernays, "Opinion Molders Appraise Nursing," *American Journal of Nursing,* 45 (1945), 1005–1011; Samuel Stouffer, "The American Soldier in World War II," Survey S-224, "Hospital Patients," June 1945, Roper Center, University of Connecticut, Storrs, Conn., and Williams College, Williamstown, Mass.: Hughes, *Twenty Thousand Nurses,* pp. 19–20.

6. Robert W. Habenstein and Edwin A. Christ, *Professionalizer, Traditionalizer, and Utilizer* (Columbia, Mo., 1955), pp. 55–64.

7. Nurses who were graduated in 1940 in Pennsylvania averaged eight years in full-time nursing by 1955; 90 percent had married, and 89 percent of the wives had become mothers. The wives who continued longer in nursing usually had only one child, however. Marvin Bressler and William Kephart, *Career Dynamics* (Harrisburg, Pa., 1957), pp. 51–55.

8. Nursing Information Bureau, *Facts About Nursing, 1944,* p. 9.

9. "The Nurses' Contribution to American Victory: Facts and Figures From Pearl Harbor to V-J Day," *American Journal of Nursing,* 45 (1945), 683.

10. Ibid., 683, and Kalisch and Kalisch, *Advancement of Nursing,* p. 482; *Congressional Record,* 78th Cong., 1st sess., July 6, 1943.

11. Bresser and Kephart, *Career Dynamics;* Stouffer, Survey S-192, "Attitude of Army Nurses," Feb. 1945.

12. Mabel Keaton Staupers, *No Time for Prejudice* (New York, 1961), chap. 5. See also Darlene Clark Hine, "Mabel K. Staupers and the Integration of Black Nurses into the Armed Forces," in John Hope Franklin and August Meier, eds., *Black Leaders of the Twentieth Century* (Urbana, Ill., 1982), pp. 241–257.

13. Roberts, *American Nursing,* chap. 36; Philip A. Kalisch and Beatrice

Kalisch, "The Cadet Nurse Corps in World War II," *American Journal of Nursing,* 76 (1976), 240–242.

14.   The Bolton Act had a significant impact on black nursing schools and the admittance of blacks to integrated schools. See Staupers, *No Time for Prejudice,* chap 5; Darlene Clark Hine, "From Hospital to College: Black Nurse Leaders and the Rise of Collegiate Nursing Schools," *Journal of Negro Education,* 51 (1982), 222–237; Hine, *Black Women in White Caps* (Urbana, forthcoming).

15.   The proposed bill would draft male nurses and make them officers; before 1955 male nurses were not allowed in the nurses corps, and if drafted held enlisted status, not necessarily in a medical unit.

16.   Kalisch and Kalisch, *Advancement of Nursing,* p. 595.

17.   On roles see Col. Julie O. Flikke, *Nurses in Action* (New York, 1943), pp. 218–221; W. P. Briggs, "Men Nurses in the U.S. Navy," *American Journal of Nursing,* 43 (1943), 39–42; Daniel M. Brown, "Men Nurses and the U.S. Navy," *American Journal of Nursing,* 42 (1942), 499–501.

18.   Mattie E. Treadwell, *The United States Army in World War II,* vol. VIII, *The Women's Army Corps* (Washington, D.C., 1954), p. 346.

19.   Norma C. Furtos, "The Navy Is My Career," *Journal of the American Medical Women's Association,* 14 (June 1959), 516; Mary Roth Walsh, "Women Physicians and World War II," *Journal of the American Medical Women's Association,* 32 (May 1977), 189–192.

20.   In 1945, 60 percent of the nurses thought that male officers of equal rank, mostly doctors, had more privileges; only 16 percent felt the army in general accepted women on a par with male officers; 48 percent felt discriminated against because of sex. Stouffer, Survey S-192A, "Nurses in the Pacific Area," Jan. 1945.

21.   "Our Girls in Uniform," *Ladies Home Journal,* 60 (Jan. 1943), 69.

22.   Stouffer, Survey S-192A.

23.   Edward J. Bernays, "The Armed Services and the Nursing Profession," *American Journal of Nursing,* 46 (1946), 167.

24.   Ibid., pp. 166–167.

25.   Bernays, "Opinion Molders Appraise Nursing," pp. 1005, 1006.

26.   Ada Taylor to Mrs. Roosevelt, Jan. 10, 1945, in Eleanor Roosevelt Papers, Correspondence 95, box 1251, Franklin Delano Roosevelt Library, Hyde Park, N.Y. See also *American Journal of Nursing,* 45 (1945), 231.

27.   Bernays, "Armed Services," pp. 166–167.

28.   Pauline Maxwell, "History of the Army Nurse Corps," manuscript, Center for Military History, Army Headquarters, Washington, D.C., vol. XIV, 322–324, vol. XII, 170–171.

29.   Edward J. Bernays, "Hospitals and the Nursing Profession," *American Journal of Nursing,* 46 (1946), 110. See also "About the Absent for Duty Nurse," *Hospitals,* 18 (Feb. 1944), 30–33; Louise M. Tattershall and Marion E. Alten-

derfer, "Paid Auxiliary Nursing Workers Employed in General Hospitals," *American Journal of Nursing,* 44 (1944), 853–858.

30. On the Red Cross see "The History of the American National Red Cross," vol. VIII, Constance McLoughlin Green, "The History of Volunteer Special Services, 1919–47," 1950, pp. 137–144, manuscript, American National Red Cross Archives, Washington, D.C.; Mrs. Walter Lippmann, "We Want the Givers, Not the Takers," *Red Cross Courier* (Sept. 1942), pp. 9–30; Mary M. Roberts, "What Lies Ahead for Nursing," *Hospitals,* 19 (April 1945), 34.

31. *The Economic Status of Registered Professional Nurses, 1946–47,* Department of Labor Bulletin 931 (Washington, D.C., 1948), p. 9 et passim; S. H. McGuire and Dorothy W. Conrad, "Postwar Plans of Army and Navy Nurses," *American Journal of Nursing,* 46 (1946), 305–306, and 45 (1945), 1021–1023; Mary Walker Randolph, "What Army Nurses Expect from the Profession," *American Journal of Nursing,* 46 (1946), 95–97; Edna E. Sharritt, "Where Are the Ex-Service Nurses?" *American Journal of Nursing,* 46 (1946), 849–851. For a radical critique see Kathleen Cannings and William Lazonick, "The Development of the Nursing Labor Force in the United States: A Basic Analysis," *International Journal of Health Services,* 5 (1975), 195–216.

32. Hughes, *Twenty Thousand Nurses,* pp. 31–33, 258–259; Kalisch and Kalisch, *Advance of Nursing,* p. 494; Department of Labor, *Economic Status of Registered Professional Nurses, 1946–47,* pp. 1–12, 48.

33. On the greatly improved status of blacks see Estelle Massey Riddle and Josephine Nelson, "The Negro Nurse Looks Toward Tomorrow," *American Journal of Nursing,* 45 (1945), 627–630; Stauper, *No Time for Prejudice;* Kalisch and Kalisch, *Advancement of Nursing,* pp. 560–572.

34. The best treatment of the postwar model is in Roberts, *American Nursing,* parts 9 and 10. For the organizational structure of nursing see Lucille E. Notter and Eugenia Kennedy Spalding, *Professional Nursing: Foundations, Perspectives, and Relationships* (Philadelphia, 1976), part 5.

35. Harold D. Smith to Senator Elbert D. Thomas, Jan. 29, 1945, and enclosures, in Franklin Delano Roosevelt Papers, Official File, box 4675F, FDR Library.

36. Kalisch and Kalisch, *Advancement of Nursing,* chap. 15.

37. Ibid., pp. 496–497; Roberts, *American Nursing,* pp. 563–571; Susan Reverby, "Hospital Organizing in the 1950's: An Interview with Lilian Roberts," *Signs,* 1 (1976), 1053–1060; David R. Denton, *The Union Movement in American Hospitals, 1846–1976,* Ph.D. diss., Boston University, 1976.

38. For a good history of the episode see Philip A. Kalisch and Beatrice Kalisch, "Nurses Under Fire: An Analysis of the World War II Experience of Military Nurses on Bataan and Corregidor," *Nursing Research,* 25 (1976), 409–429. For contemporary descriptions see Page Coopery, *Navy Nurse* (New York, 1946); Theresa Archard, *G.I. Nightingale* (New York, 1945); Edith Aynes, *From Nightingale to Eagle: The Army Nurses' History* (Englewood Cliffs, N.J., 1973); Juanita Redmond, *I Served on Bataan* (Philadelphia, 1943).

3. Volunteer, Worker, or Housewife?

1. Rates of volunteer activity and of eagerness to do volunteer work early in the war were calculated from National Opinion Research Center (NORC) nationwide surveys reported in Office of War Information, Bureau of Intelligence, "Women and the War," Report 31, Aug. 6, 1942, table 31a, in Record Group 44, box 1798, National Archives, Washington, D.C. See also OWI, "Voluntary Participation in the War Effort," 1942, pp. 6–10, in Rensis Likert Papers, box 1, Michigan Historical Collections, University of Michigan, Ann Arbor, Mich. Frances H. Williams, "Minority Groups and the OPA," *Public Administration Review,* 7 (1947), 123–128. On national policy see Imogene H. Putnam, *Volunteers in OPA* (Washington, D.C., 1947), pp. 2–3, 11.

2. OWI, "Women and the War," table 34a; Irma Gross and Evelyn Zwemer, *Management in Michigan Homes,* Michigan State Agricultural Experiment Station Technical Bulletin 196 (East Lansing, Mich., 1945), pp. 49, 73

3. OWI, "Women and the War," table 34a; Office of War Information, Bureau of Intelligence, "Civilian Aspects of the War," Report 23, May 13, 1942, pp. 24–30, Record Group 44, National Archives; Genevieve Knupfer, "Portrait of the Underdog," *Public Opinion Quarterly,* 11 (1947), 103–114; Lois Pratt and P. K. Whelpton, "Social and Psychological Factors Affecting Fertility: Extra Familial Participation of Wives," *Milbank Memorial Fund Quarterly,* 34 (1956), 44–78; Elihu Katz and Paul Lazarsfeld, *Personal Influence* (Glencoe, Ill., 1955), pp. 229, 289; Mirra Komarovsky, "The Volunteer Associations of Urban Dwellers," *American Sociological Review,* 11 (1946), 686–698.

4. OWI, "Women and the War," table 35a; Karl Drew Hartzell, *The Empire State at War: World War II* (Albany, 1949), pp. 128, 131.

5. Mary Watters, *Illinois in the Second World War,* vol. 1 (Springfield, Ill., 1950), p. 321. Putnam, *Volunteers in OPA,* pp. 1, 18, 32, 165.

6. John Morton Blum, *V Was for Victory* (New York, 1976), pp. 16–21; Watters, *Illinois,* I, 278–292; "City Gardens in Wartime," *Monthly Labor Review,* 63 (Oct. 1945), 644–650.

7. Max Parvin Cavnes, *The Hoosier Community at War* (Bloomington, Ind., 1961), pp. 150, 406–438; press release, Dec. 1, 1943, Associated Negro Press, in Claude Barnett Papers, box 38, Chicago Historical Society, Chicago, Ill.; Watters, *Illinois,* I, 153–167; Julia M. H. Carson, *Home Away from Home: The Story of the USO* (New York, 1946).

8. "The History of the American National Red Cross," vol. VIII, Constance McLoughlin Green, "The History of Volunteer Special Services, 1919–47," 1950, pp. 95–172, manuscript, American National Red Cross Archives, Washington, D.C. Bureau of the Census, *Statistical Abstract of the United States, 1946* (Washington, D.C., 1946), p. 223.

9. Associated Negro Press releases of Oct. 18, 1943, Sept. 13, 1943 (on Baptists), May 19, 1943 (on AKA), in Claude Barnett Papers; "War Programs of the Illinois Association of Colored Women: 1943–1944," in Illinois State

Council of Defense Records, Woman's Division (1944), Illinois State Archives, Springfield, Ill. Williams, "Minority Groups and the OPA," pp. 125–128; Putnam, *Volunteers in OPA;* St. Clair Drake and Horace Cayton, *Black Metropolis* (New York, 1945), pp. 536–537; Louis Coleridge Kesselman, *The Social Politics of FEPC* (Chapel Hill, N.C., 1948), pp. 87–100.

10. Ruby Bryant Yearwood, "Women Volunteers United to Serve," *Opportunity: Journal of Negro Life,* 21 (April 1943), 60–62, 88–89; "The History of the American Red Cross," vol. XXXII, Kathryn Richardson Tyler and Jesse O. Thomas, "Negro Red Cross Personnel in World War II, 1942–1946," 1950, pp. iii–vi, 16, 46, 69–107, manuscript, American National Red Cross Archives.

11. Gordon W. Allport and Leo J. Postman, "The Basic Psychology of Rumor," 1945, reprinted in Daniel Katz and others, *Public Opinion and Propaganda* (New York, 1954), pp. 394–404; Office of War Information, Bureau of Intelligence, "Rumors in Wartime," Special Report, Sept. 30, 1942, Record Group 44, National Archives.

12. *Monthly Labor Review,* 65 (Dec. 1947), 667.

13. Albert Westfeld, *Getting Started: Urban Youth in the Labor Market,* WPA Research Monograph 26 (Washington, D.C., 1943), pp. 163, 194.

14. The military reached a plateau of 11.6 million men and 300,000 women from summer 1944 to summer 1945. However, there was some turnover, with veterans beginning to return in 1944. In all, 16 million persons served in the armed forces from 1941 to 1946. Clarence D. Long, *The Labor Force in War and Transition: Four Countries* (New York, 1952), p. 52; Bureau of the Census, *Historical Statistics of the United States* (Washington, D.C., 1975), pp. 126, 1140.

15. Long, *Labor Force,* pp. 34–35; *Statistical Abstract, 1946,* pp. 200, 205, 206; federal employment in Washington doubled, but comprised only 5 percent of the growth. That is, 95 percent of the new federal employees were scattered about the country, especially at military bases and arsenals. *Statistical Abstract, 1946,* pp. 206–208.

16. Mary Elizabeth Pidgeon, *Changes in Women's Employment During the War,* Women's Bureau Special Bulletin 20 (Washington, D.C., 1944).

17. On the part-time employment of women in agriculture see D'Ann Campbell, "Wives, Workers and Womanhood: America During World War II," Ph.D. diss., University of North Carolina, 1979, pp. 103–111.

18. Erna Magnus, "Gainfully Employed Women in Chicago," *Social Security Bulletin* 6 (1943), 3–17.

19. *Community Household Employment Programs,* Women's Bureau Bulletin 221 (Washington, D.C., 1948), p. 5; *The Labor Market* (March 1947), pp. 10–12; "Wartime Job Opportunities for Women Household Workers in Washington, D.C.," *Monthly Labor Review,* 62 (March 1945), 575–584.

20. Donald S. Howard, *The WPA and Federal Relief Policy* (New York, 1943), pp. 278–296; Richard Sterner, *The Negro's Share: A Study of Income, Consumption, Housing and Public Assistance* (New York, 1943), pp. 213–323; National Resources Planning Board, *Security, Work, and Relief Policies* (Wash-

ington, D.C., 1942), pp. 111–118, 156–160; Bureau of the Census, *The Social and Economic Status of the Black Population in the United States: An Historical View, 1790–1978* (Washington, D.C., 1979), p. 14.

21. *Changes in Women's Occupations, 1940–1950,* Women's Bureau Bulletin 253 (Washington, D.C., 1954), pp. 9–11, 31–35; Seymour L. Wolfbein, "Postwar Trends in Negro Employment," *Monthly Labor Review,* 65 (Dec. 1947), 664–665; National Planning Association, *Selected Studies of Negro Employment in the South* (Washington, D.C., 1955), pp. 190–197; Herbert R. Northrup and Richard L. Rowan, *Negro Employment in Southern Industry: A Study of Racial Policies in Five Industries* (Philadephia, 1970); Karen Tucker Anderson, "Last Hired, First Fired: Black Women Workers during World War II," *Journal of American History,* 69 (1982), 82–97.

22. Truman M. Pierce and others, *White and Negro Schools in the South: An Analysis of Biracial Education* (Englewood Cliffs, N.J., 1955), p. 208; Thurgood Marshall, "Teachers' Salary Cases," in Florence Murray, ed., *The Negro Handbook, 1946–1947* (New York, 1947), pp. 40–50; *The Outlook for Women in Social Work: General Summary,* Women's Bureau Bulletins 235–238 (Washington, D.C., 1952), pp. 59–61.

23. Murray, *Negro Handbook, 1946–1947,* pp. 103–111; Gordon F. Bloom, F. Marion Fletcher, and Charles R. Perry, *Negro Employment in Retail Trade: A Study of Racial Policies in the Department Store, Drugstore, and Supermarket Industries* (Philadelphia, 1972), II, 33, III, 21, IV, 44. Wolfbein, "Postwar Trends," p. 664. On breaking the job ceiling see Drake and Cayton, *Black Metropolis,* chap. 9, and Anderson, "Last Hired, First Fired," pp. 82–97.

24. "Annual Family and Occupational Earnings of Residents of Two Negro Housing Projects in Atlanta, 1937–1944," *Monthly Labor Review,* 63 (Dec. 1945), 1061–1073.

25. Throughout the century, except in world wars and recently, the labor market has been rigidly segregated by sex, with very few androgenous jobs. Valerie Kincade Oppenheimer, *The Female Labor Force in the United States* (Berkeley, 1970), pp. 66–120. See also, Edward Gross, "Plus ca change . . . ? The Sexual Structure of Occupations over Time" *Social Problems,* 16 (1968), 198–208, and Francine D. Blau and Carol L. Jusenius, "Economists' Approaches to Sex Segregation in the Labor Market," *Signs,* 1 (1976), 181–199.

26. "Recent Occupational Trends," *Monthly Labor Review,* 65 (Aug. 1947), 141–142.

27. Pidgeon, *Changes in Women's Employment,* p. 29. Wives of soldiers and sailors behaved quite differently from other wives, in part because they were generally younger. Service wives were 13 percent more likely to enter the labor force, 17 percent more likely to stay in, and 33 percent less likely to stay out. That is, service wives were 30 percent more likely to be in the labor force than other wives (see table 6).

28. Women's Bureau, *Women As Workers* (Washington, D.C., 1953), pp. 68–82; *Women Workers in Ten War Production Areas and Their Postwar Em-*

ployment Plans, Women's Bureau Bulletin 209 (Washington, D.C., 1946), pp. 73–75; " 'Extra' Workers in the Postwar Labor Force," *Monthly Labor Review* (Nov. 1945), 845; *Statistical Abstract, 1980,* p. 403.

29. Bureau of the Census, "Monthly Report on the Labor Force," *MLRF No. 28,* Oct. 7, 1944, p. 1; Jacob Perlman, "The Continuous Work-History Sample," *Social Security Bulletin,* 14 (April 1951), 6, 7. Women's Bureau, *Women As Workers,* p. 42. A large literature exists on the issue of continuity. See, for example, Gertrude Bancroft, *The American Labor Force* (New York, 1958), pp. 100–114; James Sweet, *Women in the Labor Force* (New York, 1973), pp. 68–78; I. V. Sawhill, "The Economics of Discrimination Against Women," *Journal of Human Resources,* 8 (1973), 383–396; Theodore Caplow, *The Sociology of Work* (Minneapolis, 1954), pp. 230–247.

30. *Statistical Abstract, 1949,* p. 296; Sweet, *Women in the Labor Force,* p. 13; Perlman, "The Continuous Work-History Sample." Those least likely to have work experience were poorly educated whites, particularly from rural areas.

31. William Henry Chafe, *The American Woman: Her Changing Social, Economic, and Political Roles, 1920–1970* (New York, 1972), pp. 188–189.

32. *Statistical Abstract, 1947,* p. 42; *Historical Statistics,* p. 20; Hugh Carter and Paul Glick, *Marriage and Divorce* (Cambridge, Mass., 1970), chap. 3. The number of widows who had not remarried climbed from 5.7 million in 1940 to 6.7 million in 1950 and 7.9 million in 1960. The change was due to an older age structure, rather than to war deaths.

33. Linda J. Waite, "Working Wives: 1940–1960," *American Sociological Review,* 41 (1976), 65–80: Valerie K. Oppenheimer, *The Female Labor Force in the United States* (Berkeley, 1970); Oppenheimer, "The Sociology of Women's Economic Role in the Family," *American Sociological Review,* 42 (1977), 387–406. For a broad overview see Jessie Bernard, *The Female World* (New York, 1981), chap. 23.

34. "What About the Women?" *Ladies Home Journal,* 61 (June 1944), 23, 157. For surveys of prewar work motivations see *Women Workers in Their Family Environment,* Women's Bureau Bulletin 183 (Washington, D.C., 1941). Postwar surveys of union women revealed similar patterns: Mary Elizabeth Pidgeon, *Women Workers and Their Dependents,* Women's Bureau Bulletin 239 (Washington, D.C., 1952), pp. 45–47. A survey of employed wives in 1944 showed that 57 percent planned to continue working after the war; 79 percent of them cited the need for money, while 22 percent explained that they liked working or enjoyed the independence. *Handbook of Women Workers,* p. 33.

35. Ernest Havemann and Patricia Salter West, *They Went to College: The College Graduate in America Today* (New York, 1952), pp. 62, 70; National Federation of Business and Professional Women's Clubs, *Position of Married Women in the Economic World* (Washington, D.C., 1940); Susan M. Kingsbury, *Economic Status of University Women in the U.S.A.,* Women's Bureau Bulletin 170 (Washington, D.C., 1939).

36. Institute for Psychoanalysis, *Women in Wartime* (Chicago, 1943); Charlotte Shohan Peck, "A Survey of Women's Attitudes Toward Wartime Jobs," M.S.S. thesis, Smith College School for Social Work, 1944, pp. 16–34; Jessie Bowen, "Effects of Industrial Employment of Mothers on Child Care," M.S.S. thesis, Smith College School for Social Work, 1943, pp. 60–61; "What About the Women?" *Ladies Home Journal*, p. 157; David M. Levy, "The War and Family Life," *American Journal of Orthopsychiatry*, 15 (1945), 142–147.

37. Bureau of the Census, *Current Population Reports, Labor Force*, Series P-50, no. 38, Jan. 25, 1952 (Washington, D.C., 1952), p. 11; "What About the Women?" *Ladies Home Journal*, p. 157.

38. Roper poll 50, Oct. 1945, Roper Center, Williams College, Williamstown, Mass. (N = 3512). The eta coefficients that indicate the relative importance of the various groupings were .175 for race, .119 for education, .114 for region, .090 for occupation, .079 for socioeconomic status (whites only), .068 for age, .059 for marital status, .051 for sex, and .014 for urban-rural residence. Among women, an eta of .104 contrasted the housewives (who scored −37) and the workers (who scored −21). Interaction effects were minor.

39. Robert R. Sears, Eleanor Maccoby, and Harry Levin, *Patterns of Child Rearing* (Stanford, Ca., 1957), pp. 32–49.

40. Frances E. Merrill, *Social Problems on the Home Front* (New York, 1948), chap. 2; *Historical Statistics*, p. 64; Paul H. Jacobson, "Differentials in Divorce by Duration of Marriages and Size of Family," *American Sociological Review*, 15 (April 1950), 235–244; Jacobson, *American Marriage and Divorce* (New York, 1959); Robert F. Winch, *The Modern Family* (New York, 1971), chaps. 22 and 23; Samuel H. Preston and John McDonald, "The Incidence of Divorce Within Cohorts of American Marriages Contracted Since the Civil War," *Demography*, 16 (1979), 10–11; Thomas J. Espenshade and Rachel Eisenberg Braun, "Life Course Analysis and Multistate Demography: An Application to Marriage, Divorce and Remarriage," *Journal of Marriage and the Family*, 44 (1982), 1025–1036; A. Wade Smith and June E. G. Meitz, "Cohort Education and the Decline in Undisrupted Marriages," *Journal of Marriage and the Family*, 45 (1983), 613–622.

41. John L. Thomas, *The American Catholic Family* (Englewood Cliffs, N.J., 1956), pp. 272–277; William J. Goode, *After Divorce* (Glencoe, Ill., 1956); Harvey J. Locke, *Predicting Happiness or Divorce in Marriage* (New York, 1951).

42. In 1940, 5 percent of all husbands were unaccountably absent from home; in 1944, 4 percent were absent without leave. Pidgeon, *Changes in Women's Employment*, p. 28. See also Carter and Glick, *Marriage and Divorce*, p. 63; John Durand, *The Labor Force in the United States, 1890–1960* (New York, 1948), p. 155.

43. Herbert Fleming, "Women War Workers Look Ahead," *Survey Graphic*, 33 (Oct. 1944), 415–419. A total of 555 women responded; their median age was twenty-nine, four years younger than the median age of women workers

and eight years younger than all women. See also Hadley Cantril and Mildred Strunk, *Public Opinion 1935–1946* (Princeton, 1951), p. 803.

44. Among some wives, the increased proportion of husbands absent was enormous. For example, it rose from 7 percent in 1940 to 56 percent in 1944 for the youngest white group. Black families show quite different patterns. Younger black women were both more likely to be married than their white sisters in 1940 and also more likely to have an absent husband. By 1944 the proportion of husbands absent in military service was 21 percent for white wives (aged eighteen to thirty-four), versus 11 percent for black wives (see table 7). Hence, military service had a smaller disruptive effect on black wives. This does not suggest black men had lower military participation rates; that is a topic that must be approached from the viewpoint of males, not of wives. Durand, *Labor Force*, pp. 224–226.

45. Pidgeon, *Changes in Women's Employment*, p. 29; Samuel Stouffer and others, *The American Soldier* (Princeton, 1949), I, 165, 452–457; *Historical Statistics*, p. 1140.

46. Albemarle also claimed the nation's *youngest* soldier's mother, aged thirty-two. Gertrude Dana Parlier and others, *Pursuits of War: The People of Charlottesville and Albemarle County, Virginia, in the Second World War* (Charlottesville, Va., 1948), p. 198.

47. *Historical Statistics*, pp. 49–54, 57.

48. Wilson Grabill, Clyde Kiser, and Pascal Welpton, *The Fertility of American Women* (New York, 1958), tables 75, 76.

49. The rate of illegitimate births per 1,000 births held steady during the war at about 21 for whites and 170 for blacks—that is, for 1945, about 59,000 white and 70,000 black births. U.S. Public Health Service, "Illegitimate Births by Race, 1944," *Vital Statistics, Special Reports*, 25 (1946), 249. By 1975 the numbers were 186,000 whites, 262,000 blacks, with about the same number of legitimate births as 1944. *Statistical Abstract, 1977*, p. 61.

50. In 1939, 10.3 percent of all white births were to women who already had five or more children; by 1944, the proportion was down to 7.9 percent; by 1950, 6.2 percent; by 1960, the proportion was up to 8.9 percent, then it plunged to 1.6 percent in 1975. *Statistical Abstract, 1977*, p. 56. U.S. Public Health Service, "Births by Age," *Vital Statistics, Special Reports*, 25 (1946), 146.

51. Judith Blake, "Reproductive Ideals and Educational Attainment Among White Americans, 1943–1960," *Population Studies*, 21 (1967), 160; Blake, "Ideal Family Size Among White Americans," *Demography*, 3 (1966), 154–173.

52. Richard Easterlin, *Population, Labor Force and Long Swings in Economic Growth* (New York, 1968), pp. 103–107, 118; see also Easterlin, "Relative Economic Status and the Fertility Swing," in Eleanor Sheldon, ed., *Family Economic Behavior* (Philadelphia, 1973), pp. 170–223.

53. *Statistical Abstract, 1977*, p. 781; J. Frederic Dewhurst and Associates, *America's Needs and Resources* (New York, 1955), pp. 196–231; U.S. Department of Labor, *How American Buying Habits Change* (Washington, D.C., 1959), pp. 57–102.

54. Edgar F. Borgatta and Charles F. Westoff, "Social and Psychological Factors Affecting Fertility, XXV, The Prediction of Total Fertility," *Milbank Memorial Fund Quarterly,* 32 (Oct. 1954), 401–404; Ruth Riemer and Clyde V. Kiser, "Social and Psychological Factors Affecting Fertility, XXIII, The Prediction of Total Fertility," *Milbank Memorial Fund Quarterly,* 32 (Oct. 1954), 167–189.

55. Easterlin, *Population,* pp. 238, 241.

56. Ibid., p. 238.

57. Quoted in Eleanor Straub, "United States Government Policy Toward Civilian Women During World War II," Ph.D. diss., Emory University, 1973, p. 103; see also Josephine Chandler Holcomb, "Women in the Labor Force in the United States, 1940–1950," Ph.D. diss., University of South Carolina, 1976, pp. 30–88. For useful comparisons with Britain see Margaret Allen, "The Domestic Ideal and the Mobilization of Womanpower in World War II," *Women's Studies International Forum,* 6 (1983), 401–412.

58. Straub, "Policy Toward Civilian Women," pp. 111–116; Holcomb, "Women in the Labor Force," p. 24.

59. Office of War Information, Bureau of Intelligence, "Opinions About the Wartime Employment of Women," Report C31, May 29, 1944, pp. 2, 10, Record Group 44, box E149, National Archives.

60. Ibid., p. 232. Office of War Information, Bureau of Intelligence, "Attitudes Toward the Employment of Women in War Industries," Special Report 17, Aug. 4, 1942, Record Group 44, National Archives. Roper-*Fortune* poll 35, May 1943, Roper Center, Williams College, Williamstown, Mass.

61. Cavnes, *Hoosier Community,* p. 235 and, for an excellent overall discussion, pp. 228–245; see also, Watters, *Illinois in the Second World War,* I, 385–388.

62. That is, 5 percent of the mothers with children under fourteen. Women's Bureau, *Women Workers in Ten War Production Areas,* p. 56.

63. Women's Bureau, *Women As Workers,* pp. 53, 87; *Statistical Abstract, 1946,* p. 290. But men's income went up even faster, primarily because of heavy overtime schedules, so that women slipped from 59 percent of male pay in 1939 to 47 percent in 1945.

64. Roper-*Fortune* poll 35, May 1943; "What About the Women?" *Ladies Home Journal,* p. 159.

65. Richard Centers, *The Psychology of Social Classes* (Princeton, 1949), p. 146; Oppenheimer, *Female Labor Force,* pp. 48–51; Caplow, *Sociology of Work,* pp. 237–239.

4. Making Way for Rosie

1. "Women in Industry," *The [New York] Industrial Bulletin,* 22 (Dec. 1943), 457–460.

2. U.S. Department of Labor, *1965 Handbook on Women Workers* (Wash-

ington, D.C., 1966), p. 86; see also, Valerie Kincade Oppenheimer, *The Female Labor Force in the United States* (Berkeley, 1970), chaps. 3, 5.

3. Unless the Catholic sisterhoods are included. Women were numerically dominant in the library world, but men ran the profession.

4. "Impact of War on Teacher Placement Service," *Manpower Review* (Feb. 1943), pp. 11–13.

5. Ibid.; I. L. Kandel, *The Impact of the War Upon American Education* (Chapel Hill, N.C., 1948), p. 64.

6. *The Teacher Situation in Indiana,* Bulletin of the School of Education, Indiana University, Bureau of Cooperative Research and Field Service (Bloomington, 1944), tables IV–IX, pp. 19, 59.

7. Theodore Caplow, *The Sociology of Work* (Minneapolis, 1954), p. 231.

8. Dorothy D. Crook, "Little Business Woman What Now?" *Independent Woman,* 21 (Feb. 1942), 47; Jane Todd, "Sample Picture of Woman-Owned Small Business," *Independent Woman,* 25 (Dec. 1946), 372.

9. *Woman's Work in the War,* Women's Bureau Bulletin 193 (Washington, D.C., 1942), pp. 6–7.

10. Institute of Women's Professional Relations, *Women's Work and Education: The Clip Sheet and Newsletter of the Institute of Women's Professional Relations,* April 1943, New London, Conn.

11. Caplow, *Sociology of Work,* p. 231; National Industrial Conference Board, *Personnel Practices in Factory and Office,* II (New York, 1948), 12, 35, 37, 38.

12. "Shall We Register Women for War Service?" *Independent Woman,* 21 (March 1942), 74.

13. Ibid., p. 76. For background on twentieth-century clerical workers see Margery W. Davies, *Woman's Place Is at the Typewriter: Office Work and Office Workers, 1870–1930* (Philadelphia, 1982).

14. Gladys M. Kammerer, "The Impact of the War on Federal Personnel Administration, 1939–1945," Ph.D. diss., University of Chicago, 1946, pp. 103, 199–200, 219.

15. Ibid., p. 138.

16. "Placement of Negroes in the State," *The New York Employment Review,* 4 (May 1942), 235–239. See also, *Negro Women War Workers,* Women's Bureau Bulletin 205 (Washington, D.C., 1945), pp. 2–19; Dorothy K. Newman and others, *Protest, Politics, and Prosperity: Black Americans and White Institutions, 1940–75* (New York, 1978), pp. 99–126; Kenesaw M. Landis, *Segregation in Washington, A Report of the National Committee on Segregation in the Nation's Capital* (Chicago, 1948), pp. 60–74.

17. *Handbook of Facts on Women Workers,* Women's Bureau Bulletin 225 (Washington, D.C., 1948), tables 12, 13.

18. Testimony of Zelma Mary Watson, U.S. Senate, Committee on Education and Labor, *Wartime Health and Education*, Subcommittee of 78th Cong., 2nd sess., 1944, part 3, p. 1211.

19. C. Wright Mills, *White Collar: The American Middle Classes* (New York, 1951), pp. 76, 207.

20. Pidgeon, *Changes in Women's Employment,* pp. 5–15. W. S. Woytinski and Associates, *Employment and Wages in the United States* (New York, 1953), pp. 744–755. Lucius Flint, "Selecting and Training Female Help," *Supermarket Merchandising,* 8 (March 1943), 28–31; (April 1943), 30–33; (Jan. 1943), 12; (July 1943), 28; and " 'Butcherettes' Prove Success at Lucky's" (Aug. 1943), 32.

21. Woytinsky, *Employment and Wages,* 744–755.

22. Durward Howes and others, eds., *American Women: The Standard Biographical Dictionary of Notable Women,* vol. III, *1939–40* (Los Angeles, 1939).

23. *Women in Higher-Level Positions,* Women's Bureau Bulletin 236 (Washington, D.C., 1950); Ernest Havemann and Patricia Salter West, *They Went to College: The College Graduate in America Today* (New York, 1952).

24. National Federation of Business and Professional Women's Clubs, *Position of Married Women in the Economic World* (New York, 1940), pp. 34–35, 38, appendix.

25. *The Labor Market* (Aug.–Sept. 1947), 15–17; Mary B. Leach, "The Future of Women in Banking," 38 *Banking* (May 1946), 46–47, 126–128.

26. Babette Kass and Rose Fields, *The Economic Strength of Business and Professional Women* (New York, 1954); Rosabeth Moss Kanter, *Men and Women of the Corporation* (New York, 1977), chap. 4.

27. The labor market was also segregated by race, with blacks largely prevented by custom from taking jobs traditionally held by whites. The federal government attempted to eliminate race discrimination (but not sex discrimination) by executive order in 1941. See Horace Cayton and St. Clair Drake, *Black Metropolis* (New York, 1944), and Louis Ruchames, *Race, Jobs, and Politics: The Story of FEPC* (Chapel Hill, 1948).

28. Valerie Kincade Oppenheimer, *The Female Labor Force in the United States* (Berkeley, 1970), pp. 138–142.

29. "Employment of Women Increases in New York City's War Industries," *The [New York] Employment Review,* 4 (Feb. 1942), 102.

30. Office of War Information, Bureau of Intelligence, "Attitudes Toward the Employment of Women in War Industries," Special Report 17, Aug. 4, 1942, table II, Record Group 44, National Archives.

31. Roper-*Fortune* poll 35, May 1943, Roper Center, Williams College, Williamstown, Mass. Education and socioeconomic–racial status overlapped, but analysis of variance shows that each had a strong independent effect. Factory jobs were also very appealing to women who sought security more than high pay.

32. Frank J. Taylor, "Meet the Girls Who Keep 'Em Flying," *Saturday Evening Post,* 213 (May 30, 1942), 3. See also Marilyn Noll Clark, "Women Aircraft Workers in San Diego During the Second World War," M.A. thesis, San Diego State University, 1977.

33. "Women and Negroes, UAW Regions 1-1D," April 1943, UAW Papers Research Department, box 11, folders 8-11, Walter P. Reuther Archives of Labor and Urban Affairs, Wayne State University, Detroit, Mich.

34. Ibid.; Ruth Milkman, "Redefining 'Women's Work': The Sexual Division of Labor in the Auto Industry During World War II," *Feminist Studies,* 8 (Summer 1982), 348.

35. National Safety Council, "Transactions," *Thirty-Second National Safety Congress, October 5–7, 1943* (Chicago, 1944), p. 227; "Auxiliary Labor Reserves: Relief for Labor Shortage Areas," *Manpower Review,* 10 (June 1943), 10, 11; American Management Association, *Assimilating Women Workers: Reducing Absenteeism* (New York, 1942), Production Series 141, p. 8.

36. Interview with Marguerite Hoffman in Sherna Berger Gluck, ed., *Rosie the Riveter Revisited: Women and the World War II Work Experience,* vol. 15 (Long Beach: California State University Long Beach Foundation, 1983), p. 47; interview with Betty Boggs in Gluck, *Rosie,* vol. 3, p. 39.

37. "Women Supervisors—Pro and Con," *Independent Woman,* 21 (Oct. 1942), 393; "Womanpower in Airline Maintenance Shops," *Aviation* (Dec. 1947), last page. Taylor, "Meet the Girls," 3.

38. "Women in Factory Work," *The Conference Board, Management Record,* 4 (May 1942), 129–134; Edith Efron, "A Woman Worker Defends Her Kind," *New York Times Magazine,* March 31, 1946, pp. 259–260. See also *Your Questions as to Women in War Industries,* Women's Bureau Bulletin 194 (Washington, D.C., 1942); Bureau of Vocational Education, *Training Women for National Defense Industries* (Washington, D.C., 1943); Ruth Milkman, "The Reproduction of Job Segregation by Sex: A Study of the Changing Sexual Division of Labor in the Auto and Electrical Manufacturing Industries of the 1940's," Ph.D. diss., University of California, Berkeley, 1981, chap. 2.

39. George D. Halsey, *Handbook of Personnel Management* (New York, 1945), p. 259; *Assimilating Women Workers,* p. 7; Dorothy K. Newman, *Employing Women in Shipyards,* Women's Bureau Bulletin 192-6 (Washington, D.C., 1944), pp. 28–33.

40. Milkman, "Redefining 'Women's Work,' " pp. 338, 349–350; Karen Skold, "The Job He left Behind: Women and the Shipyard Workers in Portland, Oregon During World War II," in Carol P. Berkin and Clara M. Lovett, *Women, War and Revolution* (New York, 1980).

41. Interview with Susan Laughlin in Gluck, *Rosie,* vol. 45, part II, p. 15.

42. Ethel Erickson, *Women's Employment in the Making of Steel, 1943,* Women's Bureau Bulletin 192-5 (Washington, D.C., 1944), p. 23; "Equal Pay for the Woman Worker," *The Conference Board, Management Record,* 5 (Jan. 1943), 5; Newman, *Employing Women in Shipyards,* pp. 33–35; Milkman, "The Reproduction of Job Segregation by Sex," pp. 146–160.

43. Dorothy K. Newman and Martha J. Ziegler, *Employment of Women in the Machine-Tool Industry, 1942,* Women's Bureau Bulletin 192-4 (Washington,

D.C., 1943); "Wartime Pay of Women in Industry," *The Conference Board, Management Record,* 5 (Oct. 1943), 403; Ethel Erickson, *Women's Employment in Aircraft Assembly Plants in 1942,* Women's Bureau Bulletin 190-1 (Washington, D.C., 1942), pp. 6, 14; Sheila Trupp Lichtman, "Women at War, 1941–1945: Wartime Employment in the San Francisco Bay Area," Ph.D. diss., University of California, Davis, 1981, pp. 118–122. See also, Karen Beck Skold, "Women Workers and Child Care During World War II: A Case Study of the Portland, Oregon Shipyards," Ph.D. diss., University of Oregon, 1981. For comparable adjustments in an earlier emergency see Maurine Weiner Greenwalt, *Women, War, and Work: The Impact of World War I on Women Workers in the United States* (Westport, Conn., 1980). On reconversion employment patterns see *The Labor Market* (Feb. 1946), 26; (March 1946), 35–36, 40; (May 1946), 19; (June 1946), 14. However, in manufacturing that relied upon light semiskilled assembly work, such as electrical appliances, radios, shoes, jewelry, and plastics, there were more jobs for women than applicants. *The Labor Market* (May 1946), 11, 18; (June 1946), 18–19.

44. *Women's Wartime Hours of Work,* Women's Bureau Bulletin 208 (Washington, D.C., 1947), pp. 5–7. Women's Bureau, *"Equal Pay" for Women in War Industries,* Women's Bureau Bulletin 196 (Washington, D.C., 1942), p. 7. OWI, Bureau of Intelligence, "The War Worker's Point of View," Division of Surveys, 26. Women's Bureau, *Women Workers in Some Expanding Wartime Industries,* Women's Bureau Bulletin 197 (Washington, D.C., 1943), pp. 17, 18, 43. "Wartime Hours," *Monthly Labor Review,* p. 4. Wolfson, "Aprons and Overalls," p. 52. Interview with Clella Juanita Bowman in Gluck, *Rosie,* vol. 4, p. 89.

45. Interview with Bowman in Gluck, *Rosie,* vol. 4, p. 76.

46. Women's Bureau, *Women Workers in Some Expanding Wartime Industries,* p. 18; Marjorie Barstow Greenbie, "Women Work for Victory," *Independent Woman,* 21 (Jan. 1942), 133; "Woman's Place," *Business Week,* May 16, 1942, p. 20.

47. Interviews with Betty Boggs in Gluck, *Rosie,* vol. 3, p. 30; Clella Juanita Bowman, vol. 4, pp. 64–65; Freda Campbell, vol. 5, pp. 59–60.

48. Interviews with Freda Campbell in Gluck, *Rosie,* vol. 5, pp. 58, 74; Betty Boggs, vol. 3, p. 28; Josephine Houston, vol. 16, p. 41.

49. Interviews with Flora Chavez in Gluck, *Rosie,* vol. 7, p. 49; Norma Cantrell, vol. 6, p. 33; Clella Juanita Bowman, vol. 4, p. 68.

50. Interviews with Marie Baker in Gluck, *Rosie,* vol. 2, p. 35; Clella Juanita Bowman, vol. 4, p. 67; Freda Campbell, vol. 5, p. 61.

51. Interviews with Fanny Christiana Hill in Gluck, *Rosie,* vol. 14, pp. 57, 61; Betty Boggs, vol. 3, pp. 30–32; Josephine Houston, vol. 16, p. 46; Marguerite Hoffman, vol. 15, p. 55; Norma Cantrell, vol. 6, p. 35; Marie Baker, vol. 2, p. 35; Freda Campbell, vol. 5, p. 59.

52. Interviews with Clella Juanita Bowman in Gluck, *Rosie,* vol. 4, p. 65; Freda Campbell, vol. 5, p. 71.

53. Interviews with Betty Boggs in Gluck, *Rosie,* vol. 3, p. 41; Freda Campbell, vol. 5, p. 66; Norma Cantrell, vol. 6, p. 39; Clella Juanita Bowman, vol. 4, p. 70.

54. Interviews with Norma Cantrell in Gluck, *Rosie,* vol. 6, p. 39: Marie Fierro, vol. 12, p. 29; Betty Boggs, vol. 3, pp. 33–34, 40, 100–101.

55. Women's Bureau, *Women Workers in Some Expanding Wartime Industries,* pp. 33, 41. Interviews with Betty Boggs in Gluck, *Rosie,* vol. 3, p. 46; Videll Drake, vol. 10, p. 42; Flora Chavez, vol. 7, p. 50; Freda Campbell, vol. 5, p. 67; Clella Juanita Bowman, vol. 4, p. 87.

56. "Transactions," *Thirty-Second National Safety Congress,* p. 581; "Employment of Women in Shipyards, 1942," *Monthly Labor Review* (Feb. 1943), 381; Women's Bureau, *Women Workers in Some Expanding Wartime Industries,* p. 28. Interview with Norma Cantrell in Gluck, *Rosie,* vol. 6, p. 52.

57. "Strictly Personnel: Special Problems of Women Workers," *Personnel, American Management Association,* 20 (July 1943). Conference Board, "Wartime Pay," p. 403.

58. "Transactions," *Thirty-Second National Safety Congress,* p. 579; *Employment of Women in Army Supply Depots in 1943,* Women's Bureau Bulletin 192-8 (Washington, D.C., 1945), p. 25; Conference Board, " 'Equal Pay' for Women in War Industries," pp. 12–13.

59. Women's Bureau, *Employment of Women in Army Supply Depots in 1943,* p. 25; "Transactions," *Thirty-Third National Safety Congress,* pp. 579, 583; interview with Clella Juanita Bowman in Gluck, *Rosie,* vol. 4, p. 81.

60. Newman, *Employing Women in Shipyards,* p. 70.

61. Interviews with Freda Campbell in Gluck, *Rosie,* vol. 5, pp. 63–64; Fanny Christina Hill, vol. 14, p. 71. "Margin Now Is Womanpower," *Fortune* 27 (Feb. 1943), 222–223; "Women in Factory Work," *The Conference Board, Management Record,* 4 (May 1942), 133; "Spotlight on Women in Industry," *The Conference Board, Management Record,* 4 (Dec. 1942), 393; American Management Association, *Assimilating Women Workers,* p. 12; Mary Anderson and Mary N. Winslow, *Women at Work* (Minneapolis, 1951), p. 246; Frances E. P. Harnish, *Women's Employment in Foundries, 1943,* Women's Bureau Bulletin 192-7 (Washington, 1944), p. 22. "Transactions," *Thirty-Second National Safety Congress,* p. 232; "Transactions," *Thirty-Third National Safety Congress,* p. 580.

62. Interview with Fanny Christina Hill in Gluck, *Rosie,* vol. 14, pp. 71–72.

63. Interviews with Josephine Houston in Gluck, *Rosie,* vol. 16, p. 64; Mern Freige, vol. 13, p. 45.

64. Interviews with Marguerite Hoffman in Gluck, *Rosie,* vol. 15, p. 48; Betty Boggs, vol. 3, p. 32; Clella Juanita Bowman, vol. 4, p. 67; Josephine Houston, vol. 16, p. 47; Fanny Christina Hill, vol. 14, p. 71.

65. Women's Bureau, *Employment of Women in Army Supply Depots in*

1943, p. 30; "Transactions," *Thirty-Second National Safety Congress,* pp. 233–234.

66. American Management Association, *Assimilating Women Workers,* p. 7. "Strictly Personnel," p. 58; "Women in Men's Jobs," *The Conference Board, Management Record,* 6 (July 1944), 197. "Transactions," *Thirty-Second National Safety Congress,* p. 230. Charlotte Carr, "Conversion from Manpower to Womanpower in Industry," *Annals of the American Academy of Political and Social Science,* 227 (May 1943), 223.

67. Halsey, *Personnel Management,* p. 258. Office of War Information, Bureau of Intelligence, "Women and the War," Report of Aug. 19, 1943, p. 3, Record Group 44, National Archives; "Margin Now," *Fortune,* 233; Theresa Wolfson, "Aprons and Overalls in War," *Annals of the American Academy of Political and Social Science,* 229 (Sept. 1943), 53; Erickson, "Making of Steel," p. 30; Newman, "Women in Shipyards," p. 55.

68. Interview with Flora Chavez in Gluck, *Rosie,* vol. 7, p. 51. "A New Headache," *Business Week,* Oct. 17, 1942, p. 48; King, "Danger! Women at Work," p. 40; Taylor, "Meet the Girls," p. 3; "Transactions," *Thirty-Second National Safety Congress,* p. 231; Sheila Trupp Lichtman, "Women at War, 1941–1945; Wartime Employment in the San Francisco Bay Area," Ph.D. diss., University of California, Davis, 1981, pp. 110–112.

69. Taylor, "Meet the Girls," p. 1; OWI, "Attitudes Toward the Employment of Women in War Industries," pp. 5, 9.

70. Taylor, "Meet the Girls," p. 2; Interview with Susan Laughlin in Gluck, *Rosie,* vol. 45, part II, p. 13.

71. Interview with Clella Juanita Bowman in Gluck, *Rosie,* vol. 4, p. 79; "Strictly Personnel," pp. 92, 109; Taylor, "Meet the Girls," p. 2; OWI, "Attitudes Toward the Employment of Women in War Industries," p. 5; "Women War Workers Look Ahead," *Survey* (Oct. 1944), 415.

72. Interviews with Betty Boggs in Gluck, *Rosie,* vol. 3, p. 45; Mildred Eusebio, vol. 11, p. 44; Maria Fierro, vol. 12, p. 30; Norma Cantrell, vol. 6, p. 51.

73. Interviews with Clella Juanita Bowman in Gluck, *Rosie,* vol. 4, p. 72; Norma Cantrell, vol. 6, p. 44; Flora Chavez, vol. 7, p. 44; Flora Chavez, vol. 7, p. 51; Mildred Eusebio, vol. 11, pp. 29, 44; Josephine Houston, vol. 16, p. 73; Betty Boggs, vol. 3, p. 41.

74. Interviews with Betty Boggs in Gluck, *Rosie,* vol. 3, pp. 36, 41, 45; Freda Campbell, vol. 5, p. 72; Clella Juanita Bowman, vol. 4, p. 73; Josephine Houston, vol. 16, pp. 72, 74.

75. Interview with Clella Juanita Bowman in Gluck, *Rosie,* vol. 4, p. 80; *The [New York] Industrial Bulletin* (1943), p. 477.

76. Alexander J. Allen, "Western Electric's Backward Step," *Opportunity: Journal of Negro Life,* 22 (July–Sept. 1944), 108–111, 140–143.

77. *The [New York] Industrial Bulletin* (1943), p. 259; "Women Supervisors—Pro and Con," *Independent Woman,* p. 306; Halsey, *Personnel Manage-*

ment, p. 258; Ruby W. Koestner, "Matrons Aid Production," *Personnel Journal,* 5 (Nov. 1942), 92; "Women in Factory Work," *The Conference Board, Management Record,* 21 (May 1942), 131.

78. "Women War Workers Look Ahead," *Survey* (Oct. 1944), 415; Conference Board, "Women in Factory Work," 131; Newman, *Women in Shipyards,* 7.

79. OWI, "Attitudes Toward the Employment of Women in War Industries," p. 23. Koestner, "Matrons Aid Production," p. 86.

80. "Women Supervisors—Pro and Con," *Independent Woman,* p. 306; *Women in Higher-Level Positions,* Women's Bureau Bulletin 236 (Washington, D.C., 1950), p. 47: Wolfson, "Aprons and Overalls," p. 57; *Statistical Abstract, 1946,* p. 180.

81. "Women Supervisors—Pro and Con," *Independent Woman,* pp. 306, 318; Roper-*Fortune* poll 35, May 1943.

82. Conference Board, "Women in Factory Work," p. 13; Gardner, *Human Relations,* pp. 269–270.

83. Gardner, *Human Relations,* p. 269; Gladys F. Gove, "Looking for a War Job?" *Independent Woman,* 21 (April 1942), 260–261; Halsey, *Personnel Management,* p. 260; Strictly Personnel, p. 109; Gladys Gove, "On the Job," *Independent Woman,* 21 (Dec. 1942), 369; "Woman Supervisors—Pro and Con," *Independent Woman,* p. 318.

84. Koestner, "Matrons Aid Production," p. 269.

85. Newman, *Women in Shipyards,* p. 40; "Strictly Personnel," p. 109; Women's Bureau, *Employment of Women in Army Supply Depots,* p. 20.

86. Interviews with Susan Laughlin in Gluck, *Rosie,* vol. 45, pp. 7, 35, 36; Josephine Houston, vol. 16, p. 49.

87. Interviews with Clella Juanita Bowman in Gluck, *Rosie,* vol. 4, p. 86; Freda Campbell, vol. 5, p. 71.

88. OWI, "Attitudes Toward the Employment of Women in War Industries," p. 20. Frances B. P. Harnish, *Women's Employment in Foundries, 1943,* Women's Bureau Bulletins 192-197 (Washington, D.C., 1944), p. 23; Women's Bureau, *Employment of Women in Army Supply Depots,* p. 24; "Absenteeism: The New National Malady," *Fortune* (March 1943), p. 104; Women's Bureau, *Women Workers in Some Expanding Wartime Industries,* p. 37; "Women at Work," *Business Week,* Oct. 10, 1942, p. 90; Wolfson, "Aprons and Overalls," p. 52. "What About the Women?" *Ladies Home Journal,* 61 (June 1944), 157; "Absenteeism in War Plants," *The [New York] Industrial Bulletin,* 22 (Aug. 1943), 303–308.

89. Women's Bureau, *Employment of Women in Army Supply Depots in 1943,* p. 32; "Planning for Manpower," *Manpower Review,* 10 (March 1943), 15.

90. Interview with Emile Cook in Gluck, *Rosie,* vol. 45, part I, p. 7; Ernest Goodman to George F. Addes, Aug. 7, 1943, UAW Papers, "Research on the Women's Auxilliary," folder 32.

91. See Women's Bureau, *Women in Unions in a Mid-West War Industry Area—Trade Union Survey, Summary Booklet,* July 10, 1945, Record Group 86, box 1701, National Archives; Agnes Meyer, *Journey Through Chaos* (New York, 1944), p. 10; OWI, "Attitudes Toward the Employment of Women in War Industries," p. 20; Women's Bureau, *"Equal Pay" for Women,* pp. 10–11.

92. "Employment of Women in Shipyards, 1942," *Monthly Labor Review* (Feb. 1943), 280–281; Women's Bureau, *"Equal Pay" for Women,* pp. 5, 7; Taylor, "Meet the Girls," p. 2; Harnish, *Employment in Foundries,* p. 28; Office of War Information, Bureau of Intelligence, *War Jobs for Women* (Washington, D.C., 1943), p. 21, Record Group 44, National Archives.

93. Taylor, "Meet the Girls," p. 1; "Auxiliary Labor Reserves," *Monthly Labor Review,* p. 5.

94. OWI, "Attitudes Toward the Employment of Women in War Industries," p. 11; Women's Bureau, *"Equal Pay" for Women in War Industries,* p. 5; W. Gerard Tuttle, "Women War-Workers at Vultee Aircraft," *Personnel Journal,* 21 (June 1942), 87; "Women at Work," *Business Week,* Oct. 10, 1942, p. 2.

95. "Wartime Pay of Women in Industry," *The Conference Board, Management Record,* 5 (Oct. 1943), 405.

96. Interview with Susan Laughlin in Gluck, *Rosie,* vol. 45, part II, p. 36.

5. Sisterhood versus the Brotherhoods

1. Women's Bureau, *Women in Unions in a Mid-West War Industry Area— Trade Union Survey, Summary Booklet,* July 10, 1945, p. 3, Record Group 86, box 1701, National Archives, hereafter cited as Women's Bureau's Midwest Survey. See also International Labour Office, *The War and Women's Employment: The Experience of the United Kingdom and the United States* (Montreal, 1946), p. 237; Sheila Tobias and Lisa Anderson, "What Really Happened to Rosie the Riveter? Demobilization and the Female Labor Force, 1944–1947," MSS Modular Publications, Module 9 (1974).

2. Department of Industrial Relations, Division of Labor Statistics and Law Enforcement, *Union Labor in California* (San Francisco, 1942), p. 10.

3. Massachusetts and California were the only states that kept union records by sex. In Massachusetts, female membership grew from 62,000 in 1940 to 140,000 in 1945—from 20 percent to 27 percent of all members. The proportion of women stayed at the 25 to 28 percent level for the next thirty years, indicating a permanent shift. Massachusetts did not provide enough data to classify its unions as "friendly" or "hostile." Before 1934, women were only 13 to 14 percent of the union members. Massachusetts Department of Labor and Industries, *Directory of Labor Organizations in Massachusetts* (Boston, 1938–1975).

4. Report from UAW local 674 at the Delco plant in Norwood, Ohio,

"UAW 1944 Survey of Women in Locals," UAW Papers, Woman's Division, box 5, Walter P. Reuther Archives of Labor & Industrial Relations, Wayne State University.

5. Karen Sue Anderson, "The Impact of World War II in the Puget Sound Area on the Status of Women and the Family," Ph.D. diss., University of Washington, 1975, pp. 40–43.

6. Women's Bureau Midwest Survey, responses from Walter Douard, business agent, IAM 1796, AFL, working for the Chicago-based Minneapolis-Honeywell Regular Company; Thomas Dixon, UAW, CIO, working for Excel Curtain Company in Elkhart, Ind.; Joseph Sharp, president, International Moulders and Foundry Workers Union 233, AFL, representing Howard Foundry, University Castings Corporation, and Coremakers Company; William Cypcar, president, IAM 1696, AFL, working for Chicago-based General Electric X-Ray Corporation; Leonard Hackert, president, IUUAQA 209, AFL, working for Milwaukee-based Harley Davidson Corporation. Mark Perlman, *The Machinists: A New Study in American Trade Unionism* (Cambridge, Mass., 1961), p. 121; Constance McL. Green, *The Role of Women as Production Workers in War Plants in the Connecticut Valley,* Smith College Studies in History, 28 (Northampton, Mass., 1946), pp. 7–10 and chap. 5.

7. "Spotlight on Women in Industry," *The Conference Board, Management Record,* 4 (Dec. 1942), 394.

8. Anderson, "Impact of World War II," pp. 45, 46; Ruth Milkman, "The Reproduction of Job Segregation by Sex: A Study of the Changing Sexual Division of Labor in the Auto and Electrical Manufacturing Industries of the 1940s," Ph.D. diss., University of California, Berkeley, 1981, pp. 160–180.

9. For comments of women about unions see the Woman's Bureau Midwest Survey; on strikes, *Monthly Labor Review* (May 1944), 934; on meetings, Hjalmar Rosen and R. A. Hudson Rosen, *The Union Member Speaks* (New York, 1955), pp. 80–85; Arnold M. Rose, *Union Solidarity: The Internal Cohesion of a Labor Union* (Minneapolis, 1952), pp. 46–51, 132–136; Elizabeth Hawes, *Hurry Up Please Its Time* (New York, 1946), pp. 33–42. Quote from "UAW 1944 Survey of Women in Locals," UAW Papers.

10. Brotherhood of Railway and Steamship Clerks, *Report of George M. Harrison to the Eighteenth Regular Convention* (Cincinnati, 1947), pp. 218–223.

11. *Daily Proceedings of the Fifth Constitutional Convention of the Congress of Industrial Organizations, November 9–13, 1942* (Boston, 1942), p. 337. [UAW], *Ammunition,* 6 (Sept. 1943), 29.

12. Cap Brady to Clyde Hart, Rockford, Ill., March 23, 1944, in Office of War Information, Bureau of Intelligence, Labor Editors' Panel Reports, Record Group 44, box 1744, National Archives. See also Report from Mrs. Philip Lauer to Clyde Hart, Flemington, N.J., March 27, 1944, and other March and April Housewives Panel Reports.

13. Women's Bureau Midwest Survey, response from Oma Johnson, chief

clerk, United Farm Equipment Workers 12, CIO, working for Oliver Farm Equipment Company, South Bend, Ind.

14. Office of War Information, Bureau of Intelligence, "Women and the War," Media Division Report 62, Aug. 6, 1942, p. 6. Women's Bureau Midwest Survey, response from F. M. Darling, business agent, IBEW 1031, AFL, working for Chicago-based American Penholic Corporation; see also responses from Charles Strinz, finance secretary, UAW 590, CIO, South Bend-based Torrington Company; Charles Clements, vice-president, UAW 9, CIO, Bendix Aviation Corporation. U.S. House of Representatives, Subcommittee No. 4 of the Committee on Education and Labor, *Hearings on Equal Pay for Equal Work for Women,* 80th Cong., 2nd sess., 1948, pp. 155, 180, 181, 195, 302; response from UAW local 913, in "UAW 1944 Survey of Women in Locals," UAW Papers.

15. See Sheila Trupp Lichtman, "Women at Work, 1941–1945: Wartime Employment in the San Francisco Bay Area," Ph.D. diss., University of California, Davis, 1981, pp. 188–214; U.S. Senate, Committee on Education and Labor, *Hearings on Equal Pay for Equal Work for Women,* 79th Cong., 1st sess., 1945, pp. 34–81; response from UAW local 646 in "UAW 1944 Survey of Women in Locals," UAW Papers.

16. Sherna Berger Gluck, ed., *Rosie the Riveter Revisited: Women and the World War II Work Experience* (Long Beach: California State University Long Beach Foundation, 1983), vol. 2, p. 47. Roper-*Fortune* poll 35, 1943, Roper Center, Williams College, Williamstown, Mass.

17. Gluck, *Rosie,* vol. 2, p. 35.

18. Women held no significant positions of power in labor unions, either at the local or national level. Nor were they represented in management. In government, the Secretary of Labor was a woman, but her influence in setting priorities was minimal, perhaps because she *was* a woman. Eleanor Straub, "United States Government Policy Toward Civilian Women During World War II," Ph.D. diss., Emory University, 1973, pp. 35, 43, 48–49; Virginia A. Bergquist, "Women's Participation in Labor Organizations," *Monthly Labor Review,* 97 (Oct. 1974), 3–9; *The Woman Wage-Earner: Her Situation Today,* Women's Bureau Bulletin 172 (Washington, D.C., 1939); George Martin, *Madam Secretary: Frances Perkins* (Boston, 1976). In the Women's Bureau survey of midwestern war plants, the only union offices women held were on minor committees such as entertainment. A few all-women locals had women officers, but the affairs of their locals seemed to have been controlled by male business agents.

19. Elizabeth Faulkner Baker, *Technology and Woman's Work* (New York, 1964), p. 337. Response from UAW local 329 at Fisher Body plant, Detroit, in "UAW 1944 Survey of Women in Locals," UAW Papers.

20. Office of War Information, Bureau of Intelligence, "Opinions About the Wartime Employment of Women," Special Report C-31, May 29, 1944, p. 6, Record Group 44, file E149, National Archives.

21. Women's Bureau Midwest Survey, responses from Harry Cox, president, IBEW 713, AFL, working for Chicago-based Automatic Electric Company;

Howard Koss, executive board member, IBEW 713, AFL, working for Chicago-based Automatic Electric Company; Orville Passwater, finance secretary, Federal Labor Union 18704, AFL, Anaconda Wire and Cable Company, Anderson, Ind.

22. Tobias and Anderson, "Rosie the Riveter," p. 19; "Women in Industry," *Monthly Labor Review* (Sept. 1944), 578, 588, and (May 1944), 1031, 1032; *The [New York] Industrial Bulletin* (Oct. 1945), 1.

23. Anderson, "Impact of World War II," pp. 77–78.

24. Ibid., p. 207; Nancy Gabin, "They Have Placed a Penalty on Womanhood: The Protest Actions of Women United Auto Workers in Detroit Area UAW Locals, 1945–1947," *Feminist Studies,* 8 (1982), 373–398.

25. Women's Bureau Midwest Survey, response from UAW local 917, CIO, Singer Manufacturing Co., South Bend, Ind.; Milkman, "The Reproduction of Job Segregation by Sex," pp. 318–329.

26. "Women in Industry," *Monthly Labor Review* (Sept. 1944), 586.

27. House Committee on Education and Labor, *Hearings on Equal Pay,* p. 155; Constance Williams, "The Status of Women Workers," in Colston E. Warne, ed., *Labor in Postwar America* (Brooklyn, 1949), p. 547. See also, Philip S. Foner, *Women and the American Labor Movement: From World War I to the Present* (New York, 1980).

28. House Committee on Education and Labor, *Hearings on Equal Pay,* p. 178.

29. Green, *Women as Production Workers,* p. 62; Milkman, "The Reproduction of Job Segregation by Sex," pp. 238–251.

30. House Committee on Education and Labor, *Hearings on Equal Pay,* p. 154.

31. Mattie E. Treadwell, *The United States Army in World War II, Special Studies, The Women's Army Corps* (Washington, D.C., 1954), pp. 737–739; U.S. Army, "The Woman Veteran," Records of the War Department General and Special Staffs, Army G-1 WAC Decimal File, 1942–46, pp. 21–25, 292, National Archives.

32. See Hadley Cantril, *Public Opinion, 1935–1946* (Princeton, 1951), esp. pp. 876, 902; Philip Hastings, ed., *Survey Data for Trend Analysis* (Williamstown: Roper Center, 1975), esp. pp. 173–174; Rita James Simon, *Public Opinion in America: 1936–1970* (Chicago, 1974), pp. 16–24. Office of War Information, Bureau of Intelligence, "Women and the War, A Summary of Women's Attitudes toward Domestic and Foreign Issues in the First Eight Months of the War," Report 31, Aug. 6, 1942, tables 39a, b, c, d, Record Group 44, National Archives.

33. Roper-*Fortune* poll 35, 1943.

34. The scale was created with women preferring no form of union scoring −100 points, those favoring company unions scoring −50 points, those favoring a strong national union scoring +50 points, those favoring a closed shop scoring +100 points. Women answering "don't know" were scored 0 points. When

several other scales were tested, these results were comparable with all others. The mean answer was a −31 points, indicating a general overall antipathy toward labor unions. All the social groupings that were given in the survey (like religion, education, and class) were measured on the scale. Several hundred subgroups (such as Catholic easterners) were also studied.

35. The best values (correlates) from a multiple classification analysis were socioeconomic status (+.19), occupation (+.13, +.08 controlling for status), education (+.13, +.06 controlled), region (+.11, +.13 controlled), and size of place (+.10, +.06 controlled).

36. See also Cantril, *Public Opinion,* pp. 547, 877; Simon, *Public Opinion,* pp. 16–24; George H. Gallup, *The Gallup Poll, Public Opinion 1935–1971,* vol. 1 (New York, 1972), and "Women in Industry," *Monthly Labor Review* (May 1944), 1030.

37. Baker, *Technology and Women's Work,* p. 370.

38. *Daily Proceedings, CIO 1942 Convention,* p. 275, Resolution No. 22. See also, Foner, *Women and the American Labor Movement,* esp. chap. 19.

39. "Labor 'Dilution,' " *Business Week,* Nov. 8, 1941, pp. 59–60; Milkman, "The Reproduction of Job Segregation by Sex," pp. 172–173, 209–210.

40. See Roper-*Fortune* poll 54, April 1946, Roper Center, Williams College, Williamstown, Mass.

41. On dual labor markets see: Oppenheimer, *Female Labor Force,* pp. 138–142; Michael J. Piore, "Notes for a Theory of Labor Market Stratification," in R. C. Edwards and others, eds., *Labor Market Segmentation* (Lexington, Mass., 1975); M. J. Wachter, "Primary and Secondary Labor Markets: A Critique of the Dual Approach," *Brookings Papers on Economic Activity,* 3 (1974), 637–680; Donald J. Treiman and K. Terrell, "Women, Work and Wages: Trends in the Female Occupational Structure Since 1940," in Kenneth C. Land and Seymour Spillerman, eds., *Social Indicator Models* (New York, 1975), pp. 157–199; David Snyder, Mark Hayward, and Paula Hudis, "The Location of Change in the Sexual Structure of Occupations, 1950–1970: Insights from Labor Market Segmentation Theory," *American Journal of Sociology,* 84 (1978), 706–717.

42. W. G. Katt to R. J. Thomas, June 2, 1944, UAW Papers, War Policy Division, box 5, Walter P. Reuther Archives of Labor & Industrial Relations, Wayne State University. After the war the local secured an agreement that no married woman would be hired who had "visible means of support." Clipping from Kenosha, Wis., *Labor,* Dec. 19, 1946, UAW Papers, War Policy Division, box 5.

43. The best portrayal of this attitude is the chapter, "A Woman's Place Is with Her Kids," in Sidney M. Peck, *The Rank-and-File Leader* (New Haven, 1963), pp. 180–223; see also Katherine Archibald, *Wartime Shipyard: A Study in Social Disunity* (Berkeley, 1947), pp. 16–27.

44. Ruth Milkman, "Redefining 'Women's Work': The Sexual Division of Labor in the Auto Industry During World War II," *Feminist Studies,* 8 (Summer 1982), 368.

45. *The Labor Market* (March 1946), p. 30.

46. David Montgomery, *Workers' Control in America* (New York, 1979), pp. 139–152; see also Martha May, "The Historical Problem of the Family Wage: The Ford Motor Company and the Five Dollar Day," *Feminist Studies,* 8 (1982), 399–424; Ronald W. Schatz, *The Electrical Workers, A History of Labor at General Electric and Westinghouse, 1923–1960* (Urbana, Ill., 1983), pp. 119–131.

47. David Brody, *Workers in Industrial America* (New York, 1980), p. 163; Nelson Lichtenstein, "Conflict Over Workers' Control: The Automobile Industry in World War II," in Michael H. Frisch and Daniel J. Walkowitz, eds., *Working-Class America* (Urbana, Ill., 1983), pp. 284–311.

48. Marion G. Sobol, "Commitment to Work," in F. Ivan Nye and Lois Waldman Hoffman, *The Employed Mother in America* (Chicago, 1963), pp. 49–63.

49. Response from UAW local 196 (1600 members), in "UAW 1944 Survey of Women in Locals," UAW Papers.

6. Heroines of the Homefront

1. For the link between consumer needs and national policy see Bureau of Demobilization, Civilian Production Administration, *Industrial Mobilization for War: History of the War Production Board and Predecessor Agencies, 1940–1945,* vol. 1, *Program and Administration* (Washington, D.C., 1947), pp. 307–339, 698–700, 763–766, 895–900; and Persia Campbell, *The Consumer Interest: A Study in Consumer Economics* (New York, 1949), pp. 96–185.

2. See Victor A. Thompson, *The Regulatory Process in OPA Rationing* (New York, 1950).

3. Bureau of the Census, *Statistical Abstract of the United States, 1949* (Washington, D.C., 1949), pp. 22–25; *Statistical Abstract, 1946,* pp. 47–49; Bureau of the Census, *Historical Statistics of the United States* (Washington, D.C., 1975), pp. 41, 49, 64, and chap. 3.

4. *Historical Statistics,* 126, 166–169; Howard W. Odum, *Folk, Region, and Society* (Chapel Hill, N.C., 1964), p. 63.

5. National Opinion Research Center (NORC), Jan. 7, 1944, cited in Hadley Cantril and Mildred Strunk, eds., *Public Opinion, 1935–1946* (Princeton, 1951), p. 70; Odum, *Folk, Region, and Society,* pp. 166–169.

6. Robert J. Havighurst and H. Gerthon Morgan, *The Social History of a War-Boom Community* (New York, 1951), p. 61; Office of War Information, Bureau of Intelligence, "Housing Problems in Four Production Communities," Correspondence Panel Special Report 30, Oct. 30, 1942, pp. 1–11, Record Group 44, National Archives. There are three types of OWI reports listed in this chapter in addition to the general reports: Correspondence Panel Reports, Housewives Panel Reports, and individual housewives' reports to OWI of what

was happening in their communities. Hereafter all OWI Correspondence Panel Reports will be listed OWI, Corr. Report, title, and date, all OWI Housewives Panel Reports will be listed OWI, HW Report, title, and date, and all individual housewives' reports will be listed OWI, housewife's name, location, and date. OWI Corr. Report, "Opinions about the Housing Situation," Report C65, June 24, 1946, pp. 1–26: OWI, Corr. Report, "Housing Problems in Four Production Communities," Special Report 28, Oct. 15, 1942; OWI, "Mobile"; OWI, "Detroit," tables 1–10; OWI, "Seattle," pp. 5–7; OWI, "Massena, N.Y.," pp. 1–5.

7. Encyclopedia Britannica, *Ten Eventful Years: 1937–1947*(Chicago, 1947), vol. 2, p. 592; *Historical Statistics,* pp. 639, 642, 644; OWI, Corr. Report, "Opinions about the Housing Situation," quoting Supplement 65a, pp. 8, 9; OWI, Mrs. Samuel Perlman, Brooklyn, April 30, 1946, p. 1.

8. OWI, Corr. Report, "Housing Problems in Four Production Communities," Report 30, pp. 4, 7; OWI, "Seattle," p. 4; OWI, "Mobile," p. 5.

9. Interview with Josephine M. Keeney, Feb. 1983, Mishawaka, Ind.; Richard H. Foster, Jr., "Wartime Trailer Housing in the San Francisco Bay Area," *The Geographical Review,* 70 (1980), 276–290; Donald O. Cowgill, *Mobile Homes: A Study of Trailer Life* (Philadelphia, 1941); Richard C. Fuller and Richard R. Myers, "The Natural History of a Social Problem," *American Sociological Review,* 6 (1940), 300–309; Lowell J. Carr and James E. Sterner, *Willow Run: A Study of Industrialization and Cultural Inadequacy* (New York, 1952), has numerous photographs of trailer conditions.

10. Encyclopedia Britannica, *Ten Eventful Years,* vol. 2, p. 590; interview with June Wilmore, Dec. 26, 1978, in Denver, Col.; OWI, "Massena," pp. 4, 5; OWI, "Opinions about the Housing Situation," Report C65, p. 2.

11. Florence Murray, ed., *The Negro Handbook: 1949* (New York, 1949), pp. 191–198; J. Frederic Dewhurst and Associates, *America's Needs and Resources: A New Survey* (New York, 1955), pp. 196–231.

12. *Statistical Abstract, 1946,* p. 797. For a long-tern historical perspective and technological changes see Ruth Schwartz Cowan, *More Work for Mothers: The Ironies of Household Technology from the Open Hearth to the Microwave* (New York, 1983). For rural changes see Gunnar Myrdal, *An American Dilemma: The Negro Problem and Modern Democracy* (New York, 1944), pp. 375–379. Persia Campbell, *The Consumer Interest: A Study in Consumer Economics* (New York, 1949), p. 344. See also May L. Cowles, Mildred M. Siek, and Jean F. Myers, *Where the Money Went: Changes in Family Living from 1940 to 1942 in 106 FSA Families in Wisconsin,* Wisconsin Agricultural Experiment Station Research Bulletin 155 (Madison, Wis., 1945).

13. Laura Brown Webb, "Wartime Changes in Consumer Goods in American Markets," *Monthly Labor Review* (Nov. 1942), 893. For a more general study see U.S. Department of Labor, *How American Buying Habits Change* (Washington D.C., 1951).

14. *Consumer Research Bulletin,* 12 (Jan. 1943), 3; (March 1943), 29; (June

1943), 3; (Aug. 1943), 3; (Dec. 1943), 3; OWI, Mrs. William H. Rooney, San Pablo, Ca., Oct. 3, 1943, Mrs. Sylvester McAtee, San Francisco, Sept. 30, 1943; OWI, HR Report, Jan. 1944, p. 8.

15.   Webb, "Wartime Changes," p. 893; OWI, Mrs. John A. Ewart, Pittsburgh, Aug. 5, 1946, Mrs. Helen M. Kentonor, Taos, N.M., Jan. 12, 1944; *Consumer Research Bulletin,* 12 (April 1943), 4; Margaret G. Reid, "Food, Liquor and Tobacco," in Dewhurst, *America's Needs and Resources* (New York, 1955), p. 1041 (table).

16.   Interview with Fanny Christiana Hill in Sherna Berger Gluck, ed., *Rosie the Riveter Revisited: Women and the World War II Work Experience* (Long Beach: California State University Long Beach Foundation, 1983), vol. 14, intro. to interview; Roper-*Fortune* poll, Oct. 1937, cited in Cantril and Strunk, *Public Opinion,* p. 791: Odum, *Folk, Region, and Society,* p. 63.

17.   OWI, HR Report, July 1944, p. 3, March 1945, p. 4; OWI, "Before and After VJ Day," Nov. 1945, pp. 1, 5; OWI, Mrs. John A. Ewart, Pittsburgh, May 26, 1945, p. 1, Mrs. Margaret W. Colbourn, Baltimore, May 30, 1944, p. 2, Mrs. David Diamond, Buffalo, Jan. 25, 1944, p. 2; NORC poll, June 2, 1944, cited in Cantril and Strunk, *Public Opinion,* p. 403; J. Fred Oesterling and others, "Dry Cleaning and Laundry Services in Wartime," *Journal of Home Economics,* 35 (1943), 232–236; *Consumer Research Bulletin,* 12 (March 1943), 4; (Sept. 1943), 4; (Oct. 1943), 4.

18.   Marianne Muse, *Time Expenditures on Homemaking Activities in 183 Vermont Farm Homes,* University of Vermont Agricultural Experiment Station Bulletin 530 (Burlington, 1946), pp. 18–58; Dorothy Dickins, *Time Activities in Homemaking,* Mississippi State College Agricultural Experiment Station Bulletin 424 (State College, 1945), pp. 5–17; Joann Vanek, "Time Spent in Housework," *Scientific American* (Nov. 1974), pp. 116–121; Lee Rainwater, Richard Coleman, and Gerald Handel, *Workingman's Wife, Her Personality, World and Life Style* (New York, 1959), pp. 168–183. For a recent overview of housework see Susan Strasser, *Never Done: A History of American Housework* (New York, 1982).

19.   OWI, HR Report, Feb. 1944, pp. 5, 8, April–May 1944, p. 13, Dec. 1944, p. 7, July 1945, pp. 1, 8, Nov. 1945, p. 6; OWI, "Before and After VJ Day," p. 11; *Boot and Shoe Recorder,* 124 (July 15, 1973), 6; OWI, Mrs. William P. Yarnelle, Fort Wayne, Ind., April 13, 1945, Mrs. Philip B. Lauer, Flemington, N.J., Sept. 12, 1945, Mrs. Eleanor Fowler, Washington, D.C., Oct. 10, 1944; *Consumer Research Bulletin,* 12 (May 1943), 4; Webb, "Wartime Changes," p. 897.

20.   American Home Economics Survey cited in OWI, HR Report, May–June 1943, p. 9, Feb. 1944, p. 5, April–May 1944, p. 11, March 1945, p. 4; OWI, Mrs. Eleanor Fowler, Washington, D.C., Oct. 10, 1944, p. 3, Mrs. John A. Ewart, Pittsburgh, March 1, 1944.

21.   OWI, HR Report, Jan. 1944, p. 7, March 1945, p. 5, May 1945, pp. 4, 11, June 1945, p. 5; "Cost of Clothing of Moderate Income Families," *Monthly Labor Review* (July 1944), p. 161.

22. OWI, HR Report, June 1945, p. 5; NORC polls of Sept. 16, 1942, and April 28, 1944, cited in Cantril and Strunk, *Public Opinion*, pp. 32, 35; *Statistical Abstract 1946*, p. 527; *Ladies Home Journal*, 60 (Sept. 1943), 54.

23. *Historical Statistics*, p. 77; *Statistical Abstract, 1946*, p. 87; *Statistical Abstract, 1944–45*, p. 89. American Institute of Public Opinion (AIPO, Gallup) polls of March 19, 1941, April 15, 1942, June 30, 1942, and Dec. 12, 1944, cited in Cantril and Strunk, *Public Opinion*, pp. 354, 355, 356. *Postwar Outlook for Physicians*, U.S. Bureau of Labor Statistics, Bulletin 863 (Washington, D.C., 1946), pp. 10–11; Charles R. Hoffer, *Adjustments of Michigan Farm Families to War Conditions*, Michigan State College Agricultural Experiment Station, Special Bulletin 333 (East Lansing, May 1945), pp. 10, 11, 25. See also Monroe Lerner and Odin W. Anderson, *Health Progress in the United States: 1900–1960* (Chicago, 1963).

24. Grace L. Flagg and T. Wilson Longmore, *Trends in Rural and Urban Levels of Living*, Agriculture Information Bulletin 11 (Washington, D.C., 1949), pp. 42, 43; "How Families Use Their Incomes," Department of Agriculture, Miscellaneous Publication 653 (Washington, D.C., n.d.), p. 63.

25. U.S. Senate, Committee on Education and Labor, *Hearings on Wartime Health and Education*, 78th Cong., 2nd sess., 1944, pp. 814–816; *Annual Report of the State Department of Health of Alabama: 1950* (Montgomery, 1951), p. 55; *State Board of Health of South Carolina, 62nd Annual Report: 1941* (Columbia, S.C., 1942), p. 152.

26. NORC polls, Jan. 20 and April 28, 1943, cited in Cantril and Strunk, *Public Opinion*, p. 224.

27. NORC polls, May 7 and Oct. 22, 1943, and Roper poll, June 1943, cited in Cantril and Strunk, *Public Opinion*, p. 227; OWI, Mrs. Eleanor Fowler, Washington, D.C., Aug. 31, 1943; Office of War Information, Bureau of Intelligence, "Women's Understanding of the New Point Rationing System," Special Memorandum 33, May 1943, p. 2, Record Group 44, National Archives.

28. OWI, Mrs. John A. Ewart, Pittsburgh, Sept. 27, 1943, Mrs. Margaret S. Marshall, Norfolk, Feb. 5, 1945, Mrs. Margaret W. Colbourn, Baltimore, Oct. 22, 1945; OWI, HR Report, July 1944, p. 7; AIPO poll, July 7, 1943, and NORC poll, Dec. 10, 1943, cited in Cantril and Strunk, *Public Opinion*, p. 229.

29. OWI, Mrs. William P. Yarnelle, Fort Wayne, Ind., Aug. 2, 1945. NORC polls of May 7 and Aug. 27, 1943, Jan. 15, and April 8, 1944, AIPO polls of March 10, April 2, May 12, June 12, and Oct. 26, 1943, May 31, 1944, and May 29, 1945, all cited in Cantril and Strunk, *Public Opinion*, pp. 21, 90. 92, 228, 434, 753, 996, 997, 999. OWI, Bureau of Intelligence, "Women Appraise the Food Situation," Memorandum 57, May 1943, p. 5, National Archives; *Consumer Research Bulletin*, 12 (Oct. 1943), 3; (June 1943), 4; (Feb. 1943), 3. OWI, HR Report, March 1945, p. 11. Dorothy Dickins, *Changing Patterns of Food Preparation of Small Town Families in Mississippi*, Mississippi State College

Agricultural Experiment Station Bulletin 415 (State College, 1945), pp. 13–14, 17; Roy Hoopes, *Americans Remember the Home Front* (New York, 1977), p. 293.

30. AIPO poll, May 2, 1945, and NORC poll, June 2, 1944, cited in Cantril and Strunk, *Public Opinion,* pp. 46, 661; OWI, HR Report, Jan. 1944, p. 5, and June 1945, p. 13. OWI, Bureau of Intelligence, "Attitudes on the American Food Situation," Special Memorandum 26, Jan. 7, 1943, and "Women's Awareness of the Food Campaign," Special Memorandum 92, Nov. 22, 1943, Record Group 44, National Archives; OWI, "Women Appraise the Food Situation," p. 7.

31. OWI, Mrs. Helen M. Kentonor, Taos, Sept. 3 and 23, 1943.

32. *Food Consumption of Urban Families in the United States,* Agricultural Information Bulletin 132 (Washington, D.C., 1954), pp. 71, 88.

33. *Historical Statistics,* pp. 328–329.

34. Dickins, "Changing Pattern of Food Preparation," pp. 8–32, 47– 51.

35. Reid, "Food, Liquor and Tobacco," pp. 155, 157.

36. Ibid., p. 147; Economic Research Service, U.S. Department of Agriculture, *U.S. Food Consumption, Sources of Data and Trends, 1909–1963* (Washington, D.C., 1965), pp. 70, 72. Dickins, "Changing Pattern of Food Preparation," pp. 6–8.

37. Annabelle Desmond and Leona Baumgartner, "Health Education in Nutrition: Adapting Business Promotion Techniques to Public Health Education," *American Journal of Public Health* (Sept. 1944), 967–973; Reid, "Food, Liquor and Tobacco," p. 152.

38. NORC poll, June 1942, cited in Cantril and Strunk, *Public Opinion,* p. 299. Bureau of Agricultural Economics, *Housewives Discuss Nutrition Programs: A Study in Bridgeport, Connecticut and Richmond, Virginia* (Washington, D.C., 1944); R. W. Roskelley, *Practices and Attitudes of Rural People in Colorado in Meeting a Yardstick of Good Nutrition,* Colorado Agricultural Experiment Station Bulletin 380-A (Fort Collins, Co., 1944).

39. *Historical Statistics,* pp. 210, 323–334.

40. Elihu Katz and Paul F. Lazarsfeld, *Personal Influence* (Glencoe, Ill., 1955); Hoffer, *Adjustment of Michigan Farm Families to War Conditions,* pp. 13–23; David E. Lindstrom, "Extension Service Jumps Back to the Neighborhood," *Rural Sociology* 8 (1943), 412–415; W. Lloyd Warner and Paul S. Hunt, *The Social Life on an American Community* (New Haven, 1941), pp. 110–112, 353–355; Mary Watters, *Illinois in the Second World War* (Springfield, 1951), II, 69–77; Annabelle Bender, "Civilian Defense Block Organizations in Hyde Park," M.A. thesis, University of Chicago, 1943.

41. Rudolf Arnheim, "The World of the Daytime Serial," in Paul F. Lazarsfeld and Frank N. Stanton, eds., *Radio Research, 1942–1943* (New York, 1944), pp. 43–81.

7. War and Victory Inside the Home

1. Glen H. Elder, Jr., "History and the Family: The Discovery of Complexity," 43, *Journal of Marriage and the Family* (1981), 489–520.

2. Reuben Hill and Elise Boulding, *Families Under Stress: Adjustment to the Crises of War Separation and Reunion* (New York, 1949).

3. Carol Baumann Lefevre, "The Satisfactions and Dissatisfactions of One Hundred Servicemen's Wives," M.A. thesis, University of Chicago, 1948.

4. Robert James Havighurst and others, *The American Veteran Back Home: A Study of Veteran Readjustment* (New York, 1951).

5. Hill and Boulding, *Families Under Stress,* p. 39.

6. Lefevre, "Servicemen's Wives," p. 99.

7. Ibid., p. 46.

8. "Women: They Think of the Moment," *Time,* Feb. 26, 1945, p. 19; Evelyn Millis Duvall, "Loneliness and the Serviceman's Wife," *Marriage and Family Living,* 7 (Nov. 1945), 78; Lefevre, "Servicemen's Wives," p. 48.

9. Lefevre, "Servicemen's Wives," pp. 45, 100; Hill and Boulding, *Families Under Stress,* pp. 68–69.

10. Duvall, "Loneliness and the Serviceman's Wife," p. 77.

11. "Heartsickness," *Time,* Jan. 29, 1945, p. 65.

12. Lefevre, "Servicemen's Wives," p. 26

13. Havighurst, *American Veteran,* p. 49

14. *Time,* Feb. 26, 1945, p. 19

15. Lefevre, "Servicemen's Wives," pp. 28–29.

16. Ibid., pp. 29–30.

17. Ibid., p. 31.

18. Ibid., pp. 31, 33, 41, 66.

19. Ibid., p. 32.

20. Ibid., p. 33.

21. Duvall "Loneliness and the Serviceman's Wife," p. 79.

22. Havighurst, *American Veteran,* p. 53; Hill and Boulding, *Families Under Stress,* p. 343.

23. Lefevre, "Servicemen's Wives," p. 84; Hill and Boulding, *Families Under Stress,* pp. 64, 65, 87; Havighurst, *American Veteran,* pp. 42–43.

24. Ibid., p. 76.

25. Ibid., pp. 16–17, 69, 72–80; Howard M. Bell, *Youth Tell Their Story* (Washington, D.C., 1938), pp. 18, 44.

26. *Time,* Feb. 26, 1945, p. 19.

27. Havighurst, *American Veteran,* p. 55.

28. Nathan Sinai and Odin W. Anderson, *EMIC: A Study of Administrative Experience,* Bureau of Public Health, Economic Research Series 3 (Ann Arbor, 1948), pp. 19, 36, 38, 42, 88, 110.

29. Lefevre, "Servicemen's Wives," p. 94.

30. Havighurst, *American Veteran,* p. 41.

31. Samuel Stouffer, "The American Soldier in World War II," Survey AMS-213, Omnibus Attitude Survey, May 1945, question 3, Roper Center, Williams College, Williamstown, Mass.; U.S. Naval Administrative Histories of World War II, *Commandant's Report, 11th Naval District, Part 4* (San Diego, 1946), p. 453, manuscript, Navy Department Library, Washington, D.C.; Agnes E. Meyer, *Journey Through Chaos* (New York, 1943), p. 226.

32. Virginia Mayberry, "Draftee's Wife: A Memoir of World War II," *Indiana Magazine of History,* 79 (Dec. 1983), 320; Barbara Klaw, *Camp Follower: The Story of a Soldier's Wife* (New York, 1943), pp. 14, 110–111; Meyer, *Journey Through Chaos,* p. 300.

33. Meyer, *Journey Through Chaos,* p. 188; Stouffer, Survey AMS-213, question 54.

34. Meyer, *Journey Through Chaos,* pp. 188, 189–190; *Time,* Feb. 26, 1945, p. 19.

35. Klaw, *Camp Follower,* 35; Katharine F. Lenroot, chief, Children's Bureau, speech quoted in U.S. Senate, Subcommittee of the Committee on Education and Labor, *Hearings on Wartime Health and Education,* 78th Cong., 1st sess., 1943, 1944, p. 104.

36. Hill and Boulding, *Families Under Stress,* pp. 40, 70; Lefevre, "Servicemen's Wives," p. 28; Mary Elizabeth Pidgeon, *Changes in Women's Employment During the War,* Women's Bureau Special Bulletin 20 (Washington, D.C., 1944), p. 29.

37. Lefevre, "Servicemen's Wives," pp. 18, 28.

38. Hill and Boulding, *Families Under Stress,* p. 182

39. Ibid., p. 180.

40. Lefevre, "Servicemen's Wives," p. 73

41. Ibid., pp. 106–110.

42. Ibid., p. 114.

43. Ibid.

44. Ibid., pp. 111–118; Hill and Boulding, *Families Under Stress,* p. 142; *Time,* Feb. 26, 1945, p. 19.

45. Hill and Boulding, *Families Under Stress,* pp. 141, 177, 202; Havighurst, *American Veteran,* pp. 50–52; *Time,* Feb. 26, 1945, p. 19.

46. Lefevre, "Servicemen's Wives," p. 103; Gladys Gaylord, "Marriage Counseling in Wartime," *Annals of the American Academy of Political and Social Science,* 229 (Sept. 1943), 44.

47. Spirits appeared also in *Cabin in the Sky* (1943), with an all-black cast; *Since You Went Away* (1944); *White Cliffs of Dover* (1944); *God Is My Co-Pilot* (1945); and *It's a Wonderful Life* (1946). See also, Joyce M. Baker, *Images of Women in Film: The War Years, 1941–1945* (Ann Arbor, 1981); Leslie Halliwell, *The Filmgoer's Companion* (New York, 1974); Susan M. Hartmann, *The Home Front and Beyond: American Women in the 1940s* (Boston, 1982), chap. 10; Joe Morella, Edward Z. Epstein, and John Griggs, *The Films of World War*

II (Secaucus, N.J., 1973); and Marjorie Rosen, *Popcorn Venus* (New York, 1973), chap. 12. On songs see Richard R. Lingeman, *Don't You Know There's a War On? The American Home Front, 1941–1945* (New York, 1970), pp. 219–233.

48. Urie Bronfenbrenner, "Socialization and Social Class Through Time and Space," in Eleanor E. Maccoby and others, eds., *Readings in Social Psychology* (New York, 1958), pp. 400–425. Racial differences proved quite small. Allison Davis and Robert Havighurst, "Social Class and Color Differences in Child Rearing," *American Sociological Review,* 11 (1946), 698–710.

49. Melvin Kohn, *Class and Conformity,* 2nd ed. (Chicago, 1978); Robert Winch, *The Modern Family* (New York, 1952).

50. August Hollingshead, *Elmtown's Youth* (New York, 1949, 1975); Glen H. Elder, Jr., *Adolescent Achievement and Mobility Aspirations* (Chapel Hill, N.C., 1962).

51. Hill and Boulding, *Families Under Stress,* pp. 44–45, 67.

52. *Portland Oregon Journal* and *San Diego Union,* as quoted in Office of War Information, Bureau of Intelligence, "Analysis of Editorial Opinion," Report 33, Jan. 28, 1944, p. 21, Record Group 44, National Archives.

53. U.S. Department of Labor, Children's Bureau, "Juvenile Court Statistics, 1940–42," *The Child,* 8 (Supplement to number 6) (Dec. 1943), 3.

54. Sheldon and Eleanor Glueck, *Unraveling Juvenile Delinquency* (New York, 1950), pp. 29, 68, 80–88, 98, 109–115, 121–131.

55. Lefevre, "Servicemen's Wives," p. 16; Hill and Boulding, *Families Under Stress,* p. 37.

56. Havighurst, *American Veteran,* pp. 45–46.

57. Duvall, "Loneliness and the Serviceman's Wives," p. 81.

58. Hill and Boulding, *Families Under Stress,* p. 58; Lefevre, "Servicemen's Wives," p. 59; Havighurst, *American Veteran,* pp. 45–47.

59. Lefevre, "Servicemen's Wives," pp. 58–62.

60. Hill and Boulding, *Families Under Stress,* pp. 61–64.

61. Lefevre, "Servicemen's Wives," pp. 53, 60, 101, 145.

62. Ibid., pp. 128–133; Havighurst, *American Veteran,* p. 51.

63. Hill and Boulding, *Families Under Stress,* pp. 275–277.

64. Lefevre, "Servicemen's Wives," pp. 133–134, 116.

65. Ibid., p. 122.

66. Ibid., p. 126; Hill and Boulding, *Families Under Stress,* p. 86.

67. Havighurst, *American Veteran,* p. 83; Hill and Boulding, *Families Under Stress,* p. 86.

68. Hill and Boulding, *Families Under Stress,* pp. 126, 205.

69. Ibid., pp. 147–148; see also, Duvall, "Loneliness and the Serviceman's Wife."

70. Meyer, *Journey Through Chaos,* pp. 114–115.

71. Eliot Ness, "Sex Delinquency as a Social Hazard," *Proceedings of the National Conference of Social Work, 1944* (New York, 1944), p. 280.

72. John H. Stokes, "A Statement on Prostitution in Venereal Disease Control," *Venereal Disease Information* (May 1942), p. 195; E. W. Norris, A. F. Doyle, and Albert P. Iskrant, "Venereal Disease Epidemiology in the Army Third Service Command," *Venereal Disease Information* (Oct. 1943), p. 283.

73. Alfred C. Kinsey and others, *Sexual Behavior in the Human Female* (Philadelphia, 1953), p. 442; Paul H. Gebhard and Alan B. Johnson, *The Kinsey Data: Marginal Tabulations of the 1938–1963 Interviews Conducted by the Institute for Sex Research* (Philadelphia, 1979), p. 406.

74. Hill and Boulding, *Families Under Stress*, p. 145; "The Soldiers Think of Home," *Time*, April 16, 1945, p. 24.

75. *Time*, April 16, 1945, p. 24; Havighurst, *American Veteran*, pp. 39–40.

76. Havighurst, *American Veteran*, p. 40.

77. Ibid. *Time*, April 16, 1945, p. 24.

78. Roper-*Fortune* poll 35, May 1943, Roper Center, Williams College, Williamstown, Mass.

79. Roper-*Fortune* poll 54, April 1946, Roper Center, Williams College, Williamstown, Mass.

80. In addition, blacks and singles tended to be less equalitarian. For the detailed multivariate statistical analysis see D'Ann Campbell, "Wives, Workers and Womanhood," Ph.D. diss., University of North Carolina, 1979, pp. 212–258.

8. The War and Beyond

1. On the distinctive moral reasoning of women see Carol Gilligan, *In a Different Voice: Psychological Theory and Women's Development* (Cambridge, Mass. 1983). NORC Report S-29, "Resistance to Taking War Jobs in Three New England Cities," June 24, 1943, p. 17, copy in National Opinion Research Center Archives, University of Chicago, Chicago. Office of War Information, Bureau of Intelligence, "Women and the War," Special Report of Aug. 19, 1942, p. 4, copy in the Rensis Likert Papers, Michigan Historical Collections, University of Michigan, Ann Arbor.

2. Aileen Kraditor, *Ideas of the Women's Suffrage Movement, 1890–1920* (New York, 1965).

3. Hadley Cantril and Mildred Strunk, *Public Opinion: 1935–1946* (Princeton, 1951), pp. 508–510; Mildred A. Schwartz, *Trends in White Attitudes Toward Negroes* (Chicago, 1967).

4. Bureau of the Census, *Historical Statistics of the United States* (Washington, D.C., 1975), pp. 298–305.

5. Historians are just beginning research on minority women in the last half century. On Native Americans see Alison Bernstein, "A Mixed Record: The Political Enfranchisement of American Indian Women During the Indian New Deal," unpublished paper, Organization of American Historians, annual meet-

ing, 1983. Important anthropological studies dealing with the 1940s and early 1950s include Louise S. Spindler, *Menomini Women and Culture Change,* Memoir 91 of the American Anthropological Association (Menasha, Wis., 1962); Alice Joseph, Rosamond B. Spicer, and Jane Chesky, *The Desert People* (Chicago, 1949), on the Papago; Gordon Macgregor, *Warriors Without Weapons: A Study of the Pine Ridge Sioux* (Chicago, 1945); Dorothea C. Leighton and Clyde Kluckholn, *Children of the People: The Navajo Individual and His Development* (Cambridge, Mass., 1947); Evon Z. Vogt and Ethel M. Albert, eds., *People of Rimrock: A Study of Values in Five Cultures* (Cambridge, Mass., 1967). On the impact of the war see also Evon Z. Vogt, *Navajo Veterans: A Study of Changing Values,* Papers of the Peabody Museum, 41 (Cambridge, Mass., 1951). For contemporary perspectives see J. P. Shalloo and Donald Young, eds., "Minority People in a Nation at War," *Annals of the American Academy of Political and Social Science,* 223 (1942), esp. pp. 10–54; and Oliver Leonard and C. P. Loomis, "Culture of a Contemporary Rural Community: El Cerrito, New Mexico," Bureau of Agricultural Economics, *Rural Life Series,* 1 (Washington, D.C., 1941).

6. Harry K. Schwarzweller, James S. Brown, and J. J. Mangalam, *Mountain Families in Transition: A Case Study of Appalachian Migration* (University Park, Pa., 1971); Thomas R. Ford, ed., *The Southern Appalachian Region: A Survey* (Lexington, Ky., 1962), pp. 9–84; Gordon F. De Jong, *Appalachian Fertility Decline: A Demographic and Sociological Analysis* (Lexington, Ky., 1968), p. 36; and Jack E. Weller, *Yesterday's People: Life in Contemporary Appalachia* (Lexington, Ky., 1965).

7. Foster Rhea Dulles, *The American Red Cross* (New York, 1950), chap. 29; "The History of the American National Red Cross," vol. XXX, Robert Keith Murray, "A Study of American Public Opinion on the American National Red Cross from Newspapers and Periodicals, 1881–1948," 1950, pp. 163–172, manuscript, American National Red Cross Archives, Washington, D.C.

8. Elizabeth Hawes, *Wenches with Wrenches* (Cornwall, N.Y., 1943); Katherine Archibald, *Wartime Shipyard: A Study in Social Disunity* (Berkeley, 1947); Elizabeth Hawes, *Hurry Up Please Its Time* (New York, 1946); Robert Blauner, *Alienation and Freedom: The Factory Worker and His Industry* (Chicago, 1964), pp. 70–74, 81, 87.

9. Associate Negro Press clippings throughout the war years, Claude Barnett Papers, Chicago Historical Society, Chicago, Ill.; Philip S. Foner, *Women and the American Labor Movement: From World War I to the Present* (New York, 1980).

10. Nancy Gabin, "They Have Placed a Penalty on Womanhood: The Protest Actions of Women Auto Workers in Detroit-Area UAW Locals, 1945–1947," *Feminist Studies,* 8 (Summer 1982), 373–398. See also, Ruth Milkman, "Redefining 'Women's Work': The Sexual Division of Labor in the Auto Industry During World War II," *Feminist Studies,* 8 (Summer 1982), 337–372. Of a national sample of working women aged twenty to thirty-five in 1943, 54 percent

planned to continue the same line of work after the war, 17 percent would look for a different job, and 29 percent would quit. Roper-*Fortune* poll 35, May 1943, Roper Center, Williams College, Williamstown, Mass.

11. For excellent examples see Corrine Azen Krauss, *Grandmothers, Mothers, and Daughters: An Oral History Study of Ethnicity, Mental Health and Continuity of Three Generations of Jewish, Italian, and Slavic-American Women* (New York, 1977); Glen H. Elder, Jr., *Children of the Great Depression: Social Change in Life Experience* (Chicago, 1974).

12. Roper-*Fortune* poll 35, May 1943. In all, 12 percent of the women placed careers ahead of marriage. Only 9 percent of all the single women expected not to marry.

13. Mirra Komarovsky, *Women in the Modern World: Their Education and Their Dilemmas* (Boston, 1953), p. 13.

14. Tamara K. Hareven, *Family Time and Industrial Time* (New York, 1982); John Bodnar, Roger Simon, and Michael P. Weber, *Lives of Their Own: Blacks, Italians, and Poles in Pittsburgh, 1900–1960* (Urbana, Ill., 1982); Elder, *Children of the Great Depression;* but see also, Elyce Rotella, *From Home to Office: U.S. Women at Work, 1870–1930* (Ann Arbor, 1982), and Winifred D. Wandersee, *Women's Work and Family Values, 1920–1940* (Cambridge, Mass., 1981).

15. The classic essay remains Talcott Parsons, "Age and Sex in the Social Structure of the United States," *American Sociological Review,* 7 (1942), 604–616. The only historical treatment is Richard M. Ugland, "The Adolescent Experience During World War II: Indianapolis As a Case Study," Ph.D. diss., Indiana University, 1977. On the prewar milieu see Howard M. Bell, *Youth Tell Their Story* (Washington, D.C., 1938). Paula Fass dates the emergence of the new youth culture in elite colleges during the 1920s. *The Damned and the Beautiful: American Youth in the 1920s* (New York, 1977).

16. Dorothy Gordon, "As the Youngsters See Juvenile Delinquency," *New York Times Magazine,* Aug. 16, 1944, p. 32; Lester D. Crow and Alice Crow, *Our Teen-Age Boys and Girls,* as quoted in Ugland, "The Adolescent Experience During World War II," p. 354; H. H. Remmers and D. H. Radler, *The American Teenager* (New York, 1957), pp. 223–228.

17. August Hollingshead, *Elmtown's Youth* (New York, 1949), p. 151; see also, Glen H. Elder, Jr., *Adolescent Achievement and Mobility Aspirations* (Chapel Hill, N.C., 1962).

18. L. J. Elias, *Farm Youth's Appraisal of Their Adjustments, Compared with Other Youth,* Bulletin 513, Washington Agricultural Experiment Station, Youth Series 7 (Pullman, Wash., 1949), pp. 26–44; Mildred B. Thurow, *Interests, Activities, and Problems of Rural Young Folk: Women 15 to 29 Years of Age,* Cornell Agricultural Experiment Station Bulletin 617 (Ithaca, 1934), pp. 44–45; Glen H. Elder, Jr., "Achievement Orientation and Career Patterns of Rural Youth," *Sociology of Education,* 37 (1963), 30–58.

19. Charles S. Johnson, *Growing Up in the Black Belt* (Washington, D.C., 1941), pp. 59, 223, 236.

20. Robert J. Havighurst and Hilda Taba, *Adolescent Character and Personality* (New York, 1949).

21. Ernest W. Burgess and H. J. Locke, *The Family* (New York, 1953); Robert F. Winch, *The Modern Family* (New York, 1952); Burgess and Paul Wallin, *Engagement and Marriage* (New York, 1953); Mirra Komarovsky, *Women in the Modern World* (Boston, 1953); William Waller and Reuben Hill, *The Family* (New York, 1952); Paul L. Campisi, "Ethnic Family Patterns: The Italian Family in the United States," *American Journal of Sociology*, 53 (1948), 443–449. For a valuable comparative perspective see Joan Busfield and Michael Paddon, *Thinking About Children: Sociology and Fertility in Post-War England* (Cambridge, Eng., 1977), part III. For a negative view see Carl C. Zimmerman, *Family and Civilization* (New York, 1947).

22. Women who came of age after 1960 were even more equalitarian (71 percent), but men changed little (up only 3 percent from the war cohort). The Equal Rights Amendment was not a salient issue before the 1970s, and thus there were no differences among the cohorts. Virginia Shapiro, "Intergenerational Conflict Over the Status of Women," *Western Political Quarterly*, 33 (1980), 267.

23. Robert O. Blood and Donald M. Wolfe, *Husbands and Wives: The Dynamics of Married Living* (New York, 1960), esp. p. 156. For recent theorizing see Ronald E. Cromwell and David H. Olson, *Power in Families* (New York, 1975).

24. Donald M. Wolfe, "Power and Authority in the Family," in Robert F. Winch, ed., *Selected Studies in Marriage and the Family* (New York, 1962), pp. 582–600.

25. F. Ivan Nye and Lois Wladis Hoffman, *The Employed Mother in America* (Chicago, 1963).

26. Susan B. Anthony II, *Out of the Kitchen—Into the War* (New York, 1943), p. 133. Compare J. E. Trey, "Women in the War Economy—World War II," *Review of Radical Political Economics*, 4 (1974), 40–57.

27. Komarovsky, *Women in the Modern World*, pp. 190–194; Nye and Hoffman, *Employed Mother*, chap. 6.

28. Roper-*Fortune* poll 54, April 1946.

29. Ibid.

30. Karen Tucker Anderson, *Wartime Women: Sex Roles, Family Relations, and the Status of Women During World War II* (Westport, Conn., 1981); Leila J. Rupp, *Mobilizing Women for War: German and American Propaganda, 1939–1945* (Princeton, 1978); Grace Elizabeth Laleger, *The Vocational Interests of High School Girls* (New York, 1942).

31. *Ladies Home Journal*, 61 (July 1944), 101; Havighurst and Taba, *Adolescent Character*, p. 46; Komarovsky, *Women in the Modern World*, chap. 3; James S. Coleman, *The Adolescent Society* (New York, 1961); *It's a Wonderful Life*, Frank Capra director, screenplay by Frances Goodrich, Albert Hackett, and Capra.

32. Eleanor Roosevelt, "If You Ask Me," *Ladies Home Journal,* 61 (Aug. 1944), 33.

33. Harold Smith, "The Problem of 'Equal Pay for Equal Work' in Great Britain During World War II," *Journal of Modern History* 53 (Dec. 1981), 652–672; Margaret Allen, "The Domestic Ideal and the Mobilization of Woman-power in World War II," *Women's Studies International Forum,* 6 (1983), 401–412.

Index